D1563329

CHANGE TO CHAINS

6000 YEAR QUEST FOR CONTROL

———◆———

VOLUME I -
RISE OF THE REPUBLIC

WILLIAM J. FEDERER

CHANGE TO CHAINS
-6000 Year Quest for Control
୶

Volume I - Rise of the Republic

by William J. Federer

For other, contact: Amerisearch, Inc.
P.O. Box 20163 St. Louis, MO 63123
314-487-4395, 314-487-4489 fax 1-888-USA-WORD
www.amerisearch.net wjfederer@gmail.com

HISTORY/POLITICAL/EDUCATION
ISBN 978-0-9827101-4-2 paperback
ISBN ebook

Cover design by
DustinMyersDesign.com 573-308-6060

Free ebook
For a limited time, as owner of this book, you can get a free
ebook of this title
by sending an email to:

wjfederer@gmail.com
with subject line "Change ebook"

Amerisearch, Inc., P.O. Box 20163, St. Louis, MO 63123
1-888-USA-WORD, 314-487-4395, 314-487-4489fax
www.amerisearch.net, wjfederer@gmail.com

"What has destroyed the liberty and the rights of man in every government that has ever existed under the sun? The generalizing and concentrating of all cares and powers into one body."
-Thomas Jefferson, to Joseph C. Cabell, 1816

≈

"The tendency of power to increase itself, particularly when exercised by a single individual... would terminate in virtual monarchy."
-William Harrison, *Inaugural Address*, March 4, 1841

≈

"When a government becomes powerful it...takes bread from innocent mouths and deprives honorable men of their substance, for votes with which to perpetuate itself."
-Cicero (106-43 BC), Roman Statesman

≈

"If we don't have a proper fundamental moral background, we will finally end up with a totalitarian government which does not believe in rights for anybody except the State."
-Harry S Truman, Attorney General's Conference, 1950

≈

"The story of liberty is a history of the limitation of government power, not the increase of it."
-Woodrow Wilson, *The New York Times*, September 14, 1912

≈

"Government that is big enough to give you everything you want is more likely to simply take everything you've got."
-Ronald Reagan, St. John's University, New York, March 28, 1985

≈

"Society...must repose on principles that do not **change**."

- Montesquieu, *The Spirit of the Laws*, 1748

&

"One **change** always leaves the way open for others."

-Niccolo Machiavelli, *The Prince*, 1513

&

"Behold the insidious efforts of the partisans of

arbitrary power...to lock the strong **chains**
of domestic despotism on a country."
-Mercy Otis Warren, *Observations on the new Constitution*, 1788

&

"America is the last hope of millions of enslaved peoples...

I have seen fellow-prisoners in Communist prisons beaten,
tortured, with 50 pounds of **chains** on their legs-praying for
America....that the dike will not crumple;
that it will remain free."
-Rev. Richard Wurmbrand, 1967

&

"It is when a people forget God,

that tyrants forge their **chains**."
-Patrick Henry

&

"*Posterity - you will never know how much it has cost my generation to preserve your freedom. I hope you make good use of it.*"
-John Adams, in a letter
to his wife Abigail, April 26, 1777

∽

"*To secure the blessings of liberty to ourselves and our posterity...*"
-Preamble, U.S. Constitution

∽

"*Every step in civilization has been made possible by those who have been willing to sacrifice for posterity.*"
-William Jennings Bryan, U.S. Scretary of State

∽

"*Our forefathers passed the vast Atlantic, spent their blood and treasure, that they might enjoy their liberties, both civil and religious, and transmit them to their posterity... Now if we should give them up, can our children rise up and call us blessed?*"
-William Prescott, 1775, Colonel at Battle of Bunker Hill

∽

"*A good man leaves an inheritance to his children's children.*"
-Proverbs 13:22

∽

"People will not look forward to posterity who never look backward to their ancestors."
-Edmund Burke,
Reflections on the Revolution in France, 1790

෴

"Not to know what happened before you were born is to be a child forever."
- Cicero, *Ad M. Brutum*, 46 BC

෴

"History is an excellent teacher with few pupils."
-Will & Ariel Durant, *The Story of Civilization*, 1967

෴

"Civilization is not inherited; it has to be learned and earned by each generation anew; if the transmission should be interrupted... civilization would die, and we should be savages again."
-Will & Ariel Durant, *The Lessons of History*, 1968

෴

CONTENTS

Contents

CHANGE TO CHAINS - WILLIAM J. FEDERER

INTRODUCTION

"Always remember Frodo, the Ring is trying
to get back to its master. It wants to be found."
-Gandalf in J.R.R. Tolkien's *The Lord of the Rings*

Author J.R.R. Tolkien, in his best-selling novel, *The Lord of the Rings*, wrote of the irresistible pull of power to concentrate into the hands of Lord Sauron:

> One Ring to rule them all, One Ring to find
> them, One Ring to bring them all and in the
> darkness bind them.

This story is similar to an ancient myth, the Ring of Gyges, as retold by Plato in *The Republic* (380 BC), where a shepherd in Lydia, named Gyges, noticed a cave in the fields. Exploring it, he spotted a gold ring on the finger of a former king who had been buried there. Putting the ring on, he discovered it allowed him to become invisible, but the ring also induced him to immoral and ruthless behavior. He stole into the king's palace, seduced the queen, killed the king, and took the throne.

Tolkien's *Lord of the Rings* and the "Ring of Gyges" are metaphors for the unseen magnetic draw for power to be held in the hands of one individual who inevitably becomes corrupted by it.

"Power tends to corrupt and absolute power corrupts absolutely," wrote British statesman Lord Acton to Bishop Creighton, 1887.

Gandalf exclaimed:

> Don't...tempt me Frodo! I dare not take it.
> Not even to keep it safe. Understand, Frodo. I
> would use this ring from a desire to do good...But
> through me, it would wield a power too great and
> terrible to imagine.

George Washington warned in his *Farewell Address*, 1796:

> Usurpation...though...in one instance, may be the instrument of good, it is the customary weapon by which free governments are destroyed.

This book will examine the cycle:

1) CONCENTRATED POWER - The recurring story in history is that in times of uncertainty and crisis, power concentrates into the hands of one person, a monarch. From Indian chiefs to gang leaders, Pharaohs to Sultans, Kings to Communist Dictators, the rule by one person, historically called a "Monarch," has been the most common form of human government;

2) SEPARATED POWER – A few rare experiments exist in history of alternatives to monarchy, of which America has been the most successful. Without a monarch to enforce order by external control, order in society had to be maintained by citizens embracing voluntary internal controls. To prevent a return to monarchy, America's founders separated the power of a king into three branches, then separated it again into Federal and State levels, then tied up this new Federal Frankenstein with ten handcuffs, the First Ten Amendments, resulting in an unprecedented explosion of individual freedom, opportunity, motivation and prosperity;

3) POWER CONCENTRATED – In times of internal civil disorders, external threats and loss of public virtue, power reconcentrates, like a rubberband snapping back, resulting in a loss of freedom, opportunity, motivation and prosperity.

Concentrated –> Separated –> Concentrated

A demonstration of this progression is: a fist in one hand to represent the concentrated power of a king; an open palm with fingers apart on the other hand to represent separated power of a republican government; then a return to the fist with each recurring crisis, resulting in a reconcentration of power.

Before one can appreciate the rarity of America's experiment with separated power controlled by the will of the people, it is vital to review the world's long history of concentrated power.

~

6,000 YEARS OF RECORDED HUMAN HISTORY

"The book is written...It may...wait a century for a reader, as God has waited **6,000 years** for an observer."-Johannes Kelper, astronomer, regarding his book, *The Harmonies of the World*, 1619

There have been approximately 6,000 years of recorded human history. That is all – only about 6,000. Scholars have examined the most ancient human records:

*Sumerian cuneiform on clay tablets
*Egyptian hieroglyphics on papyrus and
    carved in stone
*Chinese characters in bamboo books
*etchings on palm leaves and birch bark in India
*markings on leather, vellum, wood veneer,
    wax and parchment
*the Epic of Gilgamesh and the Code of
    Hammurabi, written in Akkadian
*Norte Chico monuments of Peru

These records date back no further than around 4,000 BC. 4,000 BC added to 2,000 AD equals 6,000 years. 6,000 years is really not that long. It's just 60 people living 100 years each, back-to-back.

Richard Overy, editor of *The Times Complete History of the World*, stated in "The 50 Key Dates of World History" (Oct. 19, 2007):

> No date appears before the start of human civilizations about **5,500 years ago** and the beginning of a written or pictorial history.

Franklin D. Roosevelt addressed the American Youth Congress in Washington, DC, February 10, 1940:

> I knew that some day Russia would return to religion for the simple reason that **four or five thousand years of recorded history** have proven that mankind has always believed in God in spite of many abortive attempts to exile God.

In his address, "Prince of Peace," printed in the New York Times, September 7, 1913, U.S. Secretary of State William Jennings Bryan wrote:

> The miraculous birth of Christ is not more mysterious than any other conception-it is simply unlike it...Science has not yet revealed to us the secret of life...**6,000 years of recorded history** and yet we know no more about the secret of life than they knew in the beginning.

During the past 6,000 years, empires have risen and empires have fallen, empires have risen and empires have fallen, in a recurring cycle. Pulitzer Prize winning historians Will and Ariel Durant wrote an 11-volume work, *The Story of Civilization* (published 1935-1975), in which they examined the rise, flourishing and fall of major world civilizations.

More than 20 years after his death, Will Durant's quote appeared in an opening graphic of Mel Gibson's 2006 film *Apocalypto*:

> A great civilization is not conquered from without until it has destroyed itself from within.

In a companion work, *The Lessons of History* (NY: Simon and Schuster, 1968, p. 90), Will and Ariel Durant wrote:

> Civilizations begin, flourish, decline, and disappear – or linger on a stagnant pool left by once life-giving streams.

As the proverb states: "Riches are not forever, and doth the crown endure to every generation?"

Like a tetherball winding tighter around a pole, or in the opposite case, flying increasingly further from the pole, the Durants wrote in *The Lessons of History* (p. 89-90) :

> Oswald Spengler (1880-1936)...divided history into...two periods:
> -one of centripetal **organization**, unifying a culture in all its phases into a unique coherent, and artistic form;
> -the other a period of centrifugal **disorganization,** in which creed and culture decompose in division and criticism, and end in chaos.

❧

CYCLES IN CIVILIZATIONS

Civilizations typically go through stages:

1) Out of times of chaos and disorder, civilizations begin with a warrior leader who is not afraid to fight, defend, kill, and conquer.

2) Civilizations flourish with ruling leaders who are capable at managing, organizing, economics and administering justice.

3) Civilizations decline with self-indulgent leaders who are lax, proud, corrupt and naively assume their empire will continue forever.

Past empires, at their height of influence, felt an invincibility.

They could not imagine they would someday decline or disappear from the stage of human history. Jacques Attali wrote in "The West and the Tyranny of Public Debt" (*Time Magazine*, 12/27/10):

> History offers one final lesson. The power of sovereign states can foster a sense of impunity that encourages excessive debt.

It is a recurring theme in human behavior, rags to riches to rags. Out of the crises of poverty, an immigrant grandfather begins with nothing, works hard at manual labor, starts a business and accumulates savings. He sends his son to college, who learns to manage the family business causing it to flourish. Then a lazy, self-indulgent grandson comes along who squanders the family's wealth.

Human beings display behavioral traits, and since civilizations are comprised of human beings, civilizations display behavioral traits. Will and Ariel Durant wrote in *The Lessons of History* (p. 86):

> Man is a competitive animal...his State must be like himself.

Daniel Webster stated in his 4th of July Oration, 1802:

> Man, in all countries, resembles man. Wherever you find him, you find human nature in him and human frailties about him.

Thomas Jefferson wrote in his Notes on Virginia, 1782:

> Human nature is the same on each side of the Atlantic, and will be alike influenced by the same causes.

Civilizations are like athletes. Out of the chaos of competition, a young athlete begins a disciplined training with a self-denying ethic. He is focused on winning the prize, achieving his goal of being the best in the world.

After years of competition, he flourishes and becomes the champion, reigning and enjoying his status and acclaim.

Gradually, he neglects discipline, exercise, and self-restraint, declining into an indulgent lifestyle of instant self-gratification, weakening his body with overeating, sexual promiscuity, and drugs.

A new up-and-coming athlete challenges the old champ, who then enters the ring, convinced in his mind that he is as fit as he used to be, but in reality he is an overweight, potbellied, couch potato who is quickly overtaxed by physical exertion, and defeated. The new athlete reigns, beginning the cycle again.

Out of the chaos of war, unrest and crises, a civilization begins with a leader who can mobilize people to fight, work hard, be patriotic, loyal and have a self-denying moral ethic.

After years of conquest and trade, the civilization flourishes and reigns as the best in the world for a period of time.

Gradually, it neglects moral discipline, casts off restraint, indulges in luxury and an instant self-gratification lifestyle. It declines into a welfare mentality, buying on credit with no savings. Citizens weaken themselves with overeating, sexual promiscuity, and drugs.

When a new up-and-coming civilization challenges it to compete, the old civilization enters the ring convinced it is still as militarily and economically fit as it used to be, but in reality, it has overstretched its borders, overtaxed it citizens, and become overweight with debt – the "fat" of the body-politic. The new civilization becomes the world champion, beginning the cycle again.

Will and Ariel Durant, wrote in *The Story of Civilization*, Vol 3-Caesar and Christ, Epilogue-Why Rome fell:

> The essential causes of Rome's decline lay in her people, her morals, her class struggle, her failing trade, her bureaucratic despotism, her stifling taxes, her consuming wars.

Historian Arnold Joseph Toynbee provided intelligence for the British during World Wars I and II. He was a delegate to the Paris Peace Conferences. Toynbee's 12-volume *Study of History* (1934-1961), described the rise, flowering, and decline of 26 cultures from Egypt, Greece and Rome to Polynesia and Peru. Toynbee wrote:

Civilizations die from suicide, not by murder.

Abraham Lincoln warned on January 27, 1837:

At what point then is the approach of danger to be expected? I answer, if it ever reach us, it must spring up amongst us; it cannot come from abroad. If destruction be our lot we must ourselves be its author and finisher. As a nation of free men we must live through all time, or die by suicide.

"Red at night, sailors delight. Red in the morning, sailors take warning." This phenomenon in weather was noted in Matthew 16:

When it is evening, ye say, It will be fair weather: for the sky is red. And in the morning, It will be foul weather today: for the sky is red and lowring. O ye hypocrites, ye can discern the face of the sky; but can ye not discern the signs of the times?

Meteorology is the study of weather. Colder high pressure air is pulled down to mix with warmer low pressure air. At first the air movement is unnoticeable, but it gradually increases in intensity until there is a chaotic change – a clash of wind and storm, culminating in the colder higher pressure air being brought down - equalized.

After a while, another area experiences colder high pressure, resulting in the world's air rushing to equalize, repeating the cycle.

In civilizations, as one nation experiences a high level of prosperity and power, it is pulled down to mix with people from weaker, poorer countries. At first the immigration is slow and the demographic assimilation is unnoticeable; but then the intensity increases with warriors attacking in a chaotic change – a clash of cultural, economic and military storms, culminating in the powerful, prosperous civilization being brought down - equalized.

After a while, another area of the globe experiences a high level of economic power and prosperity, resulting in the world's population rushing there to equalize, repeating the cycle.

The Durants wrote in *The Lessons of History* (p. 88):

> History repeats itself...We may reasonably expect that in the future, as in the past, some new states will rise, some old states will subside.

When one civilization exits center stage, another makes its entrance. The chaotic crises of a crumbling old order are precursors to people embracing anyone who promises to rescue them, a 'man on horseback,' the next dictator.

৵

TWO TYPES OF POWER: CONCENTRATED & SEPARATED

Just like weather fluctuates between two alternatives, colder high pressure and warmer low pressure, governments fluctuates between two alternatives. Calvin Coolidge stated at the unveiling of the equestrian statue of Bishop Francis Asbury, October 15, 1924:

> There are only two main theories of government in the world. One rests on righteousness, the other rests on force. One appeals to reason, the other appeals to the sword. One is exemplified in a **republic**, the other is represented by a **despotism**.
>
> The history of government on this earth has been almost entirely a history of the **rule of force held in the hands of a few.** Under our Constitution America committed itself to the practical application of the **rule of reason, with the power in the hands of the people**.

When power is concentrated, the State is supreme, with the king as the head of the State, as France's Louis XIV, the "Sun King," is attributed with saying: "L'État, c'est moi" ("I am the State").

When power is separated, the individual is supreme. America's founders wanted to maximize the individual. It is an inverse relationship. The more power is concentrated in government - the less freedom and opportunity is experienced by the individual.

All forms of government are on a sliding scale between maximum individual liberty on one end and maximum State control on the other, called "tyranny." One end of the spectrum holds the individual supreme and the other end holds the State supreme. President Dwight Eisenhower addressed the American Legion's Back-to-God Program, February 20, 1955:

> The Founding Fathers expressed the ideal
> of Government based on the individual. That ideal
> previously had existed only in the hearts and minds
> of men...They recogniz[ed] God as the author of
> individual rights.

The most efficient form of government is a monarchy - one person says it, it happens, or heads roll. America's founders created an *inefficient* government on purpose - frustratingly slow at times to making good decisions; but thankfully slow to making irreversible bad decisions.

With absolute power in the hands of monarchs, society operates according to the patronage system: if one is friends with the king, they are more equal; if they are not friends with the king, they are less equal; and if they are an enemy of the king, they are dead – it's called treason. Franklin Roosevelt referred to this, June 27, 1936:

> In 1776, we sought freedom from the tyranny
> of a political autocracy – from the 18th century
> royalists who held special privileges from the crown.

Ronald Reagan stated in 1973:

> The classical Liberal, during the
> Revolutionary time...did not believe those rights

were dispensations granted by the king to the people, he believed that he was born with them.

The quality of citizens' lives depended on how well they would obey the monarch. It is Chicago politics, the bribe or the bullet, favors or fear. John Adams wrote in January 1776:

> Fear is the foundation of most governments; but it is so sordid and brutal a passion, and renders men in whose breasts it predominates so stupid and miserable, that Americans will not be likely to approve of any political institution which is founded on it.

When in the market for liberty, there is a "risk-return" trade-off. As in stock and bond investing: "the greater the risk-the greater the return, the lower the risk-the lower the return." In other words: the greater the liberty-the greater the risk; the lower the risk-the lower the liberty. The securest place is a prison cell, but there is no liberty. Franklin wrote in his notes for the Pennsylvania Assembly, February 17, 1775 (*Memoirs of the Life and Writings of Benjamin Franklin*, 1818):

> They who can give up essential liberty to obtain a little temporary safety, deserve neither liberty nor safety.

Ronald Reagan explained to the Students and Faculty at St. John's University in New York, March 28, 1985:

> If we've learned anything, it is that government that is big enough to give you everything you want is more likely to simply take everything you've got. And that's not freedom, that's servitude. That isn't the way Americans were meant to live.

President Woodrow Wilson explained in New York, 1912:

The history of Liberty is a history of limitations of governmental power, not the increase of it. When we resist, therefore, the concentration of power, we are resisting the powers of death, because concentration of power is what always precedes the destruction of human liberties.

Marcus Tullius Cicero (106-43 BC), an ancient Roman scholar, statesman and orator, stated:

When a government becomes powerful it is destructive, extravagant and violent; it is an usurer [a loan shark] which takes bread from innocent mouths and deprives honorable men of their substance, for votes with which to perpetuate itself.

In his 1964 speech, *A Time for Choosing*, Ronald Reagan stated:

I suggest to you there is no left or right, only an up or down. Up to the maximum of individual freedom consistent with law and order, or down to the ant heap of totalitarianism; and regardless of their humanitarian purpose those who would sacrifice freedom for security have, whether they know it or not, chosen this downward path.

As power concentrates, there is an increase of bureaucracy, political intrigue, influence peddling, intimidation, debt, pride, immorality, and suppression of dissent. Jefferson is credited with saying:

My reading of history convinces me that most bad government results from too much government.

༝
POWER TENDS TO CONCENTRATE

Throughout history, the process of concentration has started for many different reasons, in many different situations.

Concentration of power may begin with a need to unite in defense against a common enemy; or to seek economic advantage through efficient divisions of labor (as some people are naturally better at some tasks than others); or the opportunity to prosper by controlling trade routes; or the claim of divine right; or just a despotic lust to control others.

Some monarchs would submit to traditions, customs, laws or constitutions, whereas others ignore them, choosing to act as tyrannical despots, wielding absolute and arbitrary power.

The cycles of civilizations reveal after periods of chaos, power re-concentrates. Human history records that out of disorder and defeat, authoritarian rule, like gravity, inevitably coalesces into the hands of one powerful individual These individuals have been called:

Ajaw, Amir, Archduke, Archon, Autocrat, Baig, Bey, Basileus, Caesar, Caliph, Chairman, Chanyu, Chatrapati, Chief, Chieftain, Commander, Count, Czar, Dauphin, Despot, Dey, Dictator, Doge, Duke, Earl, Emir, Emperor, General Secretary, Grand Mughal, Imperator, Kaiser, Khagan, Khan, King, Lord, Maharajah, Mai, Marquess, Master, Monarch, Nawab, Padishah, Pasha, Pharaoh, Potentate, President, Prime Minister, Prince, Queen, Raja, Regent, Rex, Ruler, Sapa, Satrap, Shah, Sheikh, Shogun, Sovereign, Sultan, Suzerain, Thakur, Tlatoani, Tsar, Tyrant, Viceroy, Vizer, and Wanax.

Regardless of whether one's title is prince or president, if one dictates, they are effectively the dictator. In 732 AD, Charles Martel stopped the Muslim invasion into France. His son, Pepin the Short, the father of Charlemagne, increased Carolingian power over the Merovingian Dynasty.

In 751 AD, Pepin the Short sent a message to Pope Stephen II:

> Who ought to be the king of France—the man who has the title, or the man who has the power?

The World Future Fund Research Project wrote in its article "Totalitarianism, Past Present & Future":

> The term totalitarianism was invented by Mussolini but the philosophy it represents is

actually thousands of years old. The centralization of political power and control of citizens by an authoritarian state are political trends that date back to the dawn of history.

In the ancient world, in both the east and the west, totalitarianism evolved into highly elaborate systems of philosophy, from Plato's views in the "Republic" to the ideas of Lord Shang in ancient China to the very detailed plans for totalitarian rule described by Kautilya in ancient India...

For almost 5,000 years authoritarian rule has been the norm of the human condition...

Authoritarian rule represents the overwhelming majority of world history.

President Harry S Truman commented on the Constitution in his *Memoirs-Volume Two: Years of Trial and Hope:*

> The men who wrote the Constitution...were all well informed on the history of government from Babylon to Britain...They knew that arbitrary and even **tyrannical government had come about where the powers of government were united in the hands of one man**. The system they set up was designed to prevent a demagogue or "a man on horseback" from taking over the powers of government.

George Washington warned in his *Farewell Address*, 1796:

> **Disorders and miseries...gradually incline the minds of men to seek security** and repose **in the absolute power of an Individual**... [who] turns this disposition to the purposes of his own elevation, on the ruins of Public Liberty."

MOST COMMON FORM OF GOVERNMENT - MONARCHY

Columbia Encyclopedia, 6th Edition (Columbia University Press, 2008) gives the definition of "monarchy":

> **Monarchy has existed since the earliest history of humankind** and was often established during periods of external threat or internal crisis because it provided a more efficient focus of power than aristocracy or democracy, which tended to diffuse power.

At the Constitutional Convention in Philadelphia, 1787, Benjamin Franklin addressed the "Dangers of a Salaried Bureaucracy" (*The World's Famous Orations,* America: I:1761–1837, 1906, III):

> There is scarce a king in a hundred who would not, if he could, follow the example of Pharaoh—get first all the people's money, then all their lands, and then make them and their children servants for ever...I am apprehensive that **the government of the States may,** in future times, **end in a monarchy.**

In *The Lessons of History* (NY: Simon and Schuster, 1968), Will and Ariel Durant described monarchy as the "most natural" form of government:

> **Monarchy seems to be the most natural kind of government**...If we were to judge forms of government from their prevalence and duration in history we should have to give the palm to monarchy; democracies, by contrast, have been hectic interludes.

The Oxford Dictionary defines "Monarchy" as:

> A state having a form of government in which the supreme power is vested in a single person...absolute or despotic, a government by the absolute will of the monarch.

The Columbia Encyclopedia, 6th Edition (Columbia University Press, 2008) includes in its definition of "monarchy":

> Monarchy form of government in which sovereignty is vested in a single person whose right to rule is generally hereditary and who is empowered to remain in office for life. The power of this sovereign may vary from the absolute to that strongly limited by custom or constitution.

Franklin D. Roosevelt stated at the Dedication of the Jefferson Memorial in Washington, DC, April 13, 1943:

> Thomas Jefferson believed...that no king, no tyrant, no dictator can govern for them as well as they can govern for themselves.

Lincoln warned in Edwardsville, IL, Sept. 11, 1858:

> You have lost the genius of your own independence and become the fit subjects of the first cunning tyrant who rises among you.

Patrick Henry stated:

> It is when a people forget God, that tyrants forge their chains.

William Penn warned:

> Those who will not be governed by God will be ruled by tyrants.

Harry S Truman stated at Gonzaga University, Spokane, Washington, May 11, 1950:

> The greatest obstacle to peace is a modern tyranny led by a small group who have abandoned their faith in God. These tyrants have forsaken ethical and moral beliefs.

William Henry Harrison stated in his *Inaugural Address*, 1841:

> The danger to all well-established free governments arises from the unwillingness of the people to believe in [the] existence...of designing men.

Eisenhower stated at the Governors' Conference, June 24, 1957:

> Those who would be free must stand eternal watch against **excessive concentration of power in government**...A nation cannot be enslaved by diffused power but only by strong centralized government.

Ronald Reagan stated:

> Concentrated power has always been the enemy of liberty.

President Harrison warned in his *Inaugural Address*, 1841:

> The tendency of power to increase itself, particularly when exercised by a single individual...would terminate in virtual monarchy...**The tendencies of all such governments in their decline is to monarchy**.

George Washington stated in his *Farewell Address*, 1796:

> And of fatal tendency...to put, in the place of the delegated will of the Nation, the will of

a party; - often a small but artful and enterprising minority...

They are likely, in the course of time and things, to become potent engines, by which cunning, ambitious, and unprincipled men will be enabled to subvert the Power of the People and to usurp for themselves the reins of Government; destroying afterwards the very engines which have lifted them to unjust dominion...

This leads at length to a more formal and permanent despotism...

George Washington continued:

A free Country should inspire caution in those entrusted with its administration, to confine themselves within their respective Constitutional spheres; avoiding in the exercise of the Powers of one department to encroach upon another. **The spirit of encroachment tends to consolidate the powers of all the departments in one, and thus to create, whatever the form of government, a real despotism.**

A just estimate of that love of power, and proneness to abuse it, which predominates the human heart is sufficient to satisfy us of the truth of this position...

Real Patriots, who may resist the intrigues...are liable to become suspected and odious; while its tools and dupes usurp the applause and confidence of the people, to surrender their interests.

Eisenhower said at a Governors' Conference, June 24, 1957:

The national government was itself the creature of the States...

Yet today it is often made to appear that the creature, Frankenstein-like, is determined to destroy the creators.

Daniel Webster stated:

Miracles do not cluster, and what has happened once in 6,000 years, may not happen again. Hold on to the Constitution, for if the American Constitution should fail, there will be anarchy throughout the world.

⤸

MONARCHS IN HISTORY

For most of the 6,000 years of recorded human history, power has been held in the hands of a few. Prior to the creation of the United States, most of the world was ruled by monarchs, with just a few significant alternatives to monarchy in all the previous centuries. The "default setting" for human government was monarchy.

In *The Lessons of History* (NY: Simon and Schuster, 1968), Will and Ariel Durant noted:

Power naturally converges to a center...Hence, the centralization of power in the monarchy.

PREHISTORY: 4,000 BC to 3,200 BC, civilizations were mostly rural agricultural settlements as evidenced by artifacts in Mesopotamia, the Indus Valley, Africa, China, England, Peru, and other areas around the world.

During this time, the wheel, plow, and farming implements were invented, as well as weapons, made from stone, copper, then bronze and iron. Boats and the sail were invented.

People gravitated together, forming populations centers for protection and trade.

About 3,200 BC, writing was invented and thus the beginning of record keeping. Perhaps the oldest written story on earth is the Epic of Gilgamesh. It recounts the story of Gilgamesh, the Sumerian King of Uruk, visiting Utnapishtim and his wife, who were survivors of a great flood.

Interestingly, hundreds of ancient civilizations have accounts of an immense flood, including: Babylon, India, China, Sumatra, Wales, Scandinavia, Russia, Peru, Australia, Hawaii and Polynesia.

As cities appeared, governments developed and kings emerged. From this beginning, the pattern was consistent - power concentrated into the hands of an individual, usually during crises, internal instability, external attack, military conquest, or for economic benefit.

Perhaps the first ancient account of power concentrating was in Mesopotamia - the land between the Tigris and Euphrates rivers, known as the fertile crescent. According to the ancient story, a king named Nimrod endeavored to unite everyone to build a tower to reach heaven. This brought judgment from God and their language was confused. As no one could understand what the other was saying, as it sounded like "babel," the place was called "Babylon," and the people scattered.

In preparation for this book, kingdoms, dynasties, caliphates and empires have been examined throughout:

ANCIENT ANTIQUITY 3,200 BC - 750 BC
CLASSICAL ANTIQUITY 750 BC - 500 AD
FALL OF ROME/MIDDLE AGES/RISE OF ISLAM 500-1450
RENAISSANCE/AGE OF DISCOVERY 1450-1600
COLONIALISM/EARLY MODERN ERA 1600-1800
INDUSTRIAL REVOLUTION/MODERN ERA 1800-Present

It is evident that power in the hands of the State led by powerful dictators was the norm - the "default setting" - for human government; and power in the hands of the people was rare. The uniqueness of America's democratically-elected Constitutional Republic can be appreciated from its rare occurrence in history.

❧

MAJOR MONARCHS IN WORLD HISTORY

2500 BC	**Gilgamesh,** Sumerian King of Uruk, Mesopotamia
2500 BC	**Djoser,** Pharaoh of Egypt's 3rd Dynasty, Old Kingdom
2250 BC	**Sargon,** King of the Akkadian Empire (possible Nimrod) LARGEST EMPIRE IN THE WORLD TO THIS DATE, SURPASSING ALL PREVIOUS
2200 BC	**Kutik-Inshushinak,** King of the Old Elamite Dynasty (area of Persia/Iran)
2061 BC	**Nebhepetre Mentuhotep II,** Pharaoh of Egypt's 11th Dynasty, Middle Kingdom
1900 BC	**Bel-kap-kapu,** King of Assyria's Old Kingdom
1878 BC	**Senusret III,** Pharaoh of Egypt's 12th Dynasty, Middle Kingdom
1800 BC	**Yu the Great,** Emperor of China's Xia Dynasty
1690 BC	**Hammurabi,** King of the Babylonian Empire
1650 BC	**Nedjeh,** King of the African Kingdom of Kerma
1556 BC	**Mursilis I,** King of the Old Hittite Kingdom
1508 BC	**Hatshepsut,** Pharaoh of Egypt's 18th Dynasty, New Kingdom, LARGEST EMPIRE IN THE WORLD TO THIS DATE, SURPASSING ALL PREVIOUS
1479 BC	**Thutmose III,** Pharaoh of Egypt's 18th Dynasty, New Kingdom
1450 BC	**Artatama I,** King of the Hurrian Mitanni Empire
1353 BC	**Akhenaten,** Pharaoh, and his wife Nefertiti, of Egypt's 18th Dynasty, New Kingdom
1344 BC	**Suppiluliuma I,** King of the New Hittite Kingdom
1341 BC	**Tutankhamun,** Pharaoh of Egypt's 18th Dynasty, New Kingdom
1279 BC	**Ramesses the Great,** Pharaoh of Egypt's 18th Dynasty, New Kingdom
1285 BC	**Khumbannumena,** King of the Middle Elamite (Persian) Anzanite Dynasty
1265 BC	**Shalmaneser I,** King of the Middle Assyrian Empire

1250 BC	**Wu Ding**, Emperor of China's Shang (Yin) Dynasty LARGEST EMPIRE IN THE WORLD TO THIS DATE, SURPASSING ALL PREVIOUS
1125 BC	**Nebuchadnezzar I**, King of the 2nd Isin Dynasty, Babylonian Empire
1122 BC	**Shang Zhou**, Emperor of China's Shang Dynasty, LARGEST EMPIRE IN THE WORLD TO THIS DATE, SURPASSING ALL PREVIOUS
1080 BC	**Tiglath-Pileser I,** King of the Middle Assyrian Empire
1046 BC	**Wu of Zhao**, Emperor of China's Western Zhou Dynasty, LARGEST EMPIRE IN THE WORLD TO THIS DATE, SURPASSING ALL PREVIOUS
967 BC	**Solomon**, King of Israel
900 BC	**Po Ngbe**, Ruler of the Olmec (Rubber People) of Mesoamerica
764 BC	**Sarduri II,** King of the Urartu Empire (Kingdom of Van) Caucasus Mountains
745 BC	**Tiglath-Pileser III**, King of the Neo-Assyrian Empire, LARGEST EMPIRE IN THE WORLD AT THIS DATE, SURPASSING ALL PREVIOUS
742 BC	**Huban-nugash,** Ruler of the Neo-Elamite Empire
771 BC	**Ping**, Emperor of China's Eastern Zhou Dynasty
690 BC	**Taharqa**, Nubian Pharaoh of Egypt's 25th Dynasty, African Kush (Sudan)
611 BC	**Nebuchadnezzar II,** King of Neo-Babylonian Empire
610 BC	**Necho II**, Pharaoh of Egypt's 26th Dynasty
585 BC	**Cyaxares**, King of the Median Empire, LARGEST EMPIRE IN THE WORLD AT THIS DATE, SURPASSING ALL PREVIOUS
560 BC	**Croesus**, King of the Lydian Empire of Anatolia (world's richest man, issuing the first gold coins)
559 BC	**Cyrus the Great**, King of the Persian Empire
522 BC	**Darius the Great**, King of Kings, Persian Achaemenid Empire, LARGEST EMPIRE IN THE WORLD TO THIS DATE, SURPASSING PREVIOUS

413 BC	**Shishunaga**, King of Northern India's Shishunaga Dynasty of Magadha
400 BC	**Agesilaus II**, King of Sparta, Eurypontid Dynasty
359 BC	**Phillip II**, King of the Macedonian Empire
336 BC	**Alexander the Great**, Macedonian Empire, LARGEST EMPIRE IN THE WORLD AT THIS DATE
332 BC	**Candance of Meroe**, Queen of African Nubian Empire (halted Alexander)
321 BC	**Mahapadma,** Ruler of India's Nanda Dynasty (halted Alexander)
322 BC	**Chandragupta Maurya**, unifier of India, Emperor of Mauryan Empire, LARGEST EMPIRE IN THE WORLD AT THIS DATE
304 BC	**Ptolemy I Soter I,** of Egypt's Ptolemaic Dynasty (Alexander's General)
301 BC	**Seleucus I Nicator**, Ruler of the Seleucid Persian Empire (Alexander's General)
301 BC	**Lysimachus,** Thrace, Asia Minor (Alexander's General)
301 BC	**Cassander**, Ruler of Macedonia and Greece (Alexander's General)
297 BC	**Pyrrhus,** Ruler of the Epirus and Macedon Kingdoms
269 BC	**Ashoka**, one of India's greatest Emperors, Maurya Dynasty
222 BC	**Antiochus III the Great,** Seleucid Persian Empire
221 BC	**Qin Shi Huang**, First Emperor of a unified China, Qin Dynasty
221 BC	**Hannibal** of the North African Carthage (Phoenician) Empire
209 BC	**Modu Chanyu**, Majesty Son of Heaven, Central Asia Xiongnu Tribal Empire
206 BC	**Xiang Yu**, King of China's Western Chu Dynasty
206 BC	**Gaozu**, Emperor of China's Han Dynasty
171 BC	**Mithridates I,** Great King of Parthian Arsacid Empire
160 BC	**Menander I**, Northern India's Indo-Greek Kingdom
150 BC	**Bhagabhadra,** of India's Sunga Empire of Magadha

141 BC	**Wu,** Emperor of China's Han Dynasty, one of China's greatest emperors
100 BC	**Maues,** Ruler of the India-Scythian Saka Kingdom
83 BC	**Artaxias,** Ruler of the Armenian Empire
50 BC	**Dhanadeva,** Ruler of India's Kosala Dynasty
44 BC	**Julius Caesar,** Dictator of the Roman Republic
37 BC	**Herod the Great,** King of Judea
30 BC	**Cleopatra VII,** last Pharaoh, Egypt's Ptolemaic Dynasty
27 BC	**Caesar Augustus,** Emperor of the Roman Empire
20 BC	**Gondophares I,** Ruler of the Indo-Parthian Kingdom
10 BC	**Kharavela,** of India's Maha-Meghavahana Dynasty
1 AD	**Heraios,** Yuezhi Chief, Central Asia and Northern India's Kushan Empire
10 AD	**Wang Mang,** Emperor of China's Xin Dynasty
54 AD	**Nero,** Emperor of the Roman Empire
75 AD	**Zhang,** Emperor of China's Han Dynasty
78 AD	**Gautamiputra Satakarni,** India's Satavahana Dynasty
98 AD	**Trajan,** Emperor of the Roman Empire
100 AD	**Kanishka** of the Buddhist Kushan Empire of India
117 AD	**Hadrian,** Emperor, Roman Empire, LARGEST EMPIRE IN THE WORLD AT THIS DATE
130 AD	**Kharapallana,** Great Satrap of Northern Indo-Scythian area of Mathura
161 AD	**Marcus Aurelius,** Emperor of the Roman Empire
184 AD	**Diodotus,** Emperor of Central Asia's Bactrian Empire
221 AD	**Sun Quan,** Emperor of China's Wu Dynasty
221 AD	**Liu Bei,** Emperor of China's Shu Dynasty
263 AD	**Wen,** Emperor of China's Wei Dynasty
270 AD	**Pravarasena I,** Emperor of India's Vakataka Kingdom
297 AD	**Nobatae,** King of Lower Nubia's Christian African Nobatia Kingdom
300 AD	**Sima Yan,** Emperor of China's Western Jin Dynasty
306 AD	**Constantine the Great,** Emperor, Roman Empire
316 AD	**Liu Yao,** Emperor of China's Earlier Zhao Dynasty
329 AD	**Shi Le,** Emperor of China's Later Zhao Dynasty

330 AD	**Ezana** of Northeast Africa's Christian Asksumite (Ethiopian) Empire
347 AD	**Yuan,** Emperor of China's Eastern Jin Dynasty
350 AD	**Kaja Maja,** King of Ghana's Awkar Kingdom
358 AD	**Chak Tok Ich'aak,** Great Jaguar Paw, of the Mayan Tikal Kingdom
375 AD	**Chandragupta II the Great** of the Gupta Empire, India's Golden Age
376 AD	**Fu Jian,** Heavenly Prince, China's Former Qin Dynasty
379 AD	**Theodosius I the Great,** Roman Valetianian-Theodosian Dynasty (last ruler of east and west Empire)
395 AD	**Alaric I,** of the Visigothic Kingdom, first to sack Rome
400 AD	**Yusuf Asar Yathar,** King of Yemen's Jewish Himyarite Kingdom
405 AD	**Yujiulü Shelun,** of the Mongolian Rouran (Jwen-Jwen) Khaganate
415 AD	**Merovech,** Europe's Frankish Merovingian Dynasty
420 AD	**Liu Yu,** Emperor of China's Liu Song Dynasty
428 AD	**Genseric,** King of the Arian Vandals, (sacked Rome)
429 AD	**Atlatl Cauac** "Spearthrower Owl" of the Mayan Teotihuacan Empire
434 AD	**Attila the Hun,** "Scourge of God," King of the Hunnic Empire
450 AD	**Xiaowen,** Emperor of China's Northern Wei Dynasty
451 AD	**Ardaric,** Ruler of the Eastern European Gepid Kingdom (defeated Attila's sons)
452 AD	**Bayan I,** Khagan of the Central Asian Nomadic Avar Kingdom
471 AD	**Theodoric the Great** of the Ostrogothic Kingdom
476 AD	**Gwanggaeto the Great,** Korean Goguryeo Kingdom
481 AD	**Clovis I,** Christian Frankish Merovingian Dynasty
490 AD	**Khan Ruler** of Hepthalite (White Hun) Khanate of Central-North India
502 AD	**Wu of Liang** of China's Southern Qi Dynasty
508 AD	**Knot-eye Jaguar** "Fish-Fin," King of Bonampak, Mayan Yaxchilan, Chiapas

529 AD	**Durvinita** of India's Western of India's Western Ganga Dynasty
534 AD	**Xiaojing**, Emperor of China's Eastern Wei Dynasty
535 AD	**Yuan Baoju,** Emperor of China's Western Wei Dynasty
550 AD	**Wenxuan,** Emperor of China's Northern Qi Dynasty
550 AD	**Ishana Varman,** Southeast Asia's Maukhari Dynasty
551 AD	**Bumin Qaghan** of Central Asia's Goturk Khagnate
555 AD	**Xuan**, Emperor of China's Liang Dynasty
555 AD	**Justinian the Great,** Emperor of the Eastern Roman (Byzantine) Empire
577 AD	**Wu**, Emperor of China's Northern Zhou Dynasty
581 AD	**Wen**, Emperor of China's Sui Dynasty
581 AD	**Ishbara Qaghan** of Eastern Turkic Khaganate (north of India & China)
597 AD	**Pulakesi II** of South India's Chalukya Dynasty
606 AD	**Harsha Vardhana** of North India's Harsha Pusyabhutis Empire
615 AD	**Ajaw (King) K'inich Janaab' Pakal**, the Great, of the Mayan Empire
618 AD	**Tong Yabghu Qaghan** of Central Asia's Western Turkic Khaganate
620 AD	**Ardashir Shahanshah** of Persia's Sassanid Empire
626 AD	**Taizong**, Emperor of China's Tang Empire, one of China's greatest emperors, during a golden age of Chinese culture (Emperor Taizong had Syrian Christian Scriptures translated and built a monastery.)
629 AD	**Songtsän Gampo** of Tibet's Tufan Empire
631 AD	**Rai Sahasi II** of India's Sindh Dynasty
632 AD	**Mohammed** and **Rightly Guided Caliphs** of the Rashidun Islamic Caliphate
665 AD	**Wu Zetian,** Empress of China's Second Zhou Dynasty
697 AD	**Merkurios,** Africa's Christian Nubian Makuria Kingdom
705 AD	**Al-Walid** of the Umayyad Islamic Caliphate, 9TH LARGEST EMPIRE IN WORLD HISTORY, SURPASSING ALL PREVIOUS

724 AD	**Lalitaditya Muktapida,** Kayastha Emperor of Kashmir's Karkota Dynasty
732 AD	**Sañjaya** of Java's Sañjaya Dynasty Kingdom of Medang
734 AD	**Yik'in Chan K'awiil** of Mesoamerica's Mayan Empire
750 AD	**As-Saffah,** Caliph of the Abbasid Islamic Caliphate
759 AD	**Tengri Bögü** of the Mongolian Uyghur Khaganate of Central Asia
770 AD	**Devapala,** Emperor of India's Pala Bengal Empire
775 AD	**Dharmasetu,** Maharaja of Indonesia's Sumatra Srivijaya Malay Empire
800 AD	**Charlemagne,** Emperor of Europe's Francia Carolingian Dynasty
802 AD	**Jayavarman II** of Cambodia's Khmer Empire
805 AD	**Idris II** of Morocco's Idrisid Islamic Dynasty
814 AD	**Amoghavarsha I** of India's Rashtrakuta Dynasty
818 AD	**Seon,** King of Korea's Balhae Kingdom
820 AD	**Michael II** the Amorian, of the Byzantine Empire's Phrygian Dynasty
828 AD	**Abdullah ibn Tahir,** Persia's Tahirid Islamic Dynasty
830 AD	**Khun Borom Rachathirath "Piluoge"** of South China's Nanzhao Kingdom
836 AD	**Mihir Bhoja I the Great,** India's Gurjara Pratihara Dynasty
861 AD	**Bulan,** Great Khagan of Southern Russia's Jewish Khazar Khaganate
867 AD	**Ya'qub bin Laith as-Saffar,** Emir of Persia's Saffarid Islamic Dynasty
867 AD	**Basil I the Macedonian** of the Byzantine (Armenian) Empire
868 AD	**Ahmad ibn Tulun** of Egypt's Tulunid Islamic Emirate
892 AD	**Ismail Samani,** Amir of the Greater Khorasan Samanid Islamic Dynasty
893 AD	**Simeon I the Great,** Slavic European Bulgarian Empire
907 AD	**Zhu Wen,** Emperor of China's Later Liang Dynasty
912 AD	**Abd-ar-Rahman III** of the Umayyad Caliphate of Cordoba Al-Andalus

916 AD	**Yelü Abaoji,** Emperor of China's Liao (Khitan "Cathay") Dynasty
922 AD	**Almas,** Emir of the Volga Bulgar Islamic Khanate
923 AD	**Li Cunxu,** Emperor, China's Later Restored Tang Dynasty
936 AD	**Shi Jingtang,** Emperor of China's Later Jin Dynasty
936 AD	**Otto I the Great,** Emperor, Europe's Holy Roman Empire
941 AD	**Marzuban ibn Muhammad,** Azerbaijan Sallarid Dynasty
947 AD	**Liu Zhiyuan,** Emperor of China's Later Han Dynasty
960 AD	**Taizu,** Emperor of China's Song Dynasty
969 AD	**Abdullah al-Mahd Billah,** Fatimid Islamic Caliphate
977 AD	**Sebuktigin** of Persia's Ghaznavid Empire
980 AD	**Vladimir I** the Great of Russia's Kievan Empire
985 AD	**Chola I,** Raja Raja the Great of India's Chola Empire
987 AD	**Topiltzin Ce Acatl Quetzalcoatl** of the Nahuatl Toltec Empire
1000 AD	**Bhoj,** Raja of Central India's Kingdom of Malwa, Paramara Dynasty
1025 AD	**Mahmoud Tamgach** of Kashgar, Central Asia's Kara-Khanid Khanate
1029 AD	**Alp Arslan,** Sultan of the Great Seljuk Islamic Dynasty
1038 AD	**Li Yuanhao,** China's Western Xia (Tangut) Dynasty
1041 AD	**Laksm Karna,** Central India's Kalachuri Dynasty of Tripuri
1044 AD	**Anawrahta,** King of Burma's Pagan Kingdom
1057 AD	**Robert Guiscard,** Norman Duke of Apulia and Calabria, Italy and Sicily
1063 AD	**Eight Deer Jaguar Claw,** King of Oaxaca's Mixtec Kingdom
1066 AD	**William the Conqueror,** Norman Ruler,Saxon England
1076 AD	**Vikramaditya VI,** India's Western Chalukya Empire
1087 AD	**Kambine Diaresso,** Ghana (King) of Western Sahara's Wagadou Kingdom

1096 AD	**Duan Zhengchun,** Western China's Kingdom of Dali
1100 AD	**Tu'itatui** of Polynesia's Tu'i Tonga Empire
1108 AD	**Louis VI** of France's Capetian Dynasty
1124 AD	**Yelu Dashi** of Central Asia's Kara-Khitan (Western Liao) Khanate
1130 AD	**Bijjala II**, Mahamandalesvara of India's Kalachuri Empire
1130 AD	**Abd al-Mu'min al Kumi**, Emir of Marrakesh, Almohad Berber Dynasty
1147 AD	**Abdallah ibn Yasin,** Almoravid Islamic Dynasty
1152 AD	**Frederick I Barbarossa**, Emperor of Europe's Holy Roman Empire
1152 AD	**Narasimha I** of South India's Hoysala Empire
1161 AD	**Shizong**, Emperor, North China's Jurchen Jin Dynasty
1162 AD	**Shahabuddin Muhammad Ghauri** of Afghanistan and India's Ghorid Sultanate
1174 AD	**Saladin**, Sultan of the Ayyubid Islamic Dynasty of Egypt and Syria
1194 AD	**Baldwin IX** of the Fourth Crusade, of the Latin Byzantine Empire
1200 AD	**Singhana II** of India's Yadava (Gauli) Kingdom
1200 AD	**Ala ad-Din Muhammad II**, Shah of Persia's Khwarezmid Empire
1206 AD	**Genghis Khan** of the Mongolian Empire, 2ND LARGEST EMPIRE IN WORLD HISTORY, SURPASSING ALL PREVIOUS
1206 AD	**Anangabhima III** of India's Eastern Ganga Dynasty
1221 AD	**Dunama Dabbalemi**, Mai (King) of South Libya's Kanem Sayfawa Dynasty
1224 AD	**Lizong**, Emperor, China's Southern Song Dynasty
1227 AD	**Chagatai Khan,** Central Asia's Mongolian Chagatai Khanate
1230 AD	**Mari Djata,** Mansa of West Africa's Mali Empire
1241 AD	**Shayban** of Central Asia's Shaybanid Uzbek Dynasty
1250 AD	**Jatavarman Sundara Pandyan** of South India's Pandyan Dynasty

1250 AD	**Paramount** Chief of America's Mississippian Cahokia Indians
1250 AD	**Aybak**, Emir of Egypt's Bahriya Mamluk Sultanate
1256 AD	**Sartaq**, Christian Khan of the Golden Horde, Kipchak Khanate
1256 AD	**Hulagu Khan** of Persia's Mongolian Ilkhanate
1259 AD	**Michael VIII**, Emperor, Byzantine Palaiologos Empire
1294 AD	**Kublai Khan**, Mongol Emperor,China's Yuan Dynasty, 8TH LARGEST EMPIRE IN WORLD HISTORY (His request via Marco Polo's father and uncle for the Pope to send 100 Christian teachers went unanswered.)
1296 AD	**Alauddin Khilji,** North India's Deli Sultanate of Khilji
1299 AD	**Osman I**, Sultan of the Ottoman Empire
1320 AD	**Ghiyath al-Din Tughluq** of North India's Turkic Muslim Tughlag Dynasty
1346 AD	**Stefan Dušan**, Tsar of Serbian Empire
1347 AD	**Aladdin Hassan Bahman** Shah of India's Bahmani Islamic Sultanate
1350 AD	**Hayam Wuruk**, Rajasanagara of Indonesia's Majapahit Empire
1356 AD	**Bukka Raya I**, Emperor of India's Vijayanagara Empire, Sangama Dynasty
1368 AD	**Hongwu**, Emperor of China's Ming Dynasty
1370 AD	**Nacen-pinco**, king of South America's Andean Chimú Kingdom
1370 AD	**Timur (Tamerlane) the Great** of Central Asia's Timurid Islamic Dynasty
1375 AD	**Margaret**, Queen of Denmark and the Scandinavian Kalmar Union
1382 AD	**Barkuk**, Sultan of Egypt's Mamluk Burjiyya Dynasty
1392 AD	**Taejo Yi Seong-gye**, Emperor of Korea's Great Joseon Dynasty
1400 AD	**Tokosra of Kosraean, Pacific Micronesia Kingdom**
1419 AD	**Olugh Mokhammad**, Khan of Central Asia's Tatar Kazan Islamic Khanate

1424 AD	**Zhu Di,** Emperor of China's Ming Dynasty, his treasure ships sailed world, 1421-1423
1448 AD	**Vlad III Tepes,** The Impaler, of Romania
1449 AD	**Hajji Giray** of Crimea's Tatar Islamic Khanate
1450 AD	**K'iq'ab,** Mayan K'iche' Kingdom, Q'umarkaj, Guatemala
1451 AD	**Mehmet II** Conqueror, Sultan of the Ottoman Empire
1462 AD	**Ivan the Great of Moscow,** Grand Prince of all Rus
1469 AD	**Ferdinand and Isabella,** united Spanish Empire
1470 AD	**Lorenzo the Magnificent,** Florence's ruling Medici Family
1479 AD	**Batumöngke Dayan Khan,** Great Khan of the Yuan Mongol Empire
1490 AD	**Taibuga,** Khan, Siberia's Tatar Turkic Siber Khanate
1493 AD	**Askia the Great,** Soninke Emperor of West Africa's Songhai Empire
1493 AD	**Huayna Capac,** Sapa of South America's Andean Cozco Incan Empire
1502 AD	**Montezuma II,** Tlatoani Ruler, Mexico's Aztec Empire
1509 AD	**Henry VIII** of England's Tudor Dynasty
1509 AD	**Sri Krishna Deva Raya,** Raja of South India's Vijayanagara Empire
1517 AD	**Ibrahim Lodi,** Afghan Sultan of India's Lodi Dynasty, Delhi Sultanate
1519 AD	**King Charles V** of Spain, Emperor of Europe's Holy Roman Emperor, LARGEST EMPIRE IN THE WORLD AT THIS DATE
1521 AD	**Atahuallpa,** Emperor, South America's Incan Empire
1526 AD	**Babur,** Emperor of India's Mughal Islamic Empire
1529 AD	**Cosijopii I,** King, Mesoamerica's Zapotec Kingdom
1533 AD	**Ivan IV,** Grand Prince of Moscow, Tsar of all Russia
1540 AD	**Sher,** Pashtun (Afghan) Shah of North India's Suri Delhi Sultanate
1544 AD	**William I,** House of Orange, United Province of the Netherlands

1547 AD	**Catherine de Medici,** Queen of France
1558 AD	**Elizabeth I**, Queen of England, House of Tudor
1587 AD	**Abbas I**, Shah of Persia's Safavid Islamic Dynasty
1566 AD	**Suleiman the Magnificent,** Sultan, Ottoman Empire, 6TH LARGEST EMPIRE IN WORLD HISTORY
1588 AD	**Christian IV**, King of Denmark and the Danish Colonial Empire
1603 AD	**James I** of England's House of Tudor & Scotland's House of Stuart
1610 AD	**Louis XIII**, King of France and the First French Colonial Empire
1611 AD	**Gustav II Adolphus** of the Swedish Empire during Sweden's Golden Age
1627 AD	**Shah Jahan,** India's Mughal Empire in its Golden Age
1642 AD	**Shivaji Bhosle**, Chatrapati of India's Hindu Maratha Empire
1643 AD	**Louis XIV** "Sun King", France's Bourbon Dynasty, longest, most powerful reign of any European monarch
1644 AD	**Kangxi**, Emperor of China's Qing Manchu Dynasty
1674 AD	**Jon Sobieski**, Lion of Lehistan, King of Poland-Lithuania
1682 AD	**Peter I the Great** of the Russia's Romanov Dynasty
1720 AD	**Mir Qamar-ud-Din Siddiqi**, Nizam ul-mulk of India's Hyderabad State
1736 AD	**Nader,** Shah of Persia's Afsharid Islamic Dynasty
1740 AD	**Maria Theresa,** Habsburg Empress, Austro-Hungarian Dynasty
1740 AD	**Frederick II the Great,** German Prussian Empire
1752 AD	**Alaungpaya**, King of Burma's Konbaung Dynasty
1759 AD	**Charles III**, Bourbon King of the Spanish Empire, 5TH LARGEST EMPIRE IN WORLD HISTORY
1762 AD	**Catherine the Great** of Russia's Romanov Dynasty
1782 AD	**Rama I**, Great King of the Thai (Siam) Empire, Chakri Dynasty

1793 AD	**Maximilien Robespierre**, President of the French Convention
1794 AD	**Mohammad Khan**, Shahanshah (King of Kings) of Persia's Qajar Dynasty
1795 AD	**Qianlong**, Emperor, Manchu Qing Dynasty of China, 7TH LARGEST EMPIRE IN WORLD HISTORY
1801 AD	**Ranjit Singh**, Majaraja of Punjab's Sikh Empire
1802 AD	**Malietoa Savea**, King of the Pacific Somoan Empire
1804 AD	**Napoleon Bonaparte I**, Emperor, French Empire
1810 AD	**Kamehameha I the Great**, Kingdom of Hawaii
1812 AD	**Shaka**, Warrior King of Africa's Zulu State
1816 AD	**John VI**, King of the Portugese Empire
1822 AD	**Agustín de Iturbide**, Emperor, First Mexican Empire
1822 AD	**Pedro I**, Emperor-King of Portugal and Brazil
1837 AD	**Victoria I**, Queen of the British Empire, ONE OF THE LARGEST EMPIRES IN HISTORY
1848 AD	**Franz Joseph I**, Emperor of Austria, Bohemia, Croatia and Hungary
1848 AD	**Napoleon III** of the Second French Colonial Empire, 10TH LARGEST EMPIRE IN WORLD HISTORY
1865 AD	**Leopold II** of Belgium and the African Congo
1867 AD	**Meiji (Mutsuhito)**, Emperor, Empire of Japan
1870 AD	**Victor Emanuel**, King of united Italy
1888 AD	**Wilhem II**, Kaiser of Germany and Prussia
1895 AD	**Nicholas II,** Czar of the Russian Empire (3RD LARGEST EMPIRE IN WORLD HISTORY
1911 AD	**Osman Ali**, Nizam of India's Hyderabad State (world's richest man)
1917 AD	**Vladimir Lenin,** Communist Dictator of Bolshevik Revolution, Soviet Russia
1922 AD	**George V**, British Empire, LARGEST EMPIRE IN WORLD HISTORY, SURPASSING ALL OTHERS
1922 AD	**Benito Mussolini**, Fascist Dictator of Italy's Socialist State
1922 AD	**Josef Stalin** of the United Soviet Socialist Republic

1926 AD	**Hirohito (Showa)**, Emperor of the Empire of Japan
1928 AD	**Chiang Kai-shek**, Generalissimo of Nationalist China
1933 AD	**Adolph Hitler**, Führer of Germany's National Socialist Workers Party
1939 AD	**Francisco Franco**, Nationalist Dictator of Spain
1943 AD	**Mao Zedong**, Communist Dictator of China
1945 AD	**Ho Chi Min**, Communist Dictator of Vietnam
1946 AD	**Juan Peron**, Dictator President of Argentina
1947 AD	**Kim Il-Sung**, Communist Dictator of North Korea
1953 AD	**Josip Broz Tito**, Communist Dictator of Yugoslavia
1957 AD	**François "Papa Doc" Duvalier,** Dictator of Haiti
1959 AD	**Fidel Castro**, Communist Dictator of Cuba
1963 AD	**Pol Pot,** Communist Dictator, Cambodia Khmer Rouge
1964 AD	**Leonid Breshnev**, Communist Dictator, United Soviet Socialist Republic, 4TH LARGEST EMPIRE IN WORLD HISTORY
1965 AD	**Nicolae Ceausescu,** Communist Dictator of Romania
1971 AD	**Idi Amin**, Military Dictator of Uganda
1974 AD	**Augusto Pinochet**, Dictator of Chile
1979 AD	**Saddam Hussein**, Dictator of Iraq
1979 AD	**Ayatollah Khomeini**, Supreme Islamic Leader, Iran
1994 AD	**Kim Jong-Il**, Communist Dictator of North Korea

ᐓ

MONARCHS CLAIM DIVINE SUPERIORITY

From Roman Emperors, Norman Conquerors, Germanic Kings, African Tribal Chiefs, Byzantine Emperors, Indian Maharajas, Mongolian Khans, Ottoman Sultans, Holy Roman Emperors, to Chinese Emperors, the default setting for human government is power concentrating in the hands of one individual.

Isaac Newton's Law of Gravity, (Principia, 1687) states that objects of a lesser mass are attracted to objects of a larger mass. In the same way, people are attracted to individuals with power.

Like an invisible force, power is drawn into the hands of fewer and fewer individuals, until ultimately, absolute power is held by one.

Anyone who has built a snowman understands the momentum of accumulation. It begins with one individual snowball, and as it is rolled in the snow, more snow sticks to it. The bigger the snowball gets, the more snow sticks to it, till it becomes very large.

Historically, kings have repeatedly used a common claim to confirm their complete control.

Studies reveal consistent themes in ancient civilizations:

1) the observing of movements of the stars in the heavens, such as at England's Stonehenge, Mississippian's Woodhenge, Mayan's Calendar, Chinese and Persian astronomers;

2) the building of pyramid type structures to reach the heavens, such as Sumerian ziggurats, Egyptian pyramids, Aztec temples and Cahokia Indian mounds; and

3) a kingly mediator with heaven, who ascended the pyramid temples and, to appease the offended deities, sacrificed humans on behalf of the State. The king used his position as "divine go-between" to validate his totalitarian rule – beginning a worship of the State.

The "king-priests" of Babylon, Egypt and Assyria transitioned into Plato's "philosopher-king" in classical Greece; Rome's imperial cult of deified "August" Caesars; Chinese Emperors with a "mandate from heaven"; Inca Emperors being "delegate of the Sun god"; Islam's Mohammed being "prophet of Allah"; Indian Rajas worshipped as semi-divine; Medieval Europe's "divine right of kings"; French Revolution's Robespierre and "the cult the goddess of Reason"; and the Communist idea of Hegel, "the State is god walking on earth."

An example that cannot be overlooked is that of Moses and Ten Commandments, and Israel's divinely anointed kings. Though similar in some respects, there are substantial differences between this and other examples, as the Hebrew Law required the king to obey the same law as the commoner, and kings were consistently rebuked by prophets if they tried to place themselves above the law:

> And it shall be, when he sitteth upon the throne of his kingdom, that he shall write him a copy of this law in a book out of that which is before the priests, the Levites...and he shall read therein all the days of his life: that he may learn to fear the LORD his God, to keep all the words of this law and these statutes, to do them: **That his heart be not lifted up above his brethren**. (Deut. 17:18)

Rather than elevate the monarch, as other examples did, Hebrew Law established an equality where the king, the wealthy, the commoner and the stranger were treated the same:

> Judge righteously between every man and his brother, and the stranger that is with him.
> Ye shall not respect persons in judgment; but ye shall hear the small as well as the great; ye shall not be afraid of the face of man; for the judgment is God's. (Deut. 1:16-17);

> One ordinance shall be both for you of the congregation, and also for the stranger that sojourneth with you, an ordinance for ever in your generations: as ye are, so shall the stranger be before the LORD. One law and one manner shall be for you, and for the stranger that sojourneth with you. (Num. 15:15-16).

HISTORY OF THE
DIVINE RIGHT OF KINGS

Monarchs claimed their status as the chosen intermediary between the people and the divinity legitimized their authoritarian rule.

Such were: Gilgamesh, Nimrod, Sargon, Hammurabi, Egyptian Pharaohs, Chinese Emperors, Roman Emperors, Central Asian Xiongnu Rulers, Byzantine Emperors, Japanese Emperors, Indian Rajas, Muslim Caliphs, and Aztec Mexico's Montezuma with temples of human sacrifice to the Sun, some of whom referred to themselves as "heavenly prince," "majesty son of heaven," or "descendant of a god or goddess."

Medieval Age European monarchs claimed a "divine right of kings" with titles such as "by the grace of God" and "defender of the faith." Their reasoning went, that since it was God's will for them to be king, whatever they will must be God's will.

The Columbia Encyclopedia, 6th Edition (Columbia University Press, 2008) includes in its definition of "monarchy":

> Most monarchies appear to have been elective originally, but dynasties early became customary. In primitive times, divine descent of the monarch was often claimed. Deification was general in ancient Egypt, the Middle East, and Asia, and it was also practiced during certain periods in ancient Greece and Rome.
>
> A more moderate belief arose in Christian Europe in the Middle Ages; it stated that the monarch was the appointed agent of divine will. This was symbolized by the coronation of the king by a bishop or the pope, as in the Holy Roman Empire...

During the Renaissance and after, there emerged "new monarchs" who broke the power of the nobility and centralized the state under their own rigid rule. Notable examples are Henry VII and Henry VIII of England and Louis XIV of France. The 16th and 17th centuries mark the height of absolute monarchy, which found its theoretical justification in the doctrine of divine right.

Karl Marx, in his *Critique of Hegel's Philosophy of Right* (1843), agreed with Georg Wilhelm Friedrich Hegel that monarchy was the supreme form of government:

> In the Crown, the different powers are bound into an individual unity which is thus at once the apex and basis of the whole...
>
> This absolutely decisive moment of the whole is not individuality in general, but a single individual, the monarch...
>
> What is important to Hegel is representing the monarch as the actual, 'God-man', the actual incarnation of the Idea...Hegel concludes: 'The personality of the state is actual only as one person, the monarch.'

Jesus advanced the concept that a person's identity is as **"an individual,"** in contrast to the collectivist idea that a person's identity is as **"a unit of the State."**

Since Jesus was not an earthly political/military leader, the question is, how did Christian monarchs of the Byzantine Empire and Medieval & Renaissance Europe adopt the concept of "the divine right of kings"? Jesus' statements regarding "the Kingdom of God" were in stark contrast to a totalitarian State ruled by a powerful and wealthy "enlightened" monarch.

Matt 20:25-27 Ye know that **the princes of the Gentiles exercise dominion over them, and they that are great exercise authority upon them.** But it shall not be so among you: but whosoever will be great among you, let him be your minister; And **whosoever will be chief among you, let him be your servant.**

Mark 10:23-25 How hardly shall they that have riches enter into the **kingdom of God!** And the disciples were astonished at his words. But Jesus answereth again...Children, how hard is it for them that trust in riches to enter into the **kingdom of God! It is easier for a camel to go through the eye of a needle, than for a rich man to enter into the kingdom of God**.

Luke 17:21 The kingdom of God cometh not with observation: Neither shall they say, Lo here! or, lo there! for, behold, **the kingdom of God is within you.**

Luke 6:20 And he lifted up his eyes on his disciples, and said, **Blessed be ye poor: for yours is the kingdom of God**.

Mark 10:14-15 Suffer the little children to come unto me, and forbid them not, for of such is the **kingdom of God.** Verily I say unto you, **Whosoever shall not receive the kingdom of God as a little child, he shall not enter therein."**

Luke 9:1-2 Then he called his twelve disciples together, and gave them power and authority over all devils, and to cure diseases. And he sent them to **preach the kingdom of God**, and to heal the sick.

Matthew 21:31-32 Verily I say unto you, That the publicans and the harlots go into **the kingdom of God** before you.

Mark 11:31-34 And the scribe said unto him, Well, Master, thou hast said the truth: for there is one God; and there is none other but he: And to love him with all the heart, and with all the understanding, and with all the soul, and with all the strength, and to love his neighbor as himself, is more than all whole burnt offerings and sacrifices. And when Jesus saw that he answered discreetly, he said unto him, **Thou art not far from the kingdom of God.**

John 18:33-37 Jesus answered, **My kingdom is not of this world:** if **my kingdom** were of this world, then would my servants fight, that I should not be delivered to the Jewish leaders but now is **my kingdom not from hence.**

Luke 12:29-31 Seek not ye what ye shall eat, or what ye shall drink...For all these things do the nations of the world seek after: and your Father knoweth that ye have need of these things. But rather **seek ye the kingdom of God;** and all these things shall be added unto you.

John 3:1-5 Nicodemus, a ruler of the Jews: The same came to Jesus by night, and said unto him, Rabbi, we know that thou art a teacher come from God: for no man can do these miracles that thou doest, except God be with him. Jesus answered and said unto him, Verily, verily, I say unto thee, **Except a man be born again, he cannot see the kingdom of God.**

In the first three centuries, Christians made no effort to change the political structure of Roman government, similar to Jews of the dispora who were scattered in countries around the world after Jerusalem was destroyed in 70 AD. They refused to get involved in their host country's politics, a decision which was unfortunately interpreted as being disloyal, resulting in suspicion, contempt, and often terrible persecutions by all political parties.

In the first three centuries, thousands of Christians were killed in 11 major persecutions:

Nero 64-68 AD
Domitian 89-96 AD
Trajan 109-117 AD
Marcus Aurelius 161-180 AD
Septimius Severus 193-211 AD
Maximinus the Thracian 235-238 AD
Decius 249-251 AD
Valerian 253-260 AD
Diocletian 285-305 AD
Galerius 305-313 AD
Julian the Apostate 361-363 AD

Christians were tied to poles and burned as Nero's torches, sewn into animal skins and fed to lions, or killed by gladiators in Rome's Coliseum. Despite all this, Christianity continued to spread, as the hedonistic, sensual Romans were impressed by the Christians' love, charity and willingness to die for their unseen God.

Roman Emperors claimed to be gods, sprinkled gold dust in their hair and demanded their image be worshipped. When Christians refused to burn incense to the Roman Emperors, they were considered unpatriotic and enemies of the State.

Reminiscent of today's marriage controversy, Emperor Claudius II allegedly banned marriage among his legions, as he thought single soldiers fought better. This was followed by Emperor Diocletian, who first purged the Roman military of all Christians, similar to the possible fallout of the current repeal of "Don't Ask Don't Tell."

Diocletian then surrounded himself with enemies of Christianity, and was reputed to have erected a memorial to the extermination of Christianity. He then went systematically, province by province, burning scriptures, and arresting and killing church leaders.

The prayers of the persecuted were seemingly heard, as Diocletian abdicated the throne, May 1, 305 AD, as a result of a painful intestinal illness. When the next Emperor, Galerius, died suddenly, there was a fight among the Roman Generals: Licinius, Maximinus (and his son, Maxentius), and Constantine, over who should be the next Emperor.

It came down to the Battle of the Milvian Bridge between Constantine and Maxentius. On October 28, 312 AD, the day before the battle, something happened. Constantine claimed to have seen the sign of Christ in the sky with the words, translated into Latin, "in hoc signo vinces," (in this sign you shall win.) Constantine put this sign on his flags and standards, and went on to win the battle. This sign was the first two letters of the name of Christ, "X-P," called in Greek the Chi-Rho, or as it was shortened in the Middle Ages to just "X," the "Christ's Cross" or "Criss-Cross."

In 313 AD, Emperor Constantine issued the Edict of Milan, ending the persecution of Christians.

Shortly thereafter, Arius began the Arian Heresy, a doctrinal division which split not only the Church, but also the Roman Empire. In response, Constantine ordered all the Bishops to Nicea in 325 AD to settle the controversy, which they did by writing the Nicene Creed.

In 380 AD, Emperor Theodosius made Christianity the official religion in the Roman Empire, and by the 390's, Theodosius outlawed paganism, temple prostitutes, human sacrifice, divination, and ended the Olympic Games.

As more heresies arose, the Roman government took an increased role in maintaining doctrinal unity, edging into the arena of governing individual rights of conscience.

By 563 AD, Emperor Justinian was acting, in effect, as the head of the Church as well as the head of the State. Justinian compiled the "Justinian Code" of laws and rebuilt the Hagia Sophia Church in

Constantinople, the largest church in Christendom for nearly a thousand years, till Sultan Mehmet II turned it into a mosque in 1453.

The Christian Roman Emperor Justinian was the significant example of "the divine right of kings," whom Europe's monarchs held in high esteem as an exemplary ruler.

KINGS SIT UPON GOD'S THRONE?

King James I of England (1603-1625) considered himself above the law and defended the divine rights of kings.

King James I stated to Parliament, 1609-1610 (*Select Statutes & Other Constitutional Documents Illustrative of the Reigns of Elizabeth and James I*, 3rd ed., G.W. Prothero, Oxford; Clarendon Press, 1906, pp. 400-401, 293-294; James Harvey Robinson, *Readings in European History,* 2 vols, Boston: Ginn & Co., 1906, 219-220):

> The state of monarchy is the supremest thing upon earth, for **kings are not only God's lieutenants upon earth and sit upon God's throne**, but even by God himself they are called gods.
>
> There be three principal [comparisons] that illustrate the state of monarchy: one taken out of the word of God, and the two other out of the grounds of policy and philosophy.
>
> In the Scriptures kings are called gods, and so their power after a certain relation compared to the Divine power. Kings are also compared to fathers of families; for a king is truly parens patriae [parent of the country], the politic father of his people. And lastly, kings are compared to the head of this microcosm of the body of man...
>
> I conclude then this point touching the power of kings with this axiom of divinity, that as to dispute what God may do is blasphemy...so is

it sedition in subjects to dispute what a king may do in the height of his power.

But just kings will ever be willing to declare what they will do, if they will not incur the curse of God. I will not be content that my power be disputed upon, but I shall ever be willing to make the reason appear of all my doings, and rule my actions according to my laws...

King James continued:

I am not to find fault that you inform yourselves of the particular just grievances... But...do not meddle with the main points of government; that is my craft...to meddle with that, were to lessen me. I am now an old king...I must not be taught my office...

I would not have you meddle with such ancient rights of mine as I have received from my predecessors, possessing them more (as ancestral customs)...

All novelties are dangerous as well in a politic as in a natural body, and therefore I would be loath to be quarreled in my ancient rights and possessions: for that were to judge me unworthy of that which my predecessors had and left me.

England's King James I stated in *True Law of Free Monarchies*:

In the parliament (which is nothing else but the head court of the king and his vassals) the laws are but craved by his subjects, and only made by him at their [proposal] and with their advice; for albeit the king make daily statutes and ordinances, [imposing] such pains thereto as he thinks [fit], without any advice of parliament or estates, yet it lies in the power of no parliament to make any kind of law or statute, without his scepter [that is, authority] be to it, for giving it the force of a law...

And as ye see it manifest that the king is overlord of the whole land, so is he master over every person that inhabiteth the same, having power over the life and death of every one of them; for although a just prince will not take the life of any of his subjects without a clear law, yet the same laws whereby he taketh them are made by himself or his predecessors, and so the power flows always from himself...

King James concluded:

Where he sees the law doubtsome or rigorous, he may interpret or mitigate the same, lest otherwise summum jus be summa injuria [the greatest right be the greatest wrong], and therefore general laws made publicly in parliament may upon...[the kings] authority be mitigated and suspended upon causes only known to him.

As likewise, although I have said a good king will frame all his actions to be according to the law, yet is he not bound thereto but of his good will and for good example—giving to his subjects...

So as I have already said, a good king, though he be above the law, will subject and frame his actions thereto, for example's sake to his subjects, and of his own free will, but not as subject or bound thereto.

Thomas Jefferson, just ten days before he died, opposed "the divine right of kings" in writing sarcastically to the mayor of Washington, DC, Roger Chew Weightman, June 24, 1826:

> The mass of mankind has not been born with saddles on their backs, nor a favored few booted and spurred, ready to ride them legitimately, by the grace of God.

President William Henry Harrison stated in his *Inaugural Address*, March 4, 1841:

> We admit of no government by divine right, believing that so far as power is concerned the Beneficent Creator has made no distinction amongst men; that all are upon an equality, and that the only legitimate right to govern is an express grant of power from the governed.

∂

RIGHTS COME FROM CREATOR, NOT GOVERNMENT

Does power flow FROM the Deity TO the rulers then TO the people, as ancient, medieval and post-Renaissance monarchs claimed, or does power flow FROM the Deity TO the people, then TO the rulers, as America's founders claimed?

Jefferson explained in the Declaration, that power flowed from the Creator to the people, and that government derived it power "from the consent of the governed":

> All Men...are endowed by their Creator with certain unalienable Rights...That to secure these Rights, Governments are instituted among Men, **deriving their just Powers from the Consent of the Governed...**

The Declaration states that government's purpose was to secure to individuals their Creator-given rights, as reflected in the Resolution passed by the Massachusetts Provincial Congress, 1774:

> Nobly defend those rights which Heaven gave and no man ought to take from us.

If one likes rights the State cannot take away, there must be a source for those rights higher than the State. President Eisenhower told the American Legion's Back-to-God Program, Feb. 20, 1955:

> The Founding Fathers... recognizing God as the author of individual rights, declared that the purpose of government is to secure those rights...
>
> In many lands the State claims to be the author of human rights...If the State gives rights, it can - and inevitably will - take away those rights.

Dwight D. Eisenhower wrote in an article published in the *Episcopal Churchnews Magazine*:

> The founding fathers had to refer to the Creator in order to make their revolutionary experiment make sense; it was because "all men are endowed by their Creator with certain inalienable rights" that men could dare to be free.

Clarence E. Manion, Professor of Constitutional Law and dean of the Notre Dame College of Law, as quoted in Verne Paul Kaub's book, *Collectivism Challenges Christianity* (1946), stated:

> Look closely at these self-evident truths, these imperishable articles of American Faith upon which all our government is firmly based.
>
> First and foremost is the existence of God. Next comes the truth that all men are equal in the sight of God. Third is the fact of God's great gift of unalienable rights to every person on earth.

Then follows the true and single purpose of all American Government, namely, to preserve and protect these God-made rights of God-made man.

Jefferson wrote in his *Notes on the State of Virginia*, 1781, Query 18, portions of which are on the Jefferson Memorial, Washington, DC:

God who gave us life gave us liberty. And can the liberties of a nation be thought secure when we have removed their only firm basis, a conviction in the minds of the people that these liberties are of the Gift of God?

That they are not to be violated but with His wrath? Indeed, I tremble for my country when I reflect that God is just; that His justice cannot sleep forever.

Alexander Hamilton wrote in *The Farmer Refuted*, February, 1775:

The sacred rights of mankind are not to be rummaged for among old parchments or musty records. They are written, as with a sunbeam, in the whole volume of human nature, by the Hand of the Divinity itself, and can never be erased or obscured by mortal power.

President Calvin Coolidge, unveiling the Equestrian Statue of Bishop Francis Asbury, Washington, DC, October 15, 1924, stated:

Our government rests upon religion. It is from that source that we derive our reverence for truth and justice, for equality and liberty, and for the rights of mankind. Unless the people believe in these principles they cannot believe in our government.

President Truman told the Attorney General's Conference, 1950:

The fundamental basis of this nation's laws was given to Moses on the Mount.

The fundamental basis of our Bill of Rights comes from the teachings we get from Exodus and St. Matthew, from Isaiah and St. Paul.

I don't think we emphasize that enough these days. **If we don't have a proper fundamental moral background**, we will finally end up with a **totalitarian government which does not believe in rights for anybody except the State**.

Warren Gamaliel Harding, November 12, 1921, opening a Conference in the Continental Memorial Hall, Washington, DC, stated:

Inherent rights are of God, and the tragedies of the world originate in their attempted denial.

Ronald Reagan, April 27, 1984, stated in Beijing, China:

I have seen the rise of fascism and communism. Both philosophies glorify the arbitrary power of the state...But both theories fail. Both deny those God-given liberties that are the inalienable right of each person on this planet, indeed, they deny the existence of God.

IF NO GOD, THE STATE BECOMES GOD

John F. Kennedy stated in his *Inaugural Address*, 1961:

The rights of man come not from the generosity of the state, but from the hand of God.

But if there is no God, where do rights come from, except "the generosity of the State."

Without a God as the source for citizens' rights, the State becomes the source of rights. The State, then, becomes the new god, and what the State "giveth," the State can "taketh awayeth."

This was espoused by Hobbes, Rousseau, Fichte, Hegel, and philosophers of the State, who influenced Karl Marx and Adolf Hitler.

The Nazi Holocaust, Soviet purges, Mao Zedong's "Cultural Revolution," Pol Pot's killing fields, all of which killed millions of people, did not happen in a vacuum. There was a philosophical background preceding them, which taught the State was the ultimate authority. Obedience to the State was the excuse made by Hitler's officers at the Nuremberg Trials:

> Hermann Goering, Chief of the Nazi Luftwaffe (Air Force) stated December 11, 1945: "We had orders to obey the head of State."
>
> Alfred Jodl, Chief of Operations for the German High Command, stated November 1, 1945: "I don't see how they can fail to recognize a soldier's obligation to obey orders. That's the code I've lived by all my life."
>
> Ernst Kaltenbrunner, Chief of the Gestapo, stated April 11, 1946: "When I saw the newspaper headline 'Gas Chamber Expert Captured' and an American lieutenant explained it to me, I was pale in amazement. How can they say such things about me?...I have only done my duty."
>
> Wilhelm Keitel, Chief of Staff of the German High Command, stated December 25, 1945: "We all believed so much in Hitler...He gave us the orders. He kept saying that it was all his responsibility."
>
> Fritz Sauckel, Chief of Slave Labor Recruitment, stated February 23, 1946: "I was given this assignment which I could not refuse."

Nazism, Fascism and **Communism** taught that **citizens exist for the State's benefit;** whereas **America's founders** believed that **the State existed for the citizens' benefit.**

Without God, government transitions from being the policeman protecting your property to the policeman owning your property. **Without God, government transitions from being the servant of the people to their master.**

Franklin D. Roosevelt commented on Adolph Hitler's National Socialist Workers' Party (Nazi) in his Radio Address on the 150th Anniversary of the Bill of Rights, December 15, 1941:

> **Government** to him is **not the servant** and the instrument of the people **but their absolute master** and the dictator of their every act.

&

WORSHIP OF STATE
– PAGANISM REVISITED

Reminiscent of ancient pagan State worship, Hegel wrote in *Philosophy of Law* (Jacob Loewenberg, editor, *Hegel: Selections*, NY: C. Scribner's Sons, 1929, pp. 443-444, 447):

> The State is the march of God through the World...We must worship the State as the manifestation of the Divine on Earth.

Political scientist Carl Friedrich described monarchy's makeover in 1939:

> In a slow process that lasted several generations, the modern concept of the State was...forged by political theorists as a tool of propaganda for absolute monarchs. They wished to give the king's government a corporate halo roughly equivalent to that of the Church.

Thomas Hobbes (1588-1679) in *Leviathan*, 1651, described the State as "our mortal god."

Jean Jacque Rousseau (1712-1778) was a friend of Voltaire (1694-1778), known for his irreverent wit, and Denis Deiderot (1713-1784), who was a critic of the Church. Jean Jacque Rousseau wrote:

The State, in relation to its members, is master of all their goods by the social contract, which, within the State, is the basis of all rights.

In *The Social Contract,* Rousseau wrote:

The citizen is no longer the judge of the dangers to which the law desires him to expose himself; **and when the prince says to him: 'It is expedient for the State that you should die,' he ought to die,** because it is only on that condition that he has been living in security up to the present, and because his life is no longer a mere bounty of nature, but a gift made conditionally by the State.

On a proposed constitution for Corsica, Rousseau wrote:

I want the property of the state to be as great and powerful, and that of the citizens as small and weak, as possible. With private property being so weak and so dependent, the Government will need to use very little force, and will lead the people, so to speak, with a movement of the finger.

Johann Gottlieb Fichte (1762-1814) lived through Napoleon's conquest and occupation of the German states. Fichte deified the state in order to give it the power to drive the French out of German lands. In his *Addresses to the German Nation,* 1809, Fichte wrote:

The State is the superior power, ultimate and beyond appeal, absolutely independent.

George Wilhelm Frederich Hegel (1770-1831), served as the Royal Prussian Court Philosopher at the University of Berlin.

His political system, as described by German philosopher Ernst Cassirer, "is an entirely new type of absolutism."

Hegel could not prove the existence of God, so he proposed that the closest anyone could come to attaining eternal life was to create and perpetuate a State which would continue to exist after their death. Ronald Reagan said on August 8, 1992:

> Nothing lasts longer than a temporary government program.

Hegel wrote:

> The State is god walking on earth.

> The State is the Divine Idea as it exists on earth.

> State is Objective Spirit.

> All the worth which the human being possesses – all spiritual reality, he possesses only through the State.

> The State is the self-certain absolute mind which recognizes no authority but its own, which acknowledges no abstract rules of good and bad, shameful and mean, cunning and deceit.

> The State is...the ultimate end which has the highest right against the individual, whose highest duty is to be a member of the State.

> In considering the idea of the State, one must not think of particular states, nor of particular institutions, but one must contemplate the idea, this actual God, by itself.

Hegel wrote in *Philosophy of Law* (Section 331):

> The Nation State...is therefore the absolute power on earth.

Hegel wrote in *Philosophy of Law* (Section 70L):

> A single person, it hardly needs saying, is something subordinate, and as such he must dedicate himself to the ethical whole [this whole being the Nation].

Hegel wrote in *Philosophy of Law* (Jacob Loewenberg, editor, Hegel: Selections, NY: C. Scribner's Sons, 1929, p. 465):

> True bravery consists in the readiness to give oneself wholly to the service of the State...
> The individual counts but as one among many...The important aspect lies in self-subordination to the universal cause.

Historian F.S.C. Northrup wrote in *The Meeting of East and West*:

> The development of German thought and culture following Kant clearly shows the individual person becomes swallowed up in the Absolute.

Benito Mussolini, the Italian dictator, stated in 1932:

> The foundation of Fascism is the conception of the State, its character, its duty and its aim. Fascism conceives of the State as an absolute, in comparison with which all individuals or groups are relative, only to be conceived of in their relation to the State.

Columbia University Professor Carmen Haider wrote in 1933:

> The Fascists draw their right of government control from the theory of the superiority of the State...From it flow the principles of authority, hierarchy, discipline and control.

Author James Bovard wrote in *How the State Became Immaculate* (October 2000):

> The State became portrayed as the equivalent of Nietzsche's Superman, exempt from traditional rules of good and evil. Yet this was a parody of Nietzsche (1844-1900) who saved his sharpest contempt for the State, declaring that "whatever it says it lies; and whatever it has it has stolen...It even bites with stolen teeth."

In 1928, Lenin supporter, Grigori Pyatakov, declared:

> According to Lenin, the Communist Party is based on the principle of coercion which doesn't recognize any limitations or inhibitions...the absence of any limitation whatsoever — moral, political, and even physical.

John Dewey stated in 1916:

> No ends are accomplished without the use of force...Squeamishness about [the State's use of] force is the mark not of idealistic but of moonstruck morals.

Bertrand Russell wrote in *Proposed Roads to Freedom*:

> Marxian Socialism, I fear, would give far too much power to the State.

Ronald Reagan commented:

> How do you tell a communist? Well, it's someone who reads Marx and Lenin. And how do you tell an anti-Communist? It's someone who understands Marx and Lenin.

PLATO'S PHILOSOPHER KING

Monarchy's State power was defended by the Greek philosopher, Plato. After witnessing the chaotic democracy of Athens, Plato described the ideal society as a body, with the **abdomen being the working class (with souls of iron and bronze)**; the **chest and arms being the military class (with souls of silver)**; and the **head being a philosopher king (with a soul of gold.)**

In his *The Republic* (380 BC), Plato recounts a conversation with Socrates on how a crisis of a State leads to power in the hands of one. He outlined how government devolves in stages:

1st. ARISTOCRAY - rule by the best, the most capable, successful property owners and experienced entrepreneurs.

2nd. TIMOCRACY - vain people who covet honor, public adulation and fame are attracted to leadership and are tempted to use their positions for their own benefit;

3rd. OLIGARCHY - rule by the few, a clique who are in leadership because of hereditary family ties, royalty, or are military leaders, but are not necessarily gifted at ruling. A rich and poor divide develops, causing poor commoners to either beg from the rich or become criminals and steal from the rich. The rich struggle to protect their wealth and become defensive.

4th. DEMOCRACY - As the socioeconomic divide widens, the middle class disappears. Tensions arise resulting in inexperienced oligarchs being overthrown and poor commoners being granted more rights and freedoms in a democracy. Commoners, unaccustomed to leadership, become drunk with power, yield to selfishness, vote money out of the treasury, and confusion reigns.

5th. TYRANNY - rule by one, the tyrant. Commoners having democratic freedom without moral restraint results in chaos. Society divides into three socioeconomic classes: the dominating class, the elites and the poor commoners. Conflicts between the dominating class and the elites cause the poor commoners to seek out someone who will protect their interests.

They find a visually appealing demagogue and invest in him all their power in the hopes he will be their champion against the other classes.

The demagogue becomes corrupted by power and turns into a tyrant with no check on his arbitrary and absolute control over the people. The tyrant surrounds himself with a small entourage of supporters for protection.

The Durants wrote in *The Lessons of History* (p, 75):

Plato's reduction of political evolution [is] a sequence of...aristocracy, democracy, and dictatorship.

When poor, uneducated, and undisciplined citizens, called "the proletariat," get the right to vote in a democracy, the chaos that will result gradually gives way to the rise of a communist dictator, as French Socialist Jean Jaures (1859-1914) explained:

The proletariat will come to power...under the universal right to vote...Our society will gradually develop toward Communism.

George Washington explained that when citizens yield to undisciplined and immoral behavior, called "licentiousness," a dictator will arise exercising arbitrary power:

Arbitrary power is most easily established on the ruins of liberty abused to licentiousness.

Jerry Coniker, founder of FamilyLand TV (Bloomingdale, OH), wrote in his March, 2011, Newsletter:

What I didn't realize then is that the moral breakdown was not the 'goal' of the death culture, it was simply the means. The real goal of the social revolutionaries is always power and control.

They try to sell their 'change' of the social order as the way to uptopia, to earthly happiness.

So why promote moral degradation? Because they can't gain control over a self-controlled people.

However, when the people are ruled by their passions, chaos ensues. Then society willingly surrenders its freedoms in order to gain peace, which leads to dictatorship by mandate of the people.

Plato's hope was that someday a "philosopher king" would rule unselfishly, being more 'enlightened' and 'intelligent' than the poor, uneducated masses. Plato wrote in *The Republic:*

> There will be no end to the troubles of states...till philosophers become kings.

In *The Laws*, Plato proposed the "idea" that in his imaginary society, "the private and individual is banished from life," and all private property and worldly possessions, including wives and children, would belong to the State.

Plato inspired totalitarian monarchs and communist theorists, such as Karl Marx and Friedrich Engels, who wrote in their *Communist Manifesto*, 1848:

> The theory of the Communists may be summed up in the single sentence: Abolition of private property.

Roger Baldwin, founder of the ACLU, wrote in the Harvard reunion book, 1935:

> I seek social ownership of property, the abolition of the propertied class, and sole control of those who produce wealth. Communism is the goal.

Communist ownership of property is completely opposite from the wishes of America's founders, as Noah Webster wrote in the preface of his *American Dictionary of the English Language* (1841):

> The liberty of the press, trial by jury, the Habias Corpus writ, even Magna Carta itself, although justly deemed the palladia of freedom, are all inferior considerations, when compared with a general distribution of **real property** among every class of people.
>
> The power of entailing estates is more dangerous to liberty and republican government than all the constitutions that can be written on paper, or even than a standing army.
>
> **Let the people have property and they will have power** - a power that will forever be exerted to prevent a restriction of the press, and abolition of trial by jury, or the abridgment of any other privilege...
>
> The production of genius and the imagination are if possible more really and exclusively property than houses and lands, and are equally entitled to legal security.

Plato explained that in his utopia, ignorant peasants are led to believe a "noble lie." The Durants wrote in *The Lessons of History* (p. 77):

> Ignorance...lends itself to manipulation by the forces that mold public opinion.

Machiavelli wrote:

> One who deceives will always find those who allow themselves to be deceived.

Jefferson wrote to Samuel Smith, 1798 (*The Jeffersonian Cyclopedia*, John P. Foley, ed., New York & London, Funk & Wagnalls Co., 1900, No. 2172, iv, 24; Paul Leicester Ford, ed., vii, 277):

Warring against the principles of the great body of the American people, **the delusion of the people is necessary to the dominant party.** I see the extent to which that delusion has been already carried, and I see there is no length to which it may not be pushed by a party in possession of the revenues and the legal authorities of the United States, for a short time, indeed, but yet long enough to admit much particular mischief.

There is no event, therefore, however atrocious, which may not be expected.

Jefferson wrote to John Dickinson, March 1801 (*The Jeffersonian Cyclopedia,* John P. Foley, ed., New York & London, Funk & Wagnalls Co., 1900, No. 2173, iv, 366; Paul Leicester Ford, ed., viii, 7):

Our fellow citizens have been led hood-winked from their principles, by a most extraordinary combination of circumstances.

Peasants allow themselves to be controlled by the enlightened despot who they blindly trust, as Plato explained:

When the true philosopher kings are born in a State, one or more of them, despising the honors of this present world which they deem mean and worthless, esteeming above all things right and the honor that springs from right, and regarding justice as the greatest and most necessary of all things...they [will] set in order their own city.

How will they proceed? They will begin by sending out into the country all the inhabitants of the city who are more than ten years old, and will take possession of their children, who will be unaffected by the habits of their parents; these they will train in their own habits and laws.

Communism, apart from its rhetoric, is just a method of regime change back to a despotic monarchy – a communist dictator. As citizens allow the State to own their property and redistribute their wealth, they loose the incentive to create, invent and work hard, as it will not be to their individual benefit. This results in falling production, increased poverty, and more dependence on the State.

As control concentrates to the State, **Communist Party members effectively become the new royalty,** and **the head of the Party acts as the new monarch.**

Jamie Glazov was born in the USSR in 1966. He fled with his parents in 1972 and settled in Halifax, Nova Scotia. Glazov earned a Ph.D. in history, and is the managing editor of Frontpage Magazine. A review of Jamie Glazov's book, *United in Hate: The Left's Romance with Tyranny and Terror* (WND Books, 2009), was written by George Jochnowitz in the article, "Why Totalitarians Hate Jews," (March 11, 2011, FrontPageMag.com):

> Plato **expressed an idea that is related to thought control: he called for the Noble Lie**, a contradiction in terms if ever there was one.
>
> In particular, he said that **the people should be taught that Rulers were made with gold, Auxiliaries with silver, and craftsmen with iron and brass.**
>
> **Chairman Mao also divided people into three categories. The first was Mao himself; the second was the Party; the third was the laobaixing, the ordinary people** (literally the "old 100 surnames").
>
> When I was teaching in China in 1989, during Beijing Spring, passers-by approached me and

asked questions...One man asked me whether, if Plato were alive today, he would consider Chairman Mao an example of the Philosopher King...Since I disapprove of the politics of both Plato and Chairman Mao, I said yes.

The Durants wrote in *The Lessons of History* (p. 72):

Violent revolutions do not so much redistribute wealth as destroy it. There may be a re-division of land, but the natural inequality of men soon re-create an inequality of possessions and privileges, and **raises to power a new minority with essentially the same instincts as in the old**.

Ronald Reagan phrased it this way:

Governments tend not to solve problems, only to rearrange them.

With each new generation, communism's advocates are convinced that previous efforts to achieve a utopia failed because past communist leaders were flawed or not committed enough.

But Plato's utopia can never be manifested as human nature has not changed - "philosopher kings" are themselves human beings susceptible to errors in judgment and selfishness, and they inevitably become monarchical despots.

A "despot," as defined in Webster's Dictionary, is one who has "absolute and arbitrary authority...independent of the control of men." President Dwight Eisenhower addressed a Governors' Conference, June 24, 1957, Williamsburg, Virginia:

In other lands **over the centuries, millions, helpless before concentrated power,** have been born, have lived and have died all in slavery, or they have lost their lives and their liberty to despots.

Instead of trusting Plato's "philosopher king," America's founders held views in line with British statesman Lord Acton, who wrote to Bishop Creighton, 1887:

> Power tends to corrupt and absolute power corrupts absolutely.

Thomas Jefferson wrote in the Declaration of Independence, 1776:

> When a long train of abuses and usurpations, pursuing invariably the same object evinces a design to reduce them under **absolute despotism**, it is their right, it is their duty, to throw off such government...
>
> The history of the present King of Great Britain is a history of repeated injuries and usurpations, all having in direct object the establishment of an **absolute tyranny**...
>
> He has made judges dependent on his will alone...He has erected a multitude of new offices, and sent hither swarms of officers to harass our people, and eat out their substance...
>
> Abolishing the free system of English laws...establishing therein an **arbitrary** government...so as to render it at once an example and fit instrument for introducing the same **absolute rule**...
>
> A prince whose character is thus marked by every act which may define a **tyrant**, is unfit to be the ruler of a free people.

An interesting note is that Plato's student was Aristotle (384-322 BC), and Aristotle's student was Alexander the Great (356-323 BC), who, instead of being a benevolent "philosopher king," was an ambitious military commander conquering from

Greece to Egypt and Persia, creating the largest empire to that time, then dying after a two-week drinking binge at the age of 32.

In his work, *Politics*, Aristotle explained that for a government of the people to work, the citizens needed to have internal virtue. If the virtue of the citizens deteriorates, then, as a last resort, a monarch could assume control. Aristotle argued that a monarchy could only be justified if the virtue of the monarch was greater than the combined virtue of all the citizens. Unfortunately, every unvirtuous tyrannical monarch who seizes power claims they, and their agenda, are more virtuous than the people.

Aristotle tactfully included Philip of Macedon and his young prince, Alexander the Great, in this virtuous category. Aristotle counseled Alexander that he should be "a leader to the Greeks and a despot to the barbarians, to look after the former as after friends and relatives, and to deal with the latter as with beasts or plants."

᪐

MONARCH MAKEOVERS: COMMUNIST & ISLAMIC DICTATORS

Throughout history, the 'enlightened' leader - the man who happened to be in power, would crush dissent, employ slave labor, erect monuments to his royal greatness, build elaborate tombs and cities of the dead, and undertake disastrous central planning schemes.

Ling Cangzhou's book, *Dragon Blood, Wolf Smoke* (Workers' Publishing House), examines history from the unification of China under the Qin dynasty in 256 BC to the fall of the Qing dynasty in 1912. In an article by Tang Qiwei for RFA's Mandarin service, Ling Cangzhou stated:

> A lot of people in contemporary China right now have a dream that China can return to the glory of the Han and Tang dynasties...
> I am telling them that in reality those

dynasties were stained with blood and behaved in a despicable manner...In ancient times, they said hell had 18 levels. Chinese history has been played out all along on the 17th level of hell, that of cruel dictatorships and barbarous conquests.

Frank Dikotter commented on the absolute power of China's Mao Zedong, in an interview with NTDTV, November 13, 2010, regarding his book, *Mao's Great Famine*:

> Mao Zedong's Communist Party of China is the one that must be held responsible for this enormous catastrophe that ranks probably as the greatest man made disaster in human history, with a minimum of 45 million people who died unnecessarily...
>
> Fundamentally the system remains the same and becomes a culture of violence. So it is not very surprising to see that many people to this day are being tortured violently for their religious views, for their political views, for whatever reason by 'the man who happens to be in power.'
>
> (http://www.ntdtv.com/xtr/gb/2010/11/13/a455321.html#video)

George Jochnowitz wrote in his review of Jamie Glazov's book, *United in Hate: The Left's Romance with Tyranny and Terror*:

> Glazov...said that the left had joined with Islamism to oppose Jews since Jews were linked to...capitalism. But there is a more profound factor in the hostility that totalitarians feel toward Jews: Jews...think dangerous thoughts.
>
> Marxist regimes reject thinkers and intellectuals. Chairman Mao exiled teachers and

writers to the countryside to learn from the peasants. Pol Pot simply killed them...

Totalitarians hate Jews. Hitler's decision to try to eradicate Jews from the world was nevertheless irrational...Einstein fled Germany; Edward Teller and Szilard fled Germany's ally, Hungary. Enrico Fermi, who was not Jewish but was married to a Jew, fled Europe when Mussolini extended Hitler's racial laws to Italy.

Today, Mahmoud Ahmadinejad is echoing the irrationality that Hitler put into effect 70 years ago...In the annual Al-Quds (Jerusalem) sermon given on December 14, 2001, Rafsanjani said that if one day the world of Islam comes to possess nuclear weapons, Israel could be destroyed...

George Jochnowitz continued:

Plato said that literature should be altered so that people should not fear death: "The poets must be told to speak well of that other world. The gloomy descriptions they now give must be forbidden, not only as untrue, but as injurious to our future warriors."

We are reminded of the perpetrators of 9/11, who willingly died so that they could kill, even though their dramatic and well-coordinated plan could not in any conceivable way have helped the cause of Islam. And as Glazov writes, "Palestinian children blew themselves into smithereens while their parents celebrated, proud that their offspring had become shahid (martyrs)."

George Jochnowitz explained:

The idea of limiting and censoring music is at least as old as the 4th century BC, when Plato wrote that in the Republic he envisioned, the flute and other instruments "capable of modulation into all the modes" would be banned. We don't think of Plato as a totalitarian, but he shared the totalitarian rulers' fear of the power of music to unleash the human spirit...It was no accident that Mao and Plato both wanted to ban certain kinds of music...

Glazov informs us, "The Taliban illegalized music completely in Afghanistan, and Ayatollah Khomeini banned most music from Iranian radio and television." Lenin did not ban music, but he wouldn't listen to it. "It makes you want to say stupid, nice things and stroke the heads of people who could create such beauty while living in this vile hell."...

George Jochnowitz concluded:

Totalitarians love death, unlike Jews, which may be another factor in explaining why totalitarians are so anti-Semitic. "Two of the most outstanding Jewish characteristics are the love of life and the enduring struggle to survive. For Islamists, as for Nazis and communists, this is an egregious transgression against their faith."

Genocide was Hitler's primary goal. Stalin engineered a famine in his war against the kulaks that killed millions. Mao caused the greatest famine in all human history.

Pol Pot killed about a third of his own people. The Kim Dynasty has caused years and years of starvation in North Korea. Ahmadinejad is looking forward to fighting a nuclear war against Israel.

Totalitarianism is about death. Life is about learning more every day. Those who fear learning also hate life. As Glazov shows us, that is why totalitarians are united in hate.

(http://frontpagemag.com/2011/03/11/ why-totalitarians-hate-jews/)

Richard Pipes commented on the absolute power of Russia's Josef Stalin in his book, *Communism-A History* (Random House, 2001):

> Collectivization's...consequences were catastrophic: it ruined Russian agricultural, first by deporting the most enterprising farmers, and secondly by depriving the kolkhoz peasant of a stake in the land, the crops of which no longer belonged to him. Russia, which before the revolution had been one of the world's leading cereal exporters, henceforth could barely feed itself...
>
> To break the resistance of the peasants in the Ukraine, the North Caucasus, and the Kazakhstan, Stalin inflicted on these areas in 1932-33 an artificial famine, shipping out all the food from entire districts and deploying the army to prevent the starving peasants from migrating in search of nourishment.
>
> It is estimated that between 6 and 7 million people perished in this man-made catastrophe."

The more power concentrates in a State, the more corruption exists, because human nature has not changed. A person's worth sinks to his or her practical usefulness to the monarch or the State, not rooted in any idealistic concept, such as being created equal by a Creator.

Franklin D. Roosevelt commented on Adolph Hitler's National Socialist Workers' Party (Nazi) in his Radio Address on the 150th Anniversary of the Bill of Rights, December 15, 1941:

> The rights to life, liberty, and the pursuit of happiness which seemed to the Founders of the Republic inalienable, were, to Hitler and his fellows, empty words...
>
> Hitler advanced: That the individual human being has no rights whatsoever in himself...That the individual human being has no right to a soul of his own, or a mind of his own, or a tongue of his own, or a trade of his own; or even to live where he pleases or to marry the woman he loves; **That his only duty is the duty of obedience**, not to his God, not to his conscience, but **to Adolf Hitler;** and that **his only value is his value**, not as a man, but **as a unit of the Nazi state.**

FDR continued in his critique of Hitler:

> To Hitler, the church, as we conceive it, is a monstrosity to be destroyed by every means...
>
> To Hitler, the freedom of men to think as they please and speak as they please and worship as they please is...most desperately to be feared...
>
> This proposed return to tyranny; this effort to impose again upon the peoples of the world **doctrines of absolute obedience, of dictatorial rule, of the suppression of truth, of the oppression of conscience**...is nothing more nor less than an attempt to overthrow and to cancel out the great upsurge of human liberty of which the American Bill of Rights is the fundamental document: to force the peoples of the earth, and

among them the peoples of this continent and this Nation, **to accept again the absolute authority and despotic rule** from which the courage and the resolution and the sacrifices of their ancestors liberated them many, many years ago.

It is an attempt which could succeed only if those who have inherited the gift of liberty had lost the manhood to preserve it.

Lev Navrozov, an immigrant from the U.S.S.R. who has worked with the Center for the Survival of Western Democracies, stated in his article, "Nationalism in the Slave States of Soviet Russia, Nazi Germany and now, China," December 23, 2010 :

> Once upon a time it was assumed that a slave should fulfill the slave-owners' order as efficiently as a machine.
>
> But after Stalin, Hitler, and Mao, it began to be assumed that a perfect slave fulfills the order not like a machine but like a musical instrument, giving an expected accord. The slaves must relive the order, and hence scream in their delight to kill and be killed.
> (http://www.worldtribune.com/worldtribune/WTARC/2010/lev1282_12_23.asp)

Vladimir Lenin tried to disguise his absolute control by calling it "the dictatorship of the proletariat," yet, as he was the one making decisions, his communist government functioned as "the dictatorship of Lenin." Lenin defined "dictatorship" as:

> Power that is limited by nothing, no laws, that is restrained by absolutely no rules, that rests directly on coercion.

President Harry S Truman addressed a Conference of the

Federal Council of Churches of Christ given in Deshler-Wallick Hotel in Columbus, Ohio, March 6, 1946:

> Dictatorship, by whatever name, is founded on the doctrine that **the individual amounts to nothing;** that **the State is the only thing that counts**; and that men and women and children were put on earth solely for the purpose of serving the State.

&

LESSONS OF HISTORY

Will and Ariel Durant wrote in their book, *The Lessons of History* (NY: Simon and Schuster, 1968, p. 90), examples from past civilizations which are applicable to current situations. A proverb states: "Past behavior is the best indicator of future performance."

Harvard Professor George Santayana wrote in *Reason in Common Sense, Volume I of The Life of Reason* (1905):

> Those who cannot remember the past are condemned to repeat it.

History is boring, unless you see it from the right perspective. Perspective is important.

Corn growing in a field appears orderless, till one turns the corner and sees the rows line up. A pixelized photo is unrecognizable, till one zooms out. All the numbers are on a combination lock but it will not open till they are in the right sequence.

So it is with history - all the names, dates and places are there, but it is not until they are seen from the right perspective that lessons become clear. History is boring, until it comes into focus.

A recurring lesson from history is that totalitarian control of a State over its subjects is the norm. Will and Ariel Durant wrote in *The Lessons of History* (p. 59-60):

> In Sumeria about 2100 BC, the economy was organized by the State. Most of the arable

land was the property of the crown; laborers received rations from the crops delivered to the royal storehouses...

Records were kept of all deliveries and distributions of rations. Tens of thousands of clay tablets inscribed with such records were found in the capital Ur.

The Durants continued:

In Babylonia (c. 1750 BC) the law code of Hammurabi fixed wages for the herdsmen and artisans, and the charges to be made by physicians for operations.

The Durants described Egypt from the death of Alexander the Great to the death of Cleopatra VII:

In Egypt under the Ptolemies (323-30 BC) the State owned the soil and managed the agriculture; the peasant was told what land to till, what crops to grow; his harvest was measured and registered by government scribes, was threshed on royal threshing floors, and was conveyed by a living chain of fellaheen into the granaries of the king.

The government owned the mines and appropriated the ore. It nationalized the production and sale of oil, salt, papyrus, and textiles. All commerce was controlled and regulated by the State; most retail trade was in the hands of State agents selling State-produced goods. Banking was a government monopoly...

Taxes were laid upon every person, industry, process, product, sale, and legal document. To keep track of taxable transactions and income, the government maintained a swarm of scribes and a complex system of personal and property registration. The revenue of this system made the Ptolemaic the richest State of the time.

The Durants told what ended Egypt's rule under the Ptolemies:

The Pharaohs took to expensive wars, and after 246 BC, they gave themselves to drink and venery, allowing administration of the State and the economy to fall into the hands of rascals who ground every possible penny out of the poor.

Generation after generation the government's exaction grew. Strikes increased in number and violence. In the capital, Alexandria, the populace was bribed to peace by bounties and spectacles, but it was watched by a large military force, was allowed no voice in the government, and became in the end a violent mob.

Agriculture and industry decayed through lack of incentive; moral disintegration spread.

The Durants wrote of Rome:

Emperor Diocletian, faced with increasing poverty and restlessness among the masses, and with imminent danger of barbarian invasion, issued in AD 301 an Edictum de pretiis, which denounced monopolists for keeping goods from the market to raise prices, and set maximum prices and wages for all important articles and services. Extensive public works were undertaken to put the unemployed to work, and food was distributed gratis, or at reduced prices, to the poor. The government – which already owned most mines, quarries and salt deposits – brought nearly all major industries and guilds under detailed control.

'In every large town,' we are told, 'the State became a powerful employer...standing head and shoulders above the private industrialists, who were in any case crushed by taxation.'

When businessmen predicted ruin, Diocletian explained that the barbarians were at the gate, and that individual liberty had to be shelved until collective liberty could be made secure. The socialism of Diocletian was a war economy, made possible by fear of foreign attack.

The Durants explained what happened to Diocletian's rule:

The task of controlling men in economic detail proved too much for Diocletian's expanding, expensive, and corrupt bureaucracy. To support this officialdom – the army, the court, public works, and the dole – **taxation rose to such heights that men lost incentive to work or earn,** and an erosive contest began between lawyers finding devices to evade taxes and lawyers formulating laws to prevent evasion.

Thousands of Romans, to escape the tax gatherer, fled over the frontiers to seek refuge among the barbarians. Seeking to check this elusive mobility, and to facilitate regulation and taxation, **the government issued decrees binding the peasant to this field** and the worker to his shop until all his debts and taxes had been paid. **In this and other ways medieval serfdom began.**

China had similar experiences, as the Durants wrote in *The Lessons of History* (p. 61-62):

Szuma Ch'ien (c. 146 BC) informs us that

to prevent private individuals from 'reserving to their sole use the riches of the mountains and the sea in order to gain a fortune, and from putting the lower class into subjection to themselves,' the **Emperor Wu Ti** of the Han Dynasty (reigning 140-87 BC) **nationalized the resources of the soil, extended governmental direction over transport and trade, laid a tax upon incomes, and established public works,** including canals that bound the rivers together and irrigated the fields.

The State accumulated stockpiles of goods, sold these when prices were rising, bought more when prices were falling, thus says Szuma Ch'ien, 'the rich merchants and large shopkeepers would be prevented from making big profits...and prices would be regulated in the Empire.'

The Durants explained what happened to Wu Ti's China:

A combination of 'acts of God' with human deviltry put an end to the experiment after the death of the Emperor. Floods alternated with droughts, created tragic shortages, and raised prices beyond control. Businessmen protested that taxes were making them support the lazy and the incompetent.

Harassed by the high cost of living, the poor joined the rich in clamoring for a return to the old ways, and some proposed that the inventor of the new system be boiled alive.

China's Xin Dynasty (9-23 AD) was described by the Durants:

Emperor Wang Mang...nationalized the land, divided it into equal tracts among the peasants, and...tried to control prices by the accumulation or release of stockpiles.

During the Song Dynasty (960-1279), China attempted similar programs:

> Wang An-shih, as premier (1068-1085) undertook a pervasive governmental domination of the Chinese economy. 'The State,' he held, 'should take the entire management of commerce, industry, and agriculture into its own hands...' He rescued the peasants from the moneylenders by loans at low interest...He organized great engineering works...Commerce was nationalized. Pensions were provided for the aged, the unemployed, and the poor.

The Durants explained what happened to Premier Wang An-shih and China's Song Dynasty:

> What undermined the experiment? First, **high taxes** laid upon all to finance a **swelling band of government employees.** Second, conscription of a male in every family to man his armies made necessary by barbarian invasion. Third, **corruption in the bureaucracy**; China, like other nations, was faced with **a choice between private plunder or public graft...**
>
> Wang An-shih's brother argued that human corruptibility and incompetence make governmental control of industry impractical, and that the best economy is laissez-faire system that relies on the natural impulses of men...
>
> High taxation...monopoly of commerce by the government...drought and flood...the appearance of a terrifying comet...dismissed Wang An-shih.

The Durants describe the Incas in Peru:

> The longest-lasting regime of socialism yet known to history was set up by the Incas in what we now call Peru, at some time in the 13th century. Basing their power largely on popular belief that the earthly sovereign was a delegate of the Sun God, the Incas organized and directed all agriculture labor, and trade.
>
> A governmental census kept account of materials, individuals, and income; professional "runners," using a remarkable system of roads, maintained the network of communication indispensable to such detailed rule over so large a territory. **Every person was an employee of the State.**

The end of the Inca Empire began with a civil war in 1532 between the Emperor Huayna Capac's sons Huascar and Atahualpa. Tens of thousands of discontented natives sought relief from Inca control and allied themselves with the Spanish conquistador Pizarro.

Through diplomacy and deceit, Pizarro and his small force of 168 men, 1 cannon and 27 horses, conquered the enormous Inca Empire. Spaniards then used the organized Inca mandatory public service system (mita) to work natives to death in the silver mines of Potosi. This, plus a lack of immunity to European diseases, ie., smallpox, typhus, influenza, diphtheria, and measles, ended the Inca Empire.

These stories recounted by Will and Ariel Durant underscore the continual drive for States to control citizens' lives, and highlight the truly unusual alignment of circumstances and beliefs which allowed for the formation of the United States of America.

❧

A PRIME TRUTH – MAN IS SELFISH

"To be a saint is the exception...Sin is a gravitation."
- Victor Hugo, *Les Miserables*, 1862

A prime truth is that man is selfish. Despite all the technological advancements, human nature has not evolved. Mankind has a fallen nature, or, as theologically defined, is cursed from original sin. Abraham Maslow, in *Theory of Motivation*, 1943, observed that humans seek to fulfill a hierarchy of personal needs., the first of which is self-defense. "Enlightened self-interest" is a nice way of saying that human instinct is self-centered. Mercy Otis Warren wrote in *Observations on the new Constitution and Federal and State Conventions*, 1788:

> **Self defense** is a primary law of nature, which no subsequent law of society can abolish; **this primeval principle**.

This 'self-focus' of humankind was addressed by the Durants in *The Lessons of History* (p. 95):

> Since we have admitted **no substantial change in man's nature** during historic times, all technological advances will have to be written off as merely new means of achieving old ends – the acquisition of goods, the pursuit of one sex by the other, the overcoming of competition, the fighting of wars.

French political writer, Morelly, called this selfish drive "avarice" in *Le Code de la Nature*, 1755:

> The only vice which I know in the universe is avarice: all the others, whatever name one gives them, are merely forms, degrees of it...
> Analyze vanity, conceit, pride, ambition, deceitfulness, hypocrisy, villainy; break down the majority of our sophisticated virtues themselves, [they] all dissolve in this subtle and pernicious element, **the desire to possess.**

"The love of money is the root of all evil." (I Tim. 6:10)

From a baby taking a rattle from another baby, to a bully taking a ball on a playground, to a gang leader ruling a hood, to a king conquering a neighboring kingdom, to a usurper plotting a political coup, to a candidate engaging in voter fraud, to the politics of personal destruction, to a "robber baron" industrialist committing a hostile corporate takeover, to global elites cornering international financial markets - since the dawn of history there has been a relentless selfish drive in some to accumulate and have power over others.

Niccolo Machiavelli wrote:

> **The wish to acquire more** is admittedly a very natural and common thing; and when men succeed in this they are always praised rather than condemned.

President Harry S Truman stated December 24, 1946:

> **Selfishness and greed**, individual or national, cause most of our troubles.

As irresistible as the desire for the forbidden fruit in the Garden of Eden, or Cain's jealous murdering of his brother Abel, or Nimrod's Tower of Babel, each generation sees the reemergence of leaders who succumb to the irresistible ambition to accumulate and concentrate power, convinced in their minds that they will use it for good.

This is like the scene in Arnold Schwarzenegger's *Terminator 2*, where the killer "terminator" sent from the future is finally destroyed into a thousand metal fragments. But just when the audience breathes a sigh of relief, the metal fragments melt into droplets, roll back together and reform the terminator, who starts killing again. President Harry S Truman described man's selfish motivation in a personal memorandum, April 16, 1950:

> There is a lure in power. It can get into a man's blood just as gambling and lust for money have been known to do.

Harvard Professor George Santayana wrote in *Winds of Doctrine:*

The worship of power is an old religion.

Alexander Hamilton wrote in The Farmer Refuted, 1775:

A fondness for power is implanted in most men and it is natural to abuse it, when acquired.

President William Henry Harrison stated in his *Inaugural Address*, March 4, 1841:

Republics can commit no greater error than to...continue any feature in their system of government which may...create or increase the love of power in the bosoms of those [in] management of their affairs...

When this corrupting passion once takes possession of the human mind, like the love of gold it becomes insatiable. It is the never-dying worm in his bosom, grows with his growth and strengthens with the declining years of its victim...

As long as the love of power is a dominant passion of the human bosom...so long will the liberties of a people depend on their constant attention to its preservation.

Thomas Jefferson wrote in his Notes on Virginia, 1782 (*The Jeffersonian Cyclopedia*, John P. Foley, ed., New York & London, Funk & Wagnalls Co., 1900, No. 24, viii, 362; Paul Leicester Ford, ed., iii, 224):

Nor should our Assembly be deluded by the integrity of their own purposes, and conclude that these unlimited powers will never be abused, because themselves are not disposed to abuse them.

They should look forward to a time, and that not a distant one, when corruption in this as in the country from which we derive our origin, will have seized the heads of government, and be spread by them through the body of the people; when they will purchase the voices of the people and make them pay the price. **Human nature is the same on each side of the Atlantic, and will be alike influenced by the same causes.** The time to guard against corruption and tyranny is before they shall have gotten hold of us.

It is better keep the wolf out of the fold, than to trust to drawing his teeth and talons after he shall have entered.

Examples in history of leaders resisting the temptation of power, such as the Roman Republic's Cincinnatus, or America's George Washington, are exceedingly rare.

ৎৢ

FIRST ATTEMPTS TO CHECK A MONARCH'S POWER

"The personality of the state is actual only as one person, the monarch." - Karl Marx, *Critique of Hegel's Philosophy of Right*, 1843

The first limit on a monarch's arbitrary power was tradition and custom, followed by powerful, wealthy landowners, then a religious class. Next, merchants, craftsmen and tradesmen accumulated wealth, invented banking houses, and a "middle-class" emerged to check monarchical power. The next limit was the revolutionary concept that a king had to submit to the same rule of law that the people had to submit to.

English tradition was deeply affected by the legendary 6th century example of King Arthur's Court and the Knights of the Round Table, where the King was not a superior being, but instead "first among equals."

The Anglo-Norman poet, Wace (1110-1174), wrote:

> Because of these noble lords about his hall, of whom each knight pained himself to be the hardiest champion, and none would count him the least praiseworthy, Arthur made the Round Table so reputed of the Britons.
>
> This Round Table was ordained of Arthur that when this fair fellowship sat to meat their chairs should be high alike, their service equal, and none before or after his comrade.
>
> Thus no man could boast that he was exalted above his fellow, for all alike were gathered round the board, and none was alien at the breaking of Arthur's bread...
>
> Thus the powerful nobles were provided with a sense of power, which mollified their belligerence over submission to the authority of their king.

As individuals were allowed to create wealth and own property, they formed a nobility that could check the unlimited power of monarchs.

The most notable example of this is when English nobles surrounded King John on the fields at Runnymeade on the Thames River and forced him to sign the Magna Carta on June 15, 1215, which stated that no "freeman" could be punished except through the law of the land.

Lord Alfred Thompson Denning (1899-1999), described the Magna Carta as:

> The greatest constitutional document of all times – the foundation of the freedom of the individual against the arbitrary authority of the despot.

The Magna Carta, or The Great Charter of the Liberties of England and of the Liberties of the Forest, asserted that the

King was bound by law. These laws eventually included the Petition of Right of 1628, the Bill of Rights of 1689, Habeas Corpus Act of 1679, and the Act of Settlement of 1701.

The Magna Carta was a foundational document in the development of constitutional law, influencing the Puritans during the English Civil War, the settlers of New England and the United States Constitution. The Durants wrote in *The Lessons of History* (p. 76):

> A British heritage: Anglo-Saxon law, which, from the Magna Carta onward, had defended the citizen against the State.

The Columbia Encyclopedia, 6th Edition (Columbia University Press, 2008) includes in its definition of "monarchy":

> Although theoretically at the apex of feudal power, the medieval monarchs were in fact weak and dependent upon the nobility for much of their power...
>
> However, even the powerful monarchs of the 17th century were somewhat limited by custom and constitution as well as by the delegation of powers to strong bureaucracies.
>
> Such limitations were also felt by the "benevolent despots" of the 18th century.
>
> Changes in intellectual climate, in the demands made upon government in a secular and commercially expanding society, and in the social structure, as the bourgeoisie [middle class] became increasingly powerful, eventually weakened the institution of monarchy in Europe.
>
> The Glorious Revolution in England (1688) and the French Revolution (1789) were

important landmarks in the decline and limitation of monarchical power. Throughout the 19th century royal power was increasingly reduced by constitutional provisions and parliamentary incursions.

Though the term "monarch" or "dictator" is no longer in vogue, leaders who possess near monarchical powers try to avoid international disdain by using democratic sounding titles, such as: "chairman," "citizen," "comrade," "führer," "general secretary," "leader," "president" or "prime minister."

Commenting on lack of checks on power in the former U.S.S.R., Vice-President Richard M. Nixon stated August 21, 1960:

> Throughout the ages, among men of all nations and creeds, law has generally been thought of as a curb on arbitrary power...During most of the world's history...the questions were how the institutions of law could be shaped so that they might not be perverted into instruments of power...
>
> How, then, is law defined today in Russia? We have an authoritative answer. It is declared to be "the totality of the rules of conduct expressing the will of the dominant class, designed to promote those relationships that are advantageous and agreeable to the dominant class." Law in the Soviet Union is not conceived as a check on power, it is openly and proudly an expression of power.

&

BELIEFS CHECK MONARCH'S POWER

Judeo-Christian beliefs exercised a moderating effect on the unrestrained power of monarchs by convicting their consciences, reminding them of a future judgment before an All-Knowing God who holds all, rich and poor alike, accountable. An early example of this was Bishop of Milan, St. Ambrose, and his influence on Roman Emperor Theodosius, 379-395 AD.

Bible verses convicting the conscience of the king include: "Love your neighbor as you love yourself," "Whatever you did unto the least of these you did unto me," "Be nice to the stranger because you were once a stranger in Egypt," "Do unto other as you would have them do unto you" and "Love your enemies."

John Bouvier's Law Dictionary - Adapted to the Laws & Constitution of the United States (Revised 6th Edition, 1856), quoted French political philosopher Montesquieu (1689-1755), who observed religion's influence on princes:

> What Montesquieu says of a prince, applies equally to an individual.
>
> "A prince who LOVES RELIGION is a lion which yields to the hand that caresses him or to the voice which renders him tame.
>
> He who FEARS RELIGION is like a wild beast which gnaws the chain which restrains it from falling on those within its reach.
>
> He who HAS NO RELIGION is like a terrible animal which feels no liberty except when it devours its victims or tears them in pieces." (http://www.constitution.org/bouv/bouvier_r.htm)

Montesquieu (1689-1755) had a significant influence on the framers of America's government. In 1721 he wrote the *Persian Letters*, a satirical reflection on France's sociopolitical institutions, and in 1748, he wrote *The Spirit of the Laws*. He introduced the revolutionary concept of dividing a monarch's power into legislative, executive and judicial branches.

Donald S. Lutz of the University of Houston, together with Charles S. Hyneman, wrote an article titled "The Relative Influence of European Writers on Late 18th Century American Political Thought," published in the *American Political Review*, 1984.

Lutz and Hyneman reviewed nearly 15,000 items written between 1760 and 1805 by the Founding Fathers, including newspaper articles, monographs, books, pamphlets, and tracts. Their research found that the most frequently quoted source by the founders was the Bible (34 percent, mostly from the Laws of Moses in the Book of Deuteronomy). The second most frequently quoted source was Montesquieu.

Montesquieu wrote:

> The Christian religion, which orders men to love one another, no doubt wants the best political laws and the best civil laws for each people, because those laws are, after [religion], the greatest good that men can give and receive.

Up until the Protestant Reformation, the Christian religion's influence on government was twofold:

1) to nurture moral, honest citizens, or as Napoleon said, to keep the poor from murdering the rich;

2) to convict the conscience of the "divinely" appointed King, restraining him from being a "wild beast...falling on those within its reach."

> As a roaring lion, and a ranging bear; so is a wicked ruler over the poor people. (Proverbs 28:15)

The Durants wrote in *The Lessons of History* (p. 43):

> Even the skeptical historian develops a humble respect for religion, since he sees it function, and seemingly indispensable, in every and any age...
>
> Supernatural hope may be the sole alternative to despair. Destroy that hope, and class war is intensified.

Heaven and utopia (on earth) are buckets in a well: when one goes down the other goes up; when religion declines Communism grows.

Religion and government overlap as they both define rules of behavior regarding a person's relations with other people for the good order of society:
-Religion prescribes guidelines for man's relationship with his God and **man's relationship with his fellow man**;
-Government prescribes guidelines for **man's relationship with his fellow man**.

John Bouvier's Law Dictionary (1856 Edition), under the definition of "Religion" stated:

Real piety in practice, consisting in the performance of all known duties to God and our fellow men...Many duties are imposed by religion calculated to promote the happiness of society.

Besides, there is an infinite number of actions, which though punishable by society, may be concealed from men, and which the magistrate cannot punish. In these cases men are restrained by the knowledge that nothing can be hidden from the eyes of a sovereign intelligent Being; that the soul never dies, that there is a state of future rewards and punishments; in fact that the most secret crimes will be punished.

True religion then offers succors to the feeble, consolations to the unfortunate, and fills the wicked with dread.

U.S. Secretary of State, William Jennings Bryan, wrote in *The Prince of Peace* (New York Times, September 7, 1913):

A religion which teaches personal responsibility to God gives strength to morality. There is a powerful restraining influence in the belief that an all-seeing eye scrutinizes every thought and word and act of the individual.

After the Protestant Reformation, there arose a third dynamic of the Christian religion's influence on government, namely, that since each individual had a personal relationship with God and was equal before Him, they should have an equal relationship with the government and be equal before it.

This teaching undermined "the divine right of kings" and initiated efforts to restructure government, making the people the "king" and the politicians the servants. Each person should have equal rights and an equal vote, and politicians could only govern by the consent of the governed.

The Durants wrote in *The Lessons of History* (p. 76):

In America...protestantism...had opened the way to religious and mental liberty.

Protestantism's aversion to a religious heirarchy translated into an aversion to a political heirarchy. Its emphasis on each person being individually accountable to God facilitated a society maintaining order without a strong government overseeing and controlling everyone.

When Daniel Webster was asked what the greatest thought was that ever passed through his mind, he responded: "My accountability to God."

~

DIFFERENT RELIGIONS CHECK POWER DIFFERENTLY

Montesquieu compares governments and religions in *The Spirit of the Laws,* 1748, Book 24, Chapter 3:

A moderate Government is most agreeable

to the Christian Religion, and a despotic Government to the Mahommedan...

While the Mahommedan princes incessantly give or receive death, the religion of the Christians renders their princes less timid, and consequently less cruel. The prince confides in his subjects, and the subjects in the prince. How admirable the religion which, while it only seems to have in view the felicity of the other life, continues the happiness of this!

Montesquieu wrote of Islam in *The Spirit of the Laws*, 1748, Book 24, Chapter 4:

The Mahometan religion, which speaks only by the sword, acts still upon men with that destructive spirit with which it was founded.

Montesquieu observed that the Christian religion "has hindered despotic power" (*The Spirit of the Laws*, 1748, Bk. 24, Ch. 3):

I have always respected religion; the morality of the Gospel is the noblest gift ever bestowed by God on man. We shall see that we owe to Christianity, in government, a certain political law, and in war a certain law of nations-benefits which human nature can never sufficiently acknowledge.

The principles of Christianity, deeply engraved on the heart, would be infinitely more powerful than the false honor of monarchies, than the humane virtues of republics, or the servile fear of despotic states.

It is the Christian religion that, in spite of the extent of empire and the influence of climate, has hindered despotic power from being established in Ethiopia, and has carried into the heart of Africa the manners and laws of Europe.

The Christian religion is a stranger to mere despotic power. The mildness so frequently recommended in the Gospel is incompatible with the despotic rage with which a prince punishes his subjects, and exercises himself in cruelty.

In *The Spirit of the Laws* (1748, Bk.24, Ch.5), Montesquieu explained Europe's experience with religion:

> The Catholic Religion is most agreeable to a Monarchy, and the Protestant to a Republic.
>
> When a religion is introduced and fixed in a state, it is commonly such as is most suitable to the plan of government there established; for those who receive it, and those who are the cause of its being received, have scarcely any other idea of policy, than that of the state in which they were born.
>
> When the Christian religion, two centuries ago, became unhappily divided into Catholic and Protestant, the people of the North embraced the Protestant, and those of the south adhered still to the Catholic.
>
> The reason is plain: the people of the north have, and will forever have, a spirit of liberty and independence, which the people of the south have not; and therefore a religion, which has no visible head, is more agreeable to the independency of the climate, than that which has one.

The idea gradually developed that government should allow the "pursuit of happiness." Not only could each person choose who to marry, where to live and what career to follow, they should be free to pursue their own God-ordained destiny, personally benefiting from educating themselves, being creative, and working hard. Confucianism, Buddhism and Hinduism also provide social order, but they ideologically support a class society ruled by a despot, where equality and upward mobility are rare or nonexistent.

⁌

DO UNTO OTHERS

Technology shows what man can do, theology teaches what men should do. Franklin D. Roosevelt greeted Archbishop Rummel of New Orleans at the National Eucharistic Congress, October 1, 1938:

> I doubt if there is any problem in the world today - social, political or economic - that would not find a happy solution if approached in the spirit of the Sermon on the Mount.

Harry S Truman stated at Fordham University, May 11, 1946:

> I doubt whether there is in this troubled world today, when nations are divided by jealousy and suspicion, a single problem that could not be solved if approached in the spirit of the Sermon on the Mount.

Calvin Coolidge stated at the unveiling of the equestrian statue of Bishop Francis Asbury, October 15, 1924:

> The government of a country never gets ahead of the religion of a country. There is no way by which we can substitute the authority of law for the virtue of man...
> Real reforms which society in these days is seeking will come as a result of our religious convictions, or they will not come at all. Peace, justice, humanity, charity - these cannot be legislated into being. They are the result of a Divine Grace.

Mercy Otis Warren quoted French philosopher Abbe de Mably in *Observations on the New Constitution, and on the Federal and State Conventions,* 1788:

> The virtues and vices of a people when a revolution happens in their government, are the measure of the liberty or slavery they ought to expect.

Gen. Omar Bradley stated on Armistice Day, November 11, 1948:

> We have grasped the mystery of the atom and rejected the Sermon on the Mount...The world has achieved brilliance without conscience. Ours is a world of nuclear giants and ethical infants.

Will and Ariel Durant wrote in *The Story of Civilization* (Vol. 7-The Age of Reason Begins, Simon & Schuster, 1961, p.613):

> Is Christianity dying?...If this is so, it is the basic event of modern times, for the soul of a civilization is its religion, and it dies with its faith.

~

CAPITALISM CHECKS CONCENTRATED POWER

Without a "Big Brother" controlling government, common men experienced increased freedom to pursue their dreams.

This pursuing of their dream, or enlightened self-interest, was the engine that unleashed human potential. Common men and women were allowed through individual capitalism to flourish, being only restrained by the brakes of Judeo-Christian morals.

The Durants wrote in *The Lessons of History* (p. 55):

> The concentration of wealth is a natural result of this concentration of ability, and regularly recurs in history.

The rate of concentration varies with the economic freedom permitted by morals and the laws.

Personal wealth increased to the point that common citizens could challenge the power of the monarch and the hereditary aristocracy. As the Durants wrote in *The Lessons of History* (p. 76):

> A government that governed least was admirably suited to liberate those individualistic energies that transformed America from a wilderness to a material utopia....
>
> The American Revolution was not only a revolt of colonials against a distant government, it was also an uprising of a native middle class against an imported aristocracy.

Ronald Reagan remarked to the Heritage Council, Warren, Michigan, October 10, 1984:

> We recognize that after all this time, Henry David Thoreau was right: that government is best which governs least.

Thomas Jefferson stated in his *Inaugural Address*, March 4, 1801:

> What more is necessary to make us a happy and prosperous people?...A wise and frugal Government, which shall restrain men from injuring one another, shall leave them otherwise free to regulate their own pursuits of industry and improvement, and shall not take from the mouth of labor the bread it has earned.

Jefferson wrote to Gideon Granger, 1800 (*The Jeffersonian Cyclopedia*, John P. Foley, ed., New York & London, Funk & Wagnalls Co., 1900, No. 1414, iv, 331; Paul Leicester Ford, ed., vii, 452):

The merchants will manage commerce the better, the more they are left free to manage for themselves.

Jefferson stated in his First Annual Message, December 1801 (*The Jeffersonian Cyclopedia*, John P. Foley, ed., NY & London, Funk & Wagnalls Co., 1900, No. 1408, viii, 13; Paul Leicester Ford, ed., viii, 123):

Agriculture, manufactures, commerce, and navigation, the four pillars of our prosperity, are the most thriving when left most free to individual enterprise.

Jefferson wrote in Opinion on a National Bank, 1791 (*The Jeffersonian Cyclopedia*, John P. Foley, ed., NY & London, Funk & Wagnalls Co., 1900, No. 1417, vii, 557; Paul Leicester Ford, ed., v, 286):

The power given to Congress by the Constitution does not extend to the internal regulation of the commerce of a State (that is to say of the commerce between citizen and citizen), which remains exclusively with its own Legislature; but to its external commerce only, that is to say, its commerce with another State, or with foreign nations, or with the Indian tribes.

Theodore Roosevelt wrote on the formation of the Constitution (*The Works of Theodore Roosevelt*, National Edition, Volume VII, NY: Charles Scribner's Sons, 1916, p. 325-328):

One great truth taught by Jefferson-that in America a statesman should trust the people, and should endeavor to secure to each man all possible individual liberty, confident that he will use it aright. The old-school Jeffersonian theorists believed in "a strong people and a weak government."

As the king's control of the state was reduced, there was the necessity to proportionately increase "individual self-control." Judeo-Christian morality was instrumental in maintaining social order and its corresponding charity kept "enlightened self-interest" from returning to the domineering selfishness of would-be monarchs.

Money magnifies the influence of its possessor, and in the hands of the people, it can check a dictator's power.

To challenge basketball's greatest players like Michael Jordan, Charles Barkley, and Shaquille O'Neal, kids should be allowed to play in their backyards, alleys, and school yards. To challenge entrenched politicians, grassroots volunteers should be allowed to enter local politics. To challenge despots, individuals should be allowed to accumulate capital.

Poverty is the best way to keep citizens dependent and in submission to the State. Stalin was notorious for controlling Russians through "fear and food":

> -citizens were always kept in fear of an intrusive government dragging them away in the night;

> -and citizens were always experiencing a food shortage, which resulted in their entire mental focus being concerned on how to feed their family dinner, not how to overthrow the government.

In other words, poor, uneducated people are easier to manipulate. In the Soviet Union, homes went into disrepair, as fearful citizens witnessed neighbors who fixed them up being falsely accused and imprisoned, followed by communist party members moving in.

Capitalism was an effective means for individuals to accumulate resources to oppose a dictator. The merchants of the Netherlands, called Dutch Masters, were a prominent example of a mercantile capitalism challenging monarchies.

Capitalism is the best way to empower individuals to be free and independent. Americans were renowned for their rugged individualism, ingenuity, and entrepreneurialism.

Capitalism's most basic quality is allowing individuals to benefit from their hard work and creativity, and to save the profits for themselves, their old age, their families and the charities of their choice.

Governments do not create, individuals create. Every invention was once just a thought inside someone's head. Human creativity was unlocked because individuals had the freedom to pursue and profit from their thoughts and ideas.

Inventors believed their inventions would not only benefit humanity, but would also benefit themselves, being secure that U.S. Patent laws guaranteed their hard work would not be stolen.

Capitalism motivated inventors, such as: Benjamin Franklin, Samuel Morse, Eli Whitney, Thomas Edison, Nikola Tesla, and Henry Ford. **Inventions from America benefited the world:**

1717 Swim fins	1833 Lock-stitch sewing machine
1731 Octant for navigation	1834 Combine harvester
1742 Franklin stove	1834 Reaper (Cyrus McCormick)
1744 Mail order	1835 Relay electrical switch
1752 Lightning rod	1835 Revolver
1760 Bifocal lenses	1835 Steam shovel
1776 Swivel chair	1835 Wrench
1787 Automatic flour mill	1836 Circuit breaker
1792 Cracker	1837 Telegraph
1793 Cotton gin	1839 Corn sheller
1800 Suspension bridge	1842 Anesthetic-ether
1801 Fire hydrant	1842 Grain elevator
1805 Refrigeration (vapor)	1843 Ice cream hand-crank
1806 Coffee percolator	1843 Rotary printing press
1808 Lobster trap	1846 Printing telegraph
1813 Circular saw	1848 Chewing gum (spruce)
1815 Dental floss	1849 Gas mask
1816 Milling machine	1849 Safety pin
1830 Vulcanization rubber	1850 Inverted microscope
1831 Electric doorbell	1851 Fire alarm box
1832 Morse code	1852 Elevator (passenger)

1853 Condensed milk
1853 Potato chips
1857 Toilet paper (modern)
1858 Burglar alarm
1858 Ironing board
1858 Mason jar for canning
1858 Monkey wrench
1858 Pencil eraser
1858 Pepper shaker
1859 Escalator
1859 Oil well
1860 Repeating rifle (lever)
1861 Machine gun (cranked)
1861 Twist drill
1863 Breakfast cereal
1863 Ratchet wrench
1863 Roller skates (4 wheel)
1867 Barbed wire
1867 Paper clip
1867 Refrigerated railroad car
1867 Typewriter
1868 Paper bag
1868 Tape measure
1869 Clothes hanger
1869 Pipe wrench
1869 Plastics (Celluloid)
1870 Can opener (rotary)
1870 Electric incandescent lamp
1870 Mixer (hand-cranked)
1870 Sandblasting
1872 Railway air brake
1873 Jeans
1874 Fire sprinkler-closed-head
1874 Keyboard layout
1875 Dental drill (electric)

1875 Mimeograph
1876 Airbrush
1876 Telephone
1877 Phonograph
1878 Carbon microphone
1879 Cash register
1881 Iron (electric)
1881 Metal detector
1882 Christmas lights
1882 Fan (electric)
1883 Thermostat
1884 Dissolvable pill
1884 Pen (fountain)
1885 Photographic film
1885 Popcorn machine
1885 Skyscraper
1885 Transformer (electric)
1886 Coca-Cola invented
1886 Dishwasher
1886 Filing cabinet
1886 Telephone directory
1888 Camera (hand-held)
1888 Drinking straw
1888 AC Electric motor
1888 Revolving door
1890 Jackhammer
1890 Smoke detector
1890 Stop sign
1890 Tabulating machine
1891 Ferris wheel
1891 Tesla coil
1891 Zipper
1892 Bottle cap
1892 Carburetor spray
1892 Tractor

1893 Motion pictures
1893 Radio (Tesla)
1894 Mousetrap
1897 Charcoal briquette
1898 Installer bit (twist drill bit)
1898 Semi-automatic shotgun
1898 Sousaphone (tuba)
1900 Thumbtack
1901 Assembly line
1901 Safety razor (disposable)
1902 Air conditioning
1902 Hearing aid
1902 Periscope (collapsible)
1902 Postage meter
1902 Teddy bear
1903 Airplane
1903 Round hay baler
1903 Offset printing press
1903 Tea bag
1903 Windshield wipers
1904 AC power outlets
1904 Automatic transmission
1904 Dragline excavator
1905 Fly swatter
1905 Gyrocompass
1906 Electronic audio amplifier
1907 Electrostatic air cleaner
1907 Paper towel
1907 Vacuum cleaner (upright)
1908 Mixer (electric)
1908 Washing machine (electric)
1910 Headset (headphone/mike)
1910 Synthetic plastic
1911 Automobile self starter
1911 Road surface marking

1912 Electric blanket
1912 Fast food restaurant
1912 Long distance radio
1912 Traffic light (electric)
1913 Ford Model T assembly
1913 Moving assembly line
1913 Refrigerator (compressor)
1914 Fortune cookie
1914 Regenerative circuit (radio)
1914 Traffic cone
1915 Single-sideband modulation (radio)
1916 Cloverleaf highway exit
1916 Condenser microphone
1916 Light switch (toggle)
1916 Supermarket
1916 Tow truck
1918 Hydraulic vehicle brake
1918 Rifle (automatic)
1918 Superheterodyne receiver (radio/TV)
1919 Blender
1919 Silica gel
1919 Toaster (pop-up)
1921 Adhesive bandage
1921 Crystal oscillator (electrical signal frequency)
1921 Garage door
1921 Wirephoto by telephone
1922 Radial arm saw
1923 Bulldozer
1923 Cotton swab
1923 Instant camera
1923 Masking tape
1923 Television

1924 Frozen food
1926 Power steering (vehicle)
1926 Rocket (liquid-fueled)
1927 Bread slicer
1927 Garbage disposal
1928 Electric razor
1928 Ice cube tray
1929 Air traffic control
1929 Car radio (Motorola)
1929 Freon (refrigerant)
1929 Sunglasses
1930 Chocolate chip cookie
1930 "Scotch" tape
1930 Runway lighting
1931 Electric guitar
1931 Electric razor
1932 Golf cart
1932 Radio astronomy
       telescope
1932 Staple remover
1933 Frequency modulation (FM)
1935 Franchising (business)
1935 Parking meter
1935 pH meter
1935 Photography-Kodachrome
1935 Richter magnitude scale
       (earthquake)
1935 Surfboard fin
1936 Chair lift (aerial)
1936 EEG brain topography
1936 Phillips-head screw
1936 Programming languages
       (computer)
1936 Stock car racing
1937 Blood bank

1937 Digital computer
1937 Photosensitive glass
1937 Shopping cart
1938 Fiberglass
1938 Nylon
1938 Teflon
1941 Acrylic fiber
1941 Deodorant
1945 Microwave oven
1946 Cancer chemotherapy
1946 DEET (insect repellent)
1946 Diaper (waterproof)
1947 Acrylic paint
1947 Defibrillator (medical)
1947 Supersonic aircraft
1947 Transistor
1948 Cable television
1948 Cat litter
1948 Hair spray
1948 Video game
1950 Credit card
1951 Wetsuit (thermal)
1952 Airbag (automobile)
1952 Artificial heart
1952 Barcode
1952 Polio vaccine
1953 Apgar scale (infant
       medical)
1953 Carbonless copy paper
1953 Crossed-field amplifier
1953 Marker pen
1953 MASER (electromagnetic
       wave amplification)
1953 Measles vaccine
1953 Wheel clamp (vehicle)

1954 Acoustic suspension loudspeaker
1954 CPR-Cardiopulmonary resuscitation
1954 Door (automatic sliding)
1954 Mogen surgical clamp
1954 Radar gun (vehicle speed detection)
1954 Synthetic diamond
1954 TV dinner
1954 Zipper storage bag
1955 Hard disk drive-computer
1956 Bone marrow transplant
1956 Fortran computer language
1956 Industrial robot
1956 Operating system-batch computer processing
1956 Particle storage ring particle accelerator
1956 Videotape
1957 Air-bubble packing
1957 Borazon (fourth hardest substance)
1957 Confocal microscopy-3 dimensional images
1957 Cryotron switch - super conductivity
1957 Radioisotope Gamma camera
1957 Laser
1957 Pacemaker (internal)
1957 Skid-steer loader
1957 Sugar packet
1957 Wireless microphone

1958 Carbon fiber
1959 Fusor (nuclear fusion)
1959 Integrated computer circuit
1959 Spandex
1959 Weather satellite
1960 Artificial turf
1960 Gas laser
1960 Laser-1st working model
1960 Magnetic stripe card
1961 Frozen carbonated beverage
1961 Wearable computer
1962 Chimney starter
1962 Glucose meter
1962 Jet injector
1962 Laser diode
1962 Light-emitting diode LED
1963 Balloon catheter
1963 BASIC computer language
1963 Computer mouse
1963 Lung transplantation
1964 8-track cartridge-magnetic recording
1964 Argon laser
1964 Carbon dioxide laser
1964 Heart transplantation
1964 Liquid crystal display
1964 Moog synthesizer sound generator
1964 Permanent press fabric
1964 Plasma display
1965 Chemical laser
1965 Compact disc

1965 Cordless telephone
1965 Hypertext (computer)
1965 Kevlar fabric
1965 Minicomputer
1965 Snowboarding
1965 Space pen
1966 Dynamic random access memory
1967 Backpack (Internal frame)
1967 Calculator (hand-held)
1968 Bone marrow transplant
1968 Racquetball
1968 Virtual reality-computer
1969 Bioactive glass
1969 Charge coupled device (ultraviolet imaging)
1969 Laser printer
1969 Mousepad
1969 Taser
1969 Wide-body aircraft
1970 Wireless local area network
1971 Floppy disk
1971 Fuzzball Internet router
1971 Microprocessor
1971 Personal computer
1971 Saffir-Simpson Hurricane Scale
1971 String trimmer (weed whacker)
1971 Supercritical airfoil (delay wave drag)
1972 C programming computer language
1972 Compact disk invented by RCA

1972 PET medical scanner
1972 Video game console
1973 Catalytic converter
1973 Mobile phone
1973 Personal watercraft (jet ski)
1973 Recombinant DNA (synthetic)
1973 Voicemail
1974 Heimlich maneuver
1974 Post-it note
1974 Scanning acoustic microscope
1974 Universal Product Code
1975 Digital camera
1976 Compact fluorescent lamp
1976 Gore Tex (waterproof, breathable fabric)
1976 Hepatitis B virus vaccine
1977 Chemical oxygen iodine laser
1977 Human-powered aircraft
1977 Magnetic resonance imaging
1978 Bulletin board system
1979 Polar fleece (insulating synthetic wool fabric)
1981 Fetal surgery
1981 Graphic User Interface
1981 Paintball
1981 Space shuttle
1981 Total internal reflection fluorescence microscope
1982 Heart (artificial) implanted in human
1983 Laser turntable (audio signal playback device)

These inventions are just some of the many created by motivated Americans, not the government.

The government can help best by refusing to grant monopoly favors, and thus maintain a level playing field for businesses to compete.

Most workers are given jobs by entrepreneurial capitalists. They have the freedom to switch jobs, or learn the business and become entrepreneurs themselves. Ronald Reagan stated:

> Entrepreneurs and their small enterprises are responsible for almost all the economic growth in the United States...The best minds are not in government. If any were, business would hire them away.

☙

CAPITALISM CHECKS CAPITALISM

Just as allowing ordinary individuals to participate in politics is a check on totalitarian governments, allowing ordinary individuals to participate in capitalism is a check on monopolistic corporations.

Growth in capitalism produced a new dynamic, as Will and Ariel Durant wrote in *The Lessons of History* (p. 54):

> Agriculture becomes industry, and soon the farmer must choose between being the employee of a capitalist and being the employee of a state.

Since some people have different skill sets, abilities and motivational drives, some inevitably become more successful. Will and Ariel Durant wrote in *The Lessons of History* (p. 55):

> Concentration of wealth is a natural result of the concentration of ability, and regularly recurs in history.

Communists like Marx, Lenin and Stalin argued that because some capitalists created monopolies, charged exorbitant prices, and treated employees unfairly, that all capitalism should be abolished forever.

This is the equivalent of saying that because some athletes won by cheating, or got away with illegal tackles, or stole their opponent's play book, that all sports should be abolished forever.

Just as athletes who play fairly are good, and athletes who cheat are bad; so capitalists who treat employees and competitors fairly, are good; and capitalists who cheat, treat employees inconsiderately and use questionable business practices to eliminate competition, are bad.

Sports competition has two remedies to keep players fair, "taught" or "caught":

1) TAUGHT- the first is "internal," athletes are taught that it is more honorable to behave according to a higher moral code, an ethical standard called "sportsmanship.";

2) CAUGHT- the second is "external," referees watch the athletes, and the athletes, out of fear of being caught cheating and penalized, play fair.

Like in sports, two remedies exist to keep businessmen fair:

1) TAUGHT- the first is "internal" – the businessman is taught that it is more honorable to behave according to a higher moral code, an ethical standard called The Golden Rule - "do unto others as you would have them do unto you";

2) CAUGHT- the second is "external" – referees, such as the Better Business Bureau, trade associations, and anti-trust laws, keep watch over businessmen, who, out of fear of being caught cheating and penalized, compete fairly.

Playing sports is neutral, just as being in business is neutral. It is not sports or capitalism that is bad, it is selfish players and businessmen who do not play by virtuous ethical and moral standards.

The same question could be asked:

"Should all political parties be banned because some politicians are corrupt?"

"Should all ministries be stopped because some ministers misuse funds?"

"Should all governments be abolished because some public officials embezzled?"

&

CAPITALISM AND GOVERNMENTS

Governments can be good or bad, depending on if they respect individual rights, treat citizens equally, and do not steal from them, as compared to enslaving citizens, committing atrocities and genocide.

It just so happens that allowing concerned citizens to participate in their own government is the best way to challenge inefficiencies and inequalities of large, totalitarian governments.

Capitalism can be good or bad, depending on if those who accumulate wealth respect individual rights, treat employees and competitors fairly, and respect the environment, as compared to manipulating markets, bribing politicians to grant them unfair advantage, and charging exorbitant interest rates.

It just so happens that allowing creative, industrious individuals to participate in capitalism is the best way to challenge inefficiencies of large, monopolistic corporations.

Capitalism is, in a sense, financial democracy.

Monarchies and monopolies lend themselves to the patronage system of favoritism, influence peddling, and bribes.

William Penn wrote in his *Preface to Frame of Government for Pennsylvania*, May 5, 1682:

> Governments, like clocks, go from the motion men give them; and as governments are made and moved by men, so by them they are ruined too. Wherefore governments rather depend

upon men, than men upon governments...Let men be good, and the government cannot be bad...

That, therefore, which makes a good constitution, must keep it, vie: men of wisdom and virtue, qualities, that because they descend not with worldly inheritances, must be carefully propagated by a virtuous education of youth.

Here it is seen again that religious beliefs have their role in preserving a free society.

Most governments throughout history were monarchies, which, for the most part, controlled both financial and political power. The King of England, for example, granted monopolistic advantages to his favorites.

An example of this is the Hudson's Bay Company in Canada. Created when King Charles II granted a charter in 1670, the Hudson's Bay Company is the oldest commercial corporation in North America. It was at one time the largest landowner in the world, with an area known as "Rupert's Land" comprising 15 percent of all acreage in North America.

For centuries, the Hudson's Bay Company had a monopoly on North America's fur trade and a stranglehold on settlement in the Pacific Northwest, until American medical missionary, Dr. Marcus Whitman, led the first successful Oregon Trail wagon train there in 1843.

After thousands of Americans poured into the area, the boundary with British Canada was set at the 49th parallel in 1846.

The Dominion of Canada was formed in the late 19th century with the Hudson's Bay Company being the country's largest private landowner. With the decline of the fur trade, the company moved into a mercantile department store business selling goods to settlers.

The favoritism granted by the King to the British East India Tea Company was a contributing factor to the Boston Tea Party, as colonists objected to paying taxes while the King's authorized company did not.

In republics, financial and political power tended to split into two distinct categories, fluctuating back and forth in their pursuit of control of the county.

The Durants wrote in *The Lessons of History* (p. 54):

> The bankers, watching the trends in agriculture, industry, and trade, inviting and directing the flow of capital, putting out money doubly and trebly to work, controlling loans and interest and enterprise, running great risks to make great gains, rise to the top of the economic pyramid.
>
> From the Medici of Florence and the Fuggers of Augsburg to the Rothschilds of Paris and London and the Morgans of New York, bankers have sat in the councils of governments, financing wars and popes, and occasionally sparking a revolution. Perhaps it is one secret of their power that, having studied the fluctuations of prices, they know that history is inflationary, and that money is the last thing a wise man will hoard.

As government becomes more concentrated, business entities, unions, and foreign interests are drawn to financially benefit from it. They send courtiers, lobbyists and insiders, to procure monopolistic favors.

This results in the combining of big money and power interests with big government (ie. global finance united with global government.)

An example of a banker who yielded to selfishness was Nicholas Biddle.

Nicholas Biddle was head of the Bank of the United States, a privately owned bank in which the revenues of the Federal Government were deposited. Biddle boasted of having more power than the President, as he not only controlled the Bank, but due to bank's size, effectively controlled the interest rates for the entire country.

A combination of George Soros and Ruppert Murdoch of his day, Nicholas Biddle influenced elections by owning newspapers and directing their editorial articles and cartoons, and by being major contributor to many Congressional campaigns.

Andrew Jackson, July 10, 1832, vetoed the Bank Renewal Bill for Nicholas Biddle's bank, stating:

> Powers and privileges possessed by the existing bank are unauthorized by the Constitution, subversive to the rights of the States, and dangerous to the liberties of the people...
>
> It is easy to conceive that great evils to our country and its institutions might flow from such a concentration of power in the hands of a few men irresponsible to the people...Their power would be great whenever they might choose to exert it...to influence elections or control the affairs of the nation.
>
> But if any private citizen or public functionary should interpose to curtail its powers or prevent a renewal of its privileges, it can not be doubted that he would be made to feel its influence...

Andrew Jackson continued:

> Controlling our currency, receiving our public moneys, and holding thousands of our citizens in dependence, it would be more formidable and dangerous than the naval and military power of the enemy...It is to be regretted that the rich and powerful too often bend the acts of government to their selfish purposes...

President Jackson continued, criticizing paybacks and pork barrel projects:

In the full enjoyment of the gifts of Heaven...every man is equally entitled to protection by law; but when the laws undertake to add to these natural and just advantages artificial distinctions, to grant titles, gratuities, and exclusive privileges, to make the rich richer and the potent more powerful, the humble members of society-the farmers, mechanics, and laborers-who have neither the time nor the means of securing like favors to themselves, have a right to complain of the injustice of their Government...

Jackson explained:

Many of our rich men have not been content with equal protection and equal benefits, but have besought us to make them richer by acts of Congress. By attempting to gratify their desires we have in the results of our legislation arrayed section against section, interest against interest, and man against man, in a fearful commotion which threatens to shake the foundations of our Union...

Jackson stood against stimulus spending funneled to political supporters:

We can at least take a stand against all new grants of monopolies and exclusive privileges, against any prostitution of our Government to the advancement of the few at the expense of the many...

For relief and deliverance let us firmly rely on that kind Providence which I am sure watches with peculiar care over the destinies of our Republic.

Jefferson wrote to George Logan, November of 1816 (*The Jeffersonian Cyclopedia*, John P. Foley, ed., New York & London, Funk & Wagnalls Co., 1900, No. 464; Paul Leicester Ford, ed., x, 69):

> I hope we shall crush in its birth the aristocracy of our moneyed corporations, which dare already to challenge our government to a trial of strength and bid defiance to the laws of our country.

Another example of government resisting concentrated financial power was Lincoln's refusal to borrow money for the Civil War from internationalist European bankers. Instead, Lincoln issued the famous Greenback Bills, to be redeemed in gold after the Civil War ended.

In the early 1900's, Theodore Roosevelt championed the fight against financial monopolies run by industrialist robbers barons, such as John D. Rockefeller, Cornelius Vanderbilt, John Jacob Astor, James Fisk, Jay Gould and Edward Harriman, precursors to today's global financial manipulators like Bernie Madoff, Enron and Goldman Sachs.

An example of unrestrained corporate selfishness was Standard Oil Company's John D. Rockefeller.

Rockefeller used unscrupulous agreements with railroads to ship his oil cheaper; then he would sell it cheaper and put his competitors out of business. Once he had a monopoly, he would raise the price of oil through roof, and pay back the railroads. Rockefeller justified this as "Social Darwinism," evolution, the survival of the fittest.

President Theodore Roosevelt explained the need for Anti-Trust Legislation in a Special Message to Congress, May 4, 1906:

> In New England, the refusal of certain railway systems to prorate has resulted in keeping the Standard Oil Company in absolute monopolistic control of the field, enabling it to charge from three to four hundred thousand

dollars a year more to the consumers of oil in New England than they would have had to pay had the price paid been that obtaining in the competitive fields.

This is a characteristic example of the numerous evils which are inevitable under a system in which the big shipper and the railroad are left free to crush out all individual initiative.

Theodore Roosevelt continued, April 14, 1908:

Already the evils of monopoly are becoming manifest.

Jefferson wrote of the Bill of Rights to F. Hopkinson, March 1789 (*The Jeffersonian Cyclopedia*, John P. Foley, ed., NY & London, Funk & Wagnalls Co., 1900, No. 819, ii, 586; Paul Leicester Ford, ed., v, 76):

A bill of rights...to secure freedom in religion, freedom of the press, **freedom from monopolies...**

Will and Ariel Durant, quoting from the *Age of Louis XIV* (p. 720), stated:

Men who can manage men, manage the men who can manage only things; and the men who can manage money, manage all.

President Woodrow Wilson is quoted in *The New York Times* article, "Theodore Roosevelt Scorns Wilson's Philosophy," September 14, 1912:

The story of liberty is a history of the limitation of a government power, not the increase of it.

Theodore Roosevelt had an anti-trust crusade against industrialist robber barons. His distant cousin, Franklin D. Roosevelt, tried to continue this, only to over-correct and create another problem worse than the first – an overpowering government. "Beware, lest the dragon-slayer become the dragon."

FDR's high taxes and government regulation began the outsourcing trend. To stay competative globally, businessmen were left no choice but to go out of the country or go out of business.

Liberal anti-job policies include:

1) Burdensome government regulations;
2) Higher taxes, which effectively act as economic sanctions;
3) Higher wages and expensive worker benefits;
4) Lawsuits, driving insurance rates up;
5) Unreasonable environmental restrictions
6) Facism/crony capitalism, where the government favors certain companies in exchange for political support.

Squeeze the sponge and the water goes out. If regulations, taxes, wages, lawsuits, environmental restriction and crony capitalism are increased, do not be surprised if jobs leave the country.

CAPITALISM WITH A CONSCIENCE

"Only a virtuous people are capable of freedom."-Ben Franklin, April 17, 1787

America's successful experience with democracy and capitalism has largely been a result of its population being virtuous.

Just as democracy can be good or bad, depending on whether the people who vote are virtuous or selfish, so capitalism can be good or bad, depending on whether people who have acquired wealth are virtuous or selfish.

Allowing average citizens to participate in politics is a means of checking totalitarian governments; in the same way, allowing average citizens to participate in capitalism is a means of checking globalist corporate monopolies.

Capitalism allows an opportunity wherein the ordinary individual can educate themself, be creative, take risks, work hard and become successful enough to challenge the concentrated power of a monopolist or dictator.

If individuals empowered by capitalism have a selfish belief system, then exploitation of the less fortunate will result, competition will be squeezed out, monopolies will be created, and if left unrestrained, they would become financial dictators over a global empire.

But if individuals empowered by capitalism have a belief system which encourages care for the less fortunate, great good will result. Henry David Thoreau wrote in *Civil Disobedience* (1849):

> It is truly enough said that a corporation has no conscience; but a corporation of conscientious men is a corporation with a conscience.

John Mackey, co-founder of Whole Foods Market, is quoted in *The Morality of Capitalism-What Your Professors Won't Tell You* (2011):

> Capitalism is a source of value. It's the most amazing vehicle for social cooperation that has ever existed...From an ethical standpoint...capitalism is about creating shared value, not for the few, but for everyone.

Billionaire philanthropist Foster Friess, founder of Friess Associates asset management firm, has contributed millions to relief efforts around the globe, including the Asian tsunami, Hurricane Katrina, the Haiti earthquake, supporting orphanages, mobile medical vans for low-income neighborhoods, orthopedic surgeries for disabled children, water purification systems for mission fields, and numerous other projects.

Giving every one of the hundreds who attended his 70th birthday celebration a $70,000 check made out to each of their favorite charities, Foster Friess stated:

> I believe we are merely stewards, not owners,

of what God has given to us. I tell friends who accuse me of being generous that it's the Lord's money.

Recipient of the Benefactor of the Year Award, Foster Friess addressed the Paul Weyrich Awards Dinner in Washington, DC, February 9, 2011:

America experienced the marriage between capitalism and Christianity. The opportunity and freedom to create wealth united with the moral direction to use it to help others.

Judeo-Christian values provided a unique ingredient in the founding and development of the American Republic. They worked to restrain selfishness and encourage charity.

A prime truth is that human nature, left to itself, is selfish, but the teaching of the Gospel admonishes men to resist it.

Two threads can be traced through history, GREED and the GOSPEL.

Of the **gospel**, it is written in Matthew, chapter 25:40:

Inasmuch as ye have done it unto the one of the least of these my brethren, ye have done it unto me.

Of **greed,** Harry S Truman wrote, December 24, 1946:

Selfishness and greed, individual or national, cause most of our troubles.

In addition to preaching, Christians motivated by the GOSPEL fought to abolish slavery, built orphanages, medical clinics, shelters, hospitals, schools, universities, donated money, gave free food and clothes, took in homeless, dug wells, dispensed emergency aid, inoculated, taught farming techniques, visited those in prison, ransomed slaves, provided literacy programs and disaster relief.

People in history motivated by the GOSPEL include:

*Missionaries like Lottie Moon, who helped famine victims in China;

*Mary Slessor who helped end twin killing in Africa;
*Gladys Aylward, who helped end the binding of girls' feet in China;
*Moravian missionaries who voluntarily sold themselves into slavery in order to evangelize slaves;
*William Carey, who helped end the Hindu Sati burning of widows upon their husband's ashes;
*Dietrich Bonhoffer, who stood up to Hitler;
*Franklin Graham's Samaritan's Purse, CBN's Operation Blessing, and ministries which distribute food, clean water, clothes and medical supplies to crises victims from Haiti to the Sudan.

Even concepts like "women and children first," philanthropy, volunteerism, civil rights, and tolerance have roots traceable to Judeo-Christian thought. Ronald Reagan phrased this, August 8, 1992:

We make a living by what we get; we make a life by what we give.

Those motivated by GREED, though some may have called themselves "Christian," were so in name only, and often fought against genuine Christian work, giving the faith a bad name. The Apostle Paul referred to these people in Titus, 1:16:

They profess that they know God; but in works they deny him, being abominable, and disobedient, and unto every good work reprobate.

People in history motivated by GREED include:

*Those involved in the slave trade;
*Merchants of the British East India Tea Company that hindered British and American missionaries in India;
*Sugar plantation owners who opposed evangelizing slaves so they would not have to be treated as equal;
*British Government officials in African colonies

who favored Muslims over Christians as magistrates because of their non-compassionate efficiency in collecting taxes;
*Those who took land from Indians;
*Belgium's King Leopold who brutalized millions on his personal plantations in the Congo;
*Those who discriminated against women;
*Those who held racial prejudice;
*Those who voted their pocketbook, even though it meant electing politicians who spread corruption and sexual immorality, leading to a disregard for innocent human life;
*Candidates who claimed to be Christian to get elected.

The main concern of people motivated by greed is their job, financial security, the bottom line, government welfare, or as Bill Clinton so aptly put it in his 1992 campaign phrase: "Its the economy, stupid." **Greed's** "Whoever has the gold rules" is contrary to the **Gospel's** Golden Rule - "do unto others as you would have them do unto you" (Matt 7:12). The word "christian" means in Greek, "one who imitates Christ." Christ preached spiritual redemption and demonstrated a concern for the needy. Those motivated by GREED or the GOSPEL exist together, as seen in the parable, Matthew 13:27:

> The servants...said unto him, Sir, didst not thou sow good seed in thy field? from whence then hath it tares? He said unto them,
> An enemy hath done this...Let both grow together until the harvest: and in the time of harvest I will say to the reapers, Gather ye together first the tares, and bind them in bundles to burn them: but gather the wheat into my barn.

The divide between GREED and the GOSPEL was

illustrated in America prior to the Civil War, with the nation's moral views on slavery dividing the country into four political categories:

1) Extreme North - end slavery now;

2) Moderate North - transition out of slavery over time;

3) Moderate South - slavery is wrong, but we have to live with it and try to treat slaves fairly;

4) Extreme South - slavery is good, and attempted to justify it by twisting scriptures.

These are the four categories regarding abortion today:

1) Pro-Life supporters, which say end abortion now;

2) Pro-Life politicians, which say transition out of abortion with incremental legal advances;

3) Pro-Abortion politicians, which say abortion is wrong, but it should be legal, rare and few; and

4) Pro-Abortion supporters, which say abortion is good, and attempt to justify killing babies born alive who survived botched abortions.

Ronald Reagan drew this analogy in his article, "Abortion and the Conscience of the Nation," published in *The Human Life Review,* 1983:

Lincoln recognized that we could not survive as a free land when some men could decide that others were not fit to be free and should be slaves...

Likewise, we cannot survive as a free nation when some men decide that others are not fit to live and should be abandoned to abortion.

President Theodore Roosevelt warned in 1909:

The thought of modern industry in the hands of Christian charity is a dream worth dreaming. The thought of industry in the hands of paganism is a nightmare beyond imagining.

Christian charity correcting injustice is not to be confused with Liberation Theology, a Marxist political movement which employs the Machiavellian tactic of "the ends justifies the means" - manipulating the poor with twisted interpretations of scriptures to start a revolution and establish a communist dictatorship.

It is unfortunate that conquistadors lusted for gold, but thankfully they were followed by sincere missionaries, like Bartolome' de Las Casas, who ministered to the natives and helped end cannibalism and human sacrifice.

True Christians tried to follow Christ's teaching "whatever you have done unto the least of these my brethren, you have done unto me" (Mat. 25:40). Mother Teresa of Calcutta said:

> I see Jesus in every human being. I say to myself, this is hungry Jesus, I must feed him. This is sick Jesus. This one has leprosy or gangrene; I must wash him and tend to him. I serve because I love Jesus.

An American example of this was New York attorney, Charles Finney (1792-1875), who saw so many Scripture references in Blackstone's Law Commentaries that he bought a Bible, read it, came to faith and became an evangelist.

Founding the Broadway Tabernacle United Church of Christ, Charles Finney explained that in the Kingdom of God: "Every member must work or quit. No honorary members."

Finney's 1835 Revival Lectures inspired George Williams to found the Young Men's Christian Association (YMCA) in 1844, and William Booth to found The Salvation Army in 1865.

Charles Finney formed the Benevolent Empire, a network of volunteer organizations to aid with social problems which in 1834 had a budget rivaling the Federal Government.

While Finney was president of Oberlin College, 1851-1866, it became a station on the Underground Railroad smuggling slaves to freedom, and it also granted the first college degree in the United States to an African American woman, Mary Jane Patterson.

An abolitionist, Charles Finney wrote:

> The time has come for Christians to vote for honest men, and take consistent ground in politics or the Lord will curse them...
>
> Politics are a part of a religion in such a country as this, and Christians must do their duty to their country as a part of their duty to God...God will bless or curse this nation according to the course Christians take in politics.

∾

CAPITALISM & CHRISTIANITY IN CHINA

The Iona Institute for Religion and Society published the article, "Christianity the reason for West's success, say the Chinese," March 3, 2011, in which Tom O'Gorman wrote:

> In the West we are doing our best to destroy our Christian heritage but in China, Chinese intellectuals are coming around to the view that it is precisely this heritage that has made the West so successful.
>
> Former editor of the *Sunday Telegraph*, Dominic Lawson, in a review in the *Sunday Times* of Niall Ferguson's new book, *Civilisation: The West and the Rest*, carries a quote from a member of the Chinese Academy of Social Sciences in which he tries to account for the success of the West, to date.
>
> He said: "One of the things we were asked to look into was what accounted for the success, in fact,

the pre-eminence of the West all over the world.

"We studied everything we could from the historical, political, economic, and cultural perspective. At first, we thought it was because you had more powerful guns than we had.

"Then we thought it was because you had the best political system. Next we focused on your economic system. **But in the past twenty years, we have realised that the heart of your culture is your religion: Christianity. That is why the West is so powerful.**

"The Christian moral foundation of social and cultural life was what made possible the emergence of capitalism and then the successful transition to democratic politics. We don't have any doubt about this."

Note the source. It isn't from a religious leader, or some religious think-tank. The Chinese Academy of Social Sciences is an instrument of the Chinese Communist government which spends a not inconsiderable amount of time and money persecuting Christians and is officially atheistic.

If this is the conclusion it has come to, maybe Europe needs to reconsider whether it mightn't be an idea to encourage rather than eradicate Christianity.

Incidentally, just to drive home the point, Lawson also refers to this data point in Ferguson's book: Wenzhou, **the Chinese city which is rated as the most entrepreneurial in the country, is also home to 1,400 churches.**

Lawson refers to a quote in the book from a prominent Wenzhou business leader, a Mr.

Hanping Zhang, who argues that "an absence of trust had been one of the main factors holding China back; but he feels he can trust his fellow Christians because he knows that they will be honest in their dealings with him."

It has long been accepted that **Christianity is one of the core elements of Western civilisation; it is too little understood that it is also one of the secrets of the stunning success of that civilisation.**

(www.ionainstitute.org/index.php?id=1336)

∼

CITIZEN GUN OWNERSHIP CHECKS CONCENTRATED POWER

"To disarm the people is the best and most effectual way to enslave them."-George Mason, *Debates in the Several State Conventions* (Elliott, ed., 1836, p. 380)

Hubert Humphrey, Democrat Vice-President under Lyndon B. Johnson, was quoted by David T. Hardy, *The Second Amendment as a Restraint on State and Federal Firearms Restrictions* (Kates, ed., Restricting Handguns: *The Liberal Skeptics Speak Out*, 1979):

> The right of citizens to bear arms is just one more guarantee against arbitrary government, one more safeguard against the tyranny which now appears remote in America, but which historically has proved to be always possible.

Supreme Court Justice Joseph Story wrote in *Commentaries on the Constitution of the United States,* 2nd Edition, 1833, p. 125):

> The right of the citizens to keep and bear arms has justly been considered as the palladium

[safeguard] of the liberties of a Republic; since it offers a strong moral check against the usurpation and arbitrary power of rulers.

Michigan Supreme Court Chief Justice Thomas Cooley wrote in *The General Principles of Constitutional Law* (2nd Ed., 1891, p. 282):

> The Second Amendment...was meant to be a strong moral check against the usurpation and arbitrary power of rulers...The people...shall have the right to keep and bear arms, and they need no permission or regulation of law for the purpose.

Patrick Henry wrote (Elliott, ed., *The Debates in the Several State Conventions*, 1836, 1941, p. 378):

> Congress, by the power of taxation, by that of raising an army...has the **sword** in one hand and the **purse** in the other...
>
> Let him candidly tell me, where and when did freedom exist when the **sword** and the **purse** were given up from the people? Unless a miracle in human affairs interposed, no nation ever retained its liberty after the loss of the sword and the purse...The great object is, that every man be armed... Everyone who is able may have a gun.

Joel Barlow wrote in *Advice to the Priviledged Orders in the Several States of Europe, Resulting from the Necessity and Propriety of a General Revolution in the Principle of Government* (1792, 1956, p. 46):

> The foundation of everything is...that the people will form an equal representative government...that the people will be universally armed...A people that legislate for themselves ought to be in the habit of protecting themselves.

Madison wrote (*Letters & Writings of James Madison*, 1865, p. 406):

The advantage of being armed, which the Americans possess over the people of almost every other nation...forms a barrier against the enterprise of ambition...Kingdoms of Europe...are afraid to trust the people with arms.

Jeffrey R. Snyder, esq., wrote in "A Nation of Cowards" (*The Public Interest*, 1993, no. 113):

Classical republican philosophy has long recognized the critical relationship between personal liberty and the possession of arms by a people ready and willing to use them.

Marcus Tullius Cicero wrote (Cicero, *Selected Political Speeches*, trans. M. Grant, 1969, p. 222):

There exists a law...inborn in our hearts...that if our lives are endangered by plots or violence or armed robbers or enemies, any and every method of protecting ourselves is morally right.

Aristotle wrote in *Parts of Animals* (trans. A. Peck, 1961, p. 373):

Animals have just one method of defence and cannot change it for another...For man, on the other hand, many means of defence are available, and he can change them at any time...

Take the hand: this is as good as a talon, or a claw, or a horn, or again, a spear, or a sword, or any other weapon or tool it can be all of these.

Machiavelli wrote in *The Prince* (trans. L. Ricci, 1952, p. 73, 81):

Among evils caused by being disarmed, it renders you contemptible...It is not reasonable to suppose that one who is armed will obey willing one who is unarmed.

Cesare Beccaria wrote in *On Crimes and Punishment* (trans. H. Paolucci, 1963, p. 87-88):

> False is the idea...that would take fire from men because it burns, and water because one may drown in it...The laws that forbid the carrying of arms are laws of such a nature. They disarm those only who are neither inclined nor determined to commit crimes.
>
> Can it be supposed that those who have the courage to violate the most scared laws of humanity, will respect the less important and arbitrary ones, which can be violated with ease and impunity...
>
> Such laws...serve rather to encourage than to prevent homicides, for an unarmed man may be attacked with greater confidence than an armed man

Thomas Paine wrote (*Writings of Thomas Paine*, Conway, ed., 1894, p. 56)

> The peaceable part of mankind will be continually overrun by the vile and abandoned while they neglect the means of self defense.
>
> The supposed quietude of a good man allures the ruffian; while on the other hand, arms, like laws, discourage and keep the invader and the plunderer in awe, and preserve order.

Montesquieu wrote in *The Spirit of the Laws* (trans. T. Nugent, 1899, p. 64):

> It is unreasonable...to oblidge a man not to attempt the defence of his own life.

Thomas More wrote in *Utopia* (trans. R.M. Adams, 1975, p. 71):

Men and women alike...assiduously exercise themselves in military training...to protect their own territory or to drive an invading enemy out of their friends' land or, in pity for a people oppressed by tyranny, to deliver them by force of arms from the yoke and slavery of the tyrant.

Roman historian Livy wrote (trans. B. Foster, 1919, p. 148):

Formerly [under the reign of Servius Tullius-the 6th Roman king, 578-535 BC] the right to bear arms had belonged solely to the patricians. Now plebeians were given a place in the army...All the citizens capable of bearing arms were required to provide their own swords, spears, and other armor.

Aristotle wrote in *Politics* (trans. T. Sinclair, 1962, p. 274):

Those who possess and can wield arms are in a position to decide whether the constitution is to continue or not.

Machiavelli wrote in *On the Art of War* (trans. E. Farnsworth, 1965, p. 30):

Citizens, when legally armed...did the least mischief to any state...Rome remained free for four hundred years and Sparta eight hundred, although their citizens were armed all that time, but many other states that have been disarmed have lost their liberty in less than forty years.

Machiavelli wrote in *Discourses on the First Ten Books of Titus Livius* (trans. L. Walker, 1965, p. 492):

If any city be armed...as Rome was...all its citizens, alike in their private and official capacity...it will be found they will be of the same mind...

But, when they are not familiar with arms and merely trust to the whim of fortune...they will change with the changes of fortune.

Jefferson wrote to George Washington, 1796 (*The Jeffersonian Cyclopedia*, John P. Foley, ed., New York & London, Funk & Wagnalls Co., 1900, No. 2138, iv, 143; Paul Leicester Ford, ed., vii. 84):

One loves to possess arms, though they hope never to have occasion for them

Machiavelli wrote in *The Prince* (trans. L. Ricci, 1952, p. 73, 81):

An armed republic submits less easily to the rule of one of its citizens...

Noah Webster wrote in *An Examination into the leading Principles of the Federal Constitution*, Oct. 10, 1787, (Paul Leicester Ford, ed., *Pamphlets on the Constitution of the United States*, 1888, 1968):

Before a standing army can rule, the people must be disarmed; as they are in almost every kingdom in Europe. The supreme power in America cannot enforce unjust laws by the sword because the whole body of the people are armed.

Adam Smith wrote in *The Wealth of Nations* (ed., Cannan, p. 309):

Men of republican principles have been jealous of a standing army as dangerous of liberty...

The standing army of Caesar destroyed the Roman Republic. The standing army of Cromwell turned the Long Parliament out of doors.

Earl Warren wrote in *The Bill of Rights and the Military*, (37 N.Y.U. L. Rev. 181, 1962):

Our War of the Revolution was, in good measure, fought as a protest against standing armies...

Thus we find in the Bill of Rights, Amendment 2...specifically authorizing a decentralized militia, **guaranteeing the right of the people to keep and bear arms.**

Jeffrey R. Snyder, esq., wrote in "A Nation of Cowards" (*The Public Interest*, 1993, no. 113):

Political theorists as dissimilar as Niccolo Machiavelli, Sir Thomas More, James Harrington, Algernon Sidney, John Locke, and Jean Jacques Rousseau all shared the view that the possession of arms is vital for resisting tyranny, and that to be disarmed by one's government is tantamount to being enslaved by it.

The *Texas Declaration of Independence*, March 2, 1836, stated:

The late changes made in the government by General Antonio Lopez Santa Ana, who having overturned the constitution of his country, now offers, as the cruel alternative, either abandon our homes acquired by so many privations, or submit to the most intolerable of all tyranny...

It has demanded us to deliver up our arms, which are essential to our defense - the rightful property of freemen-and formidable only to tyrannical governments.

Mahatma Gandhi wrote in *An Autobiography of the Story of My Experiments with the Truth* (trans. M. Desai, 1927):

Among the many misdeeds of the British rule in India, history will look upon the Act depriving a whole nation of arms as the blackest.

Islamic Sharia law forbids non-Muslims from possessing arms, swords or weapons of any kind.

Adolph Hitler acted similarly with his Edict of March 18, 1938:

> The most foolish mistake we could possibly make would be to allow the subjected people to carry arms; history shows that all conquerors who have allowed their subjected people to carry arms have prepared their own fall.

German Firearm Act of 1937:

> Firearm licenses will not be granted to Jews.

Richard Munday reported in "The Monopoly of Power," presented to the American Society of Criminology, 1991, the Nazi order regarding arms, *SA Ober Führer of Bad Tolz:*

> SA [Storm Troopers], SS [para-military adjunct of the Gestapo], and Stahlhelm...
>
> Anyone who does not belong to one of the above-named organizations and who unjustifiably keeps his weapon...must be regarded as an enemy of the national government and will be brought to account without compunction and with the utmost severity.

Jefferson wrote in the Declaration on Taking Up Arms, July 1775 (*The Jeffersonian Cyclopedia,* John P. Foley, ed., New York & London, Funk & Wagnalls Co., 1900, No. 2152; Paul Leicester Ford, ed. i, 476):

> We...most solemnly, before God and the world declare that...the arms we have been compelled to assume we will use with perseverance, exerting to their utmost energies all those powers which our Creator hath given us, to preserve that liberty which He committed to us in sacred deposit.

DEMOCRACY CHECKS CONCENTRATED POWER

What is the definition of "DEMOCRACY"? George Orwell wrote in *Politics and the English Language - An Essay* (1947):

> DEMOCRACY, not only is **there no agreed definition**, but the attempt to make one is resisted from all sides.
>
> It is almost universally felt that **when we call a country democratic, we are praising it:** consequently the defenders of every kind of regime claim that it is a democracy, and fear that they might have to stop using the word if it were tied down to any one meaning.
>
> **Words of this kind are often used in a consciously dishonest way.** That is, the person who uses them has his own private definition, but allows his hearer to think he means something quite different.

President Harrison stated in his *Inaugural Address*, 1841:

> An intolerant spirit of party...seldom fails to result in **a dangerous accession to the Executive power...established amidst unusual professions of devotion to democracy...**This is the **old trick** of those who would **usurp the government** of their country. **In the name of democracy they speak.**

Democracy has two meanings, CONCEPTUAL and ACTUAL:

1) Democracy is **favorably** described as "the CONCEPT or IDEA of people ruling themselves," which, in the case of America, is

through a constitutional republic;

2) Democracy is **unfavorably** described as "an ACTUAL FORM of government" where each citizen votes on each issue without the limits of a constitution. This strict majority rule is sometimes referred to as mobocracy.

DEMOCRACY, **unfavorably** described as "an ACTUAL FORM of government," results in chaos that precedes a dictatorship. Plato wrote in *The Republic* (380 BC):

> Dictatorship naturally arises out of democracy, and the most aggravated form of tyranny and slavery out of the most extreme form of liberty.

This is referred to by author James Bovard, who wrote in *Lost Rights: The Destruction of American Liberty* (1994):

> Democracy must be something more than two wolves and a sheep voting on what to have for dinner.

Will and Ariel Durant wrote in *The Story of Civilization* (Vol. 2-The Life of Greece, Simon & Schuster, 1939, p.554):

> Class war had turned democracy into a contest in legislative looting.

Jefferson, as quoted in *Dreams Come Due: Government And Economics As If Freedom Mattered* by John Galt (1986, p. 312), stated:

> Democracy will cease to exist when you take away from those who are willing to work and give to those who would not.

Historian Sir Alexander Fraser Tytler (1747-1813), describing the Decline and Fall of the Athenian Republic, is attributed with saying:

> A democracy cannot exist as a permanent form of government. It can only exist until the voters discover that they can vote themselves money from the public treasury.

In 1961, Ronald Reagan warned of Socialized Medicine:

> We talk democracy today. And strangely we let democracy begin to assume the aspect of majority rule...Well, majority rule is a fine aspect of democracy, provided there are guarantees written in to our government concerning the rights of the individual and of the minorities.

Franklin D. Roosevelt, on the 150th Anniversary of the Congress, March 4, 1939, stated:

> Democracy to us under the Constitution [is] not democracy by direct action of the mob; but democracy exercised by representatives chosen by the people themselves.

Richard M. Nixon, the 37th President, gave an address titled the *Meaning of Communism to Americans*, August 21, 1960:

> Russia's Communist Party's holding of elections in which the electorate is given no choice may similarly be described as an attempt by communism to salve its uneasy conscience. Knowing that it cannot achieve representative democracy, it seems to feel better if it adopts its empty forms.

When democracy was introduced into the former Soviet States, often the black market and organized crime took control.

When democracy is introduced into Muslim countries, it usually results in Sharia Law, which relegates non-Muslims to a second-class status called "dhimmi," allows men to beat their wives, orders women who have been raped to be whipped 100 times and enacts the death penalty for those leaving Islam.

Anjem Choudary, leader of Islam4UK, expressed his attitude toward democracy, (*London Daily Express*, Oct. 15, 2009):

> We request all Muslims in the United Kingdom...to join us and declare that as submitters to Almighty Allah, we have had enough of democracy and man-made law and the depravity of the British culture...
>
> We will call for a complete upheaval of the British ruling system, its members and legislature, and demand the full implementation of Sharia in Britain.

DEMOCRACY, **favorably** described as "the CONCEPT or IDEA of people ruling themselves," is referred to by Henry David Thoreau in his *Civil Disobedience* (1849):

> The progress from an absolute to a limited monarchy, from a limited monarchy to a democracy, is a progress toward a true respect for the individual.

Ronald Reagan spoke to the British Parliament, June, 1982:

> The march of freedom and democracy which will leave Marxism-Leninism on the ash heap of history as it has left other tyrannies which stifle the freedom and muzzle the self-expression of the people.

President William Howard Taft told a missionary gathering, 1908:

> The spirit of Christianity is pure democracy. It is equality of man before God - the equality of man before the law, which is, as I understand it, the most God-like manifestation that man has been able to make.

Dwight Eisenhower told the National Conference on the Spiritual Foundation of American Democracy, November 9, 1954:

Democracy is nothing in the world but a spiritual conviction, a conviction that each of us is enormously valuable because of a certain standing before our own God. Now...any organization such as that is, to my mind, a dedicated, patriotic group that can well take the Bible in one hand and the flag in the other, and march ahead.

Jimmy Carter, the 39th President, stated to European Broadcast Journalists, May 2, 1977:

We strongly favor the election of leaders who are committed to freedom and democracy and who are free from Communist philosophy, which quite often has been dominated from the Soviet Union.

Ronald Reagan, the 40th President, August 23, 1984, summed up the situation at a prayer breakfast in Reunion Arena, Dallas, Texas:

Without God there is a coarsening of the society; without God democracy will not and cannot long endure...

If we ever forget that we are One Nation Under God, then we will be a Nation gone under.

Ronald Reagan stated at the Ecumenical Prayer Breakfast of the Republican National Convention in Dallas, TX:

Our government needs the church, because only those humble enough to admit they're sinners can bring democracy the tolerance it requires to survive.

Ronald Reagan toasted Indonesian President Soeharto at a State Dinner, October 12, 1982:

> The friendship between our two countries has a solid foundation because of the similarity of our two nations with regard to the noble values which we hold dearly—such as freedom and independence, democracy and humanitarianism.

&

COMMUNICATION CHECKS CONCENTRATED POWER

The equivalent of today's Internet and Talk Radio was the Committees of Correspondence formed by Samuel Adams. These were a means of communication at a time when the King controlled major venues.

Samuel Adams had three goals: (1) delineate the rights of Colonists as men; (2) detail how these rights had been violated; (3) publicize these rights and the violations thereof throughout the Colonies. His reports spread like fire through the towns and parishes, many times by an early pony express system, similar to the Internet and talk radio today. Ben Franklin, as deputy Postmaster General of the colonies, was able to help disseminate information.

William Henry Harrison stated in his *Inaugural Address*, 1841:

> The maxim which our ancestors derived from the mother country that "freedom of the press is the great bulwark of civil and religious liberty" is one of the most precious legacies which they have left us....A decent and manly examination of the acts of the Government should be not only tolerated, but encouraged.

Jefferson wrote to James Monroe, in May of 1795, regarding Alexander Hamilton's hostility to democratic societies

(*The Jeffersonian Cyclopedia*, John P. Foley, ed., New York & London, Funk & Wagnalls Co., 1900, No. 2178; Paul Leicester Ford, ed., vii, 16):

> The incredible fact that the freedom of association, of conversation, and of the press, should in the fifth year of our government, have been attacked under the form of a denunciation of the Democratic Societies, a measure which even England, as boldly as she is advancing to the establishment of an absolute monarchy, has not yet been bold enough to attempt.

✏

WHO CONTROLS INFORMATION CONTROLS DEMOCRACY

Just as Greek theater was a means to influence the mass of citizens, today's media and education exerts a similar influence.
The Durants wrote in *The Lessons of History* (p. 77):

> Democracy is the most difficult of all forms of government, since it requires the widest spread of intelligence...Ignorance is not long enthroned, for it lends itself to manipulation by the forces that mold public opinion.

Thomas Sowell wrote in "Degeneration of Democracy," 6/2010:

> A democracy needs informed citizens if it is to thrive, or ultimately even survive.

Jefferson wrote to John Adams, 1816 (*The Jeffersonian Cyclopedia*, John P. Foley, ed., New York & London, Funk & Wagnalls Co., 1900, No. 745, vii, 27):

> We are destined to be a barrier against the

return of ignorance and barbarism.

Benjamin Franklin wrote April 17, 1787:

> Only a virtuous people are capable of freedom. As nations become corrupt and vicious, they have more need of masters.

In 1786, Dr. Benjamin Rush, who signed the Declaration of Independence, wrote *Thoughts Upon the Mode of Education Proper in a Republic,* in which he referred to the religions of Confucius, Mohammed and Christianity:

> The only foundation for a useful education in a republic is to be laid on the foundation of religion. Without this there can be no virtue, and without virtue there can be no liberty, and liberty is the object and life of all republican governments.
>
> Such is my veneration for every religion that reveals the attributes of the Deity, or a future state of rewards and punishments, that I had rather see the opinions of Confucius or Mohammed inculcated upon our youth than to see them grow up wholly devoid of a system of religious principles.
>
> **But the religion I mean to recommend in this place is that of the New Testament.** It is not my purpose to hint at the arguments which establish the truth of the Christian revelation. My only business is to declare that all its doctrines and precepts are calculated to promote the happiness of society and the safety and well-being of civil government.

In 1258, Thomas Aquinas wrote in *Summa contra Gentiles* (Bk 1, Chp 6, trans. Anton C. Pegis, University of Notre Dame Press, 1975):

Mohammed...seduced the people by promises of carnal pleasure...As is not unexpected, he was obeyed by carnal men. As for proofs of the truth of his doctrine, he brought forward only such as could be grasped by the natural ability of anyone with **a very modest wisdom**...Those who believed in him were brutal men and desert wanderers, utterly ignorant...It was a shrewd decision on his part to forbid his followers to read the *Old* and *New Testaments*, lest these books convict him of falsity.

William Penn wrote in his *Preface to Frame of Government for Pennsylvania*, May 5, 1682:

That...which makes a good constitution, must keep it, vie: **men of wisdom and virtue**, qualities, that because they descend not with worldly inheritances, must be carefully propagated by a virtuous education of youth.

Theodore Roosevelt stated (August Kerber, *Quotable Quotes of Education*, p. 138):

To educate a man in mind and not in morals is to educate a menace to society.

Noah Webster stressed education in morals in a republic:

For this reason society requires that the education of youth should be watched with the most scrupulous attention. Education, in a great measure, forms the moral characters of men, and morals are the basis of government.

Education should therefore be the first care of a legislature; not merely the institution of schools, but the furnishing of them with the best men for teachers.

A good system of education should be the first article in the code of political regulations; for it is much easier to introduce and establish an effectual system for preserving morals, than to correct by penal statutes the ill effects of a bad system.

The goodness of a heart is of infinitely more consequence to society than an elegance of manners; nor will any superficial accomplishments repair the want of principle in the mind. It is always better to be vulgarly right than politely wrong...

The education of youth [is] an employment of more consequence than making laws and preaching the gospel, because it lays the foundation on which both law and gospel rest for success...

Noah Webster continued:

To give children a good education in manners, arts and science, is important; to give them a religious education is indispensable; and an immense responsibility rests on parents and guardians who neglect these duties.

In *A Manual of Useful Studies*, published in New Haven, 1839, Noah Webster stated:

In the family are formed the elements of civil governments; the family discipline is the model of all social order;...the respect for the law and the magistrate begins in the respect for parents...

Families are the nurseries of good and bad citizens. The parent who neglects to restrain and govern his child, or who, by his example, corrupts him, is the enemy of the community to which he belongs; the parent who instructs his child in good principles, and subjects him to correct discipline, is the guardian angel of his child, and the best benefactor of society...

Ronald Reagan stated on October 14, 1969:

No government at any level and for any price can afford the police necessary to assure our safety and our freedom unless the overwhelming majority of us are guided by an inner personal code of morality.

John Adams wrote October 11, 1798:

Our Constitution was made only for a moral and religious people. It is wholly inadequate to the government of any other.

The American Republic consists of citizens democratically electing representatives to vote within the guidelines of their constitution. If citizens are educated with morals and virtue, they will elect representatives who cast good votes. If citizens are left ignorant, subject to their selfish human instincts, they will elect representatives who cast bad votes, and the resulting chaos will end with a dictator restoring order through totalitarian control.

James Abram Garfield, who later became the 20th President, stated while a Congressman, July 4, 1876:

Now more than ever before, the people are responsible for the character of their Congress. If that body be ignorant, reckless, and corrupt, it is because the people tolerate ignorance, recklessness, and corruption. If it be intelligent, brave, and pure, it is because the people demand these high qualities to represent them in the national legislature.

If the next centennial does not find us a great nation...it will be because those who represent the enterprise, the culture, and the morality of the nation do not aid in controlling the political forces.

Democracy, in this sense, is not actually rule of the people, but rather rule by those who control what the people know, leaving them at the mercy of those who control public opinion. Uneducated citizens can easily be manipulated or whipped into a frenzy by those controlling what the citizens know about the issues.

Llewellyn Rockwell, Jr., wrote in "Why Hate Monarchs?" (*The Free Market*, Vol. 19, No. 8, August 2001):

Democracy has turned out to be not majority rule but rule by well-organized and well-connected minority groups who steal from the majority.

Jefferson wrote to William Branch Giles, December of 1794 (*The Jeffersonian Cyclopedia*, John P. Foley, ed., New York & London, Funk & Wagnalls Co., 1900, No. 2177; Paul Leicester Ford, ed., vi, 515):

The attempt which has been made to restrain the liberty of our citizens meeting together, interchanging sentiments on what subjects they please, and stating their sentiments in the public papers, has come upon us a full century earlier than I expected.

To demand the censors of public measures to be given up for punishment, is to renew the demand of the wolves in the fable that the sheep should give up their dogs as hostages.

The Constitution was written to separate power into executive, legislative and judicial branches, but since then other "branches" of power have emerged, such as unions, trial lawyers, lobbyists, environmental groups, financial institutions, and perhaps the most significant, education and media. In America:

> The COUNTRY is controlled by LAWS >
> LAWS are controlled by POLITICIANS >
> POLITICIANS are controlled by VOTERS >
> VOTERS are controlled by PUBLIC OPINION >
> PUBLIC OPINION is controlled by the MEDIA (News,
>   Hollywood, Internet...) & EDUCATION >
> so whoever controls MEDIA & EDUCATION,
>   controls the COUNTRY.

This identification and influencing of power is basic to human nature, as in a traditional home a child knows that father has the final say, but he complains to mommy to persuade father; or he bothers his big sister to complain to mommy to persuade father; or he bribes little brother to bother big sister to complain to mother to persuade father!

If a child can figure out where the power sits and how to get his or her way, it is not that difficult for some to figure out that in **America** the power sits with the **laws**, but to change them one must influence **politicians** by influencing **voters** by influencing **public opinion** by controlling **media and education**!

Those promoting a liberal agenda are notably left-leaning academics and ultra-rich Hollywood/media personalities, and the gullible, less educated class of people who believe them.

Those promoting a conservative agenda are the people in-between, the practical middle-class working families, too smart to believe the media, but not rich enough to own it.

Politicians fear public opinion, so those wanting to affect the direction of a country must utilize education, media and the Internet.

An illustration from the Gospel of Matthew tells of rulers being kept in check because they feared a negative public opinion spreading among the people, (chapter 21:23-27):

> And when he was come into the temple, the chief priests and the elders of the people came unto him as he was teaching, and said, "By what authority doest thou these things and who gave thee this authority?"

And Jesus answered and said unto them, "I also will ask you one thing, which if ye tell me, I in like wise will tell you by what authority I do these things. The baptism of John, whence was it? from heaven, or of men?"

And they reasoned with themselves, saying, "If we shall say, From heaven; he will say unto us, Why did ye not then believe him? But if we shall say, Of men; WE FEAR THE PEOPLE; for all hold John as a prophet."

And they answered Jesus, and said, "We cannot tell." And he said unto them, "Neither tell I you by what authority I do these things."

The Gospel of Mark tells of a political ruler swayed because he was afraid of the negative public opinion spreading among the people, (chapter 15:9-15):

But Pilate answered them, saying, "Will ye that I release unto you the King of the Jews?" For he knew that the chief priests had delivered him for envy.

BUT THE CHIEF PRIESTS MOVED THE PEOPLE, that he should rather release Barabbas unto them. And Pilate answered and said again unto them, "What will ye then that I shall do unto him whom ye call the King of the Jews?"

And they cried out again, "Crucify him." Then Pilate said unto them,

"Why, what evil hath he done?" And they cried out the more exceedingly,

"Crucify him."

And so Pilate, WILLING TO CONTENT THE PEOPLE, released Barabbas unto them, and delivered Jesus, when he had scourged him, to be crucified.

Senate Minority Leader Everett Dirksen (R-IL) once said:

> When I feel the heat, I see the light.

Around 400 BC, the Chinese leader Sun Tzu wrote in his book, *The Art of War*:

> Supreme excellence consists in breaking the enemy's resistance without fighting.

A parable of persistence affecting political leaders is in the Gospel of Luke, (chapter 18:1-5):

> He spake a parable unto them to this end, that men ought always to pray, and not to faint; saying, "There was in a city, a judge, which feared not God, neither regarded man: And there was a widow in that city; and she came unto him, saying,
>
> 'Avenge me of mine adversary.'
>
> And he would not for a while: but afterward he said within himself, 'Though I fear not God, nor regard man; YET BECAUSE THIS WIDOW TROUBLETH ME, I will avenge her, LEST BY HER CONTINUAL COMING SHE WEARY ME.' "

American humorist Josh Billings (1818-1885), wrote in his poem "The Kicker":

> The squeaky wheel gets the grease.

"Persistence wears down resistance," or as Ben Franklin wrote:

> Energy and persistence conquer all things.

Thomas Jefferson worded it this way:

> The spirit of resistance to government is so valuable on certain occasions, that I wish it always to be kept alive.

DEMOCRACY VERSUS DICTATORSHIP

"The state is made for man, not man for the state."

- Albert Einstein

Whereas democracy, without virtue, as an "ACTUAL FORM" of government is a precursor to dictatorship, democracy as a "CONCEPT or IDEA" of government is opposed to dictatorship.

Underlying the CONCEPT or IDEA of democracy is the assumption that the State exists for man's benefit.

Underlying monarchy or communist dictatorship is the assumption that man exists for the State's benefit.

John Bouvier's Law Dictionary (1914) stated:

> A monarchy is the government which is ruled by one person, who is wholly set apart from all other members of the state's (called his subjects).

President Harry S Truman in his *State of the Union Address*, January 7, 1948, said:

> We do not believe that men exist merely to strengthen the state or to be cogs in the economic machines.

Plato, in *The Republic* (380 BC), used a war economy illustration of a mutiny on board a ship, with the mutinous crew being "democracy" and the sick captain being the "tyrant." Plato argued that it is better to be ruled by a bad tyrant than by a bad democracy, since one individual committing a bad deed is better than many people committing many bad deeds.

Monarchy can be good or bad, depending on whether the king is virtuous or selfish, just as democracy can be good or bad, depending on whether the people who vote are virtuous or selfish.

America's founders believed there was "safety in numbers" – that it was safer to trust the "many" people rather than the "one" king, especially if citizens were educated, church-going, moral people.

Jefferson wrote to William Short in 1825 (*The Jeffersonian Cyclopedia*, John P. Foley, ed., New York & London, Funk & Wagnalls Co., 1900, No. 2182, vii, 391; Paul Leicester Ford, ed., x, 335):

> Democrats consider **the people as the safest depository of power** in the last resort; they cherish them, therefore, and wish to leave in them all the powers to the exercise of which they are competent.

A way to personalize this is to ask the question:

> "If you were accused of a crime and brought to court, would you rather be tried before one politically appointed judge, or before a jury of twelve of your peers?"

The answer to that question will reveal if one would prefer to live under a dictator or under a constitutional republic with democratically-elected representatives. Harry S Truman made this contrast in his *Inaugural Address*, January 20, 1949:

> We believe that all men are created equal because they are created in the image of God. From this faith we will not be moved...
>
> **Communism** is based on the belief that man is so weak and inadequate that he is unable to govern himself, and therefore requires the rule of strong masters.
>
> **Democracy** is based on the conviction that man has the moral and intellectual capacity, as well as the inalienable right, to govern himself with reason and justice.

Communism subjects the individual to arrest without lawful cause, punishment without trial, and forced labor as a chattel of the state. It decrees what information he shall receive, what art he shall produce, what leaders he shall follow, and what thoughts he shall think.

Democracy maintains that government is established for the benefit of the individual, and is charged with the responsibility of protecting the rights of the individual and his freedom...

These differences between **communism** and **democracy** do not concern the United States alone.

People everywhere are coming to realize that what is involved is material well-being, human dignity, and the right to believe in and worship God.

DEMOCRATIC CONSTITUTIONAL REPUBLIC

In America:

- **Democracy** is the *concept or idea* (people ruling themselves);
- **Republic** is the *form* (representative government);
- **Constitution** established a *set of rules* (limiting representatives).

- **Democracy** is the WHY – because people ruling themselves is better than a king;
- **Republic** is the WHO – representatives chosen by the people do the ruling;
- **Constitution** is the HOW – representatives have to follow rules.

In America, the "People" are the sailors, the ship of State is the "Republic," and the "Constitution" is the anchor, to keep then from drifting onto the rocks of despotism.

The Latin word "representative" means one who is present in the place of another.

In contrast to a democracy as "an ACTUAL FORM of government," which requires every single citizen to vote on every single issue, a "republican" form of government is one where citizens have "representatives" to look out for their interests while they work to support their families.

During the Roman Republic, representatives were called "senators." Though they represented the people, they were not elected by the people. They inherited their position from their ancestors who were heads "paters" of family clans. Over the generations, Roman Senators became a powerful, aristocratic class.

America's founders wanted representatives elected democratically – "by the people," and for them to cast their vote in Congress as the citizens would have.

An additional limit on government is a Constitution.

A "Constitutional" Republic is where elected representatives, president and appointed judges have to follow certain rules and stay within their well-defined circles of jurisdiction.

Thus, America's form of government could be described as a **democratic Constitutional Republic.**

Jefferson wrote to Joseph C. Cabell, 1816 (*The Jeffersonian Cyclopedia*, John P. Foley, ed., New York & London, Funk & Wagnalls Co., 1900, No. 3592, vi, 543):

> The elementary republics of the wards, the county republics, the State republics, and the Republic of the Union, would form a gradation of authorities, standing each on the basis of law, holding every one its delegated share of powers, and constituting truly a system of fundamental balances and checks for the government.

Where every man is a sharer in the direction of his ward-republic, or of some of the higher ones, and feels that he is a participator in the government of affairs, not merely at an election one day in the year, but every day, when there shall not be a man in the State who will not be a member of some one of its councils, great or small, **he will let the heart be torn out of his body sooner than his power be wrested from him by a Caesar or a Bonaparte.**

REPUBLIC OPPOSITE MONARCHY

"The Republican is the only form of government which is not eternally at open or secret war with the rights of mankind."

-Thomas Jefferson, 1790 (*The Jeffersonian Cyclopedia*, John P. Foley, ed., New York & London, Funk & Wagnalls Co., 1900, p. 390, No. 3554, iii, 128; Paul Leicester Ford, ed., v. 147)

John Bouvier's Law Dictionary (1914) stated that "Monarchy is contradistinguished from republic," and gives the definitions:

We call "republic" that government in which not only there exists an organism by which the opinion of the people, or of a portion of the people (as in aristocracies), passes over into public will, that is, law, but in which also the supreme power, or the executive power, returns, either periodically or at stated times (where the chief magistracy is for life), to the people, or a portion of the people, to be given anew to another person; or else, that government in which the hereditary portion (if there be any) is not the chief and leading portion of the government, as was the case in the Netherlands.

John Bouvier's Law Dictionary (1914) defined "Republic" as:

REPUBLIC: A commonwealth; that form of government in which the administration of affairs is open to all the citizens.

Thomas Jefferson wrote to Samuel Kerchival, 1816 (*The Jeffersonian Cyclopedia*, John P. Foley, ed., New York & London, Funk & Wagnalls Co., 1900, p. 391, No. 3558, vii, 10; Paul Leicester Ford, ed., x, 38):

A government is republican in proportion as every member composing it has his equal voice in the direction of its concerns (not indeed in person, which would be impractical beyond the limits of a city or small township, but) by representatives chosen by himself and responsible to him at short periods.

John Bouvier's Law Dictionary (1914) gives the definition:

REPUBLICAN GOVERNMENT: A government of the people; it is usually put in opposition to a monarchical or aristocratic government. 2. Section 4, Article 4 of the U.S. Constitution directs that "the United States shall guaranty to every state in the Union a republican form of government. See Story, Const. §1807.

According to Montesquieu, a **Monarchy** is based on **Honor**; a **Tyranny** is based on **Fear**; and a **Republic** is based on **Virtue**, as mentioned in *John Bouvier's Law Dictionary* (Revised 6th Edition, 1856):

In the state, the REPUBLIC is the proper governmental form, and VIRTUE is the mainspring...

The mainspring is that single attribute without which, the form would fail (think of a clock that has many springs, but without the main spring, the secondary springs would never have the chance to fulfill their purposes and the clock could not work)...

Montesquieu tells us that the primary forms of governance are MONARCHY, TYRANNY and REPUBLIC.

The mainsprings of MONARCHY, TYRANNY, and REPUBLIC have been proven practically uncontroversial. Writers of poetry and prose have touched on these self-evident truths for hundreds of years. In fact, even the Bible makes it clear that HONOR, FEAR and VIRTUE are the three primary mainsprings.

In other words, for **People** to rule themselves in a **Republic**, they must have **Virtue**; for a **Tyrant** to rule in a **Tyranny**, he must use **Fear.** On the sliding scale of virtue, it is an inverse relationship:

The **more power is concentrated**, the **more a tyrant must abandon virtue** and use fear and corruption to maintain order and control;

The **more power is separated, the more the people must embrace virtue** and use morals and self-control to maintain order and control.

British statesman Lord Acton wrote to Bishop Creighton, 1887:

Absolute power corrupts absolutely.

Jefferson wrote to Gideon Granger, August of 1800 (*The Jeffersonian Cyclopedia*, John P. Foley, ed., New York & London, Funk & Wagnalls Co., 1900, No. 1445, iv, 331; Paul Leicester Ford, ed., vii, 451):

I do verily believe, that **if...the General Government at once [possesses] all the powers** of the State governments, and reduces us to a single consolidated government, **it would become the most corrupt government on the earth.**

Ronald Reagan said in Los Angeles, CA, March 2, 1977:

Politics is said to be the second oldest profession. I have come to realize that it bears a very close resemblance to the first.

Oxford English Dictionary defined:

REPUBLIC: A state in which the supreme power rests in the people and their elected representatives or officers, as opposed to one governed by a king or similar ruler.

In 1786, Dr. Benjamin Rush, who signed the Declaration of Independence, wrote *Thoughts Upon the Mode of Education Proper in a Republic,* in which he stated:

A Christian cannot fail of being a republican...for every precept of the Gospel inculcates those degrees of humility, self-denial, and brotherly kindness which are directly opposed to the pride of monarchy...

A Christian cannot fail of being useful to the republic, for his religion teaches him that no man "liveth to himself."

And lastly a Christian cannot fail of being wholly inoffensive, for his religion teaches him in all things to do to others what he would wish, in like circumstances, they should do to him."

Rep. Fisher Ames, who helped write the Bill of Rights,

compared a monarchy and a republic in a speech to the House of Representatives, 1795 (attributed by R.W. Emerson in *Essays*, 1844):

> A monarchy is a merchantman which sails well, but will sometimes strike on a rock and go to the bottom; whilst a republic is a raft which would never sink, but then your feet are always in the water.

As monarchies, often tyrannical, were the normal form of human government, alternatives to monarchy were not normal. A few rare sparks of other forms of government glimmered throughout history.

✍

HISTORY OF REPUBLICS - HOW THEY ROSE & FELL

"We have gone back to ancient history for models of Government, and examined the different forms of those Republics which, having been formed with the seeds of their own dissolution, now no longer exist."

-Ben Franklin, June 28, 1787, Constitutional Convention

Prior to the United States, there were relatively few examples of alternatives to monarchy throughout all previous history. Like dandelion weeds sprouting through the pavement of totalitarianism, most republics were small city-states along trade routes or in inaccessible remote mountains or islands.

As a result of increased freedoms, Republics became successful through commerce, manufacturing and banking, being defended by disciplined, patriotic citizen-soldiers. Republics were often weakened by internal political divisions, short-sighted in-fighting and traitors. Their prosperity rendered them attractive targets for conquest by larger aggressive States.

NOTABLE REPUBLICS IN WORLD HISTORY

Phoenician Island of Arvad (c.1800-322 BC)
Israeli Tribes under the Judges (c.1270-1050 BC)
Greek city-states: Thebes; Corinth;
    Sparta; & Athens (650-322 BC)
India's city-states of: Kuru of Hastinapur &
    Licchavi of Vaishali (c.600-400 BC)
Roman Republic (509-27 BC)
Carthage of North Africa (308-146 BC)
Doric city-states of Crete (259-183 BC)
Pyu city-state of Burma (100 BC-840 AD)
Italian city-states (301 AD-Present)
India's small republics (700-1526)
Icelandic Commonwealth (930-1262)
Free Cities of Medieval Europe (962-1806)
Russian city-states: Novgorod (1136-1478);
    Pskov (1268-1510)
Confederation of Swiss Cantons (1291-1848)
Croatian city-state of Dubrovnik (Ragusa) (1358-1808)
Polish-Lithuanian Commonwealth (1569-1795)
Dutch Republic - Seven United Netherlands (1581-1795)
French city-state of Goust (1648-1900)
English Commonwealth (1649-1659)
The United States of America (1776-)

City-state republics usually survived only for short periods because they lacked the resources to defend themselves against incursions by larger states, empires and nation states. Only a few republics became great, but their large bureaucracies contributed to their being controlled by an elite political class, then, ultimately by a monarch.

❧

REPUBLIC ALTERNATIVE TO MONARCHY -

PHOENICIAN CITY-STATE OF ARVAD (c.1800-322 BC)

Arvad was a Phoenician trading city-state situated on a tiny island off the coast of modern day Syria. Ancient monuments of Egypt and Assyria mention that Arvad had a powerful navy.

Phoenician trade benefited from the invention of the Phonetic alphabet around 1200 BC in the city-state of Byblos, from where the word "Bible" is derived.

Arvad is written of in Hebrew Scriptures: Genesis 10:18; Ezekiel 27:8,11; and 1 Maccabees 15:16-23.

In 332 BC, Arvad surrendered to Alexander the Great during his invasion of Assyria, which Greeks began to call Syria.

Arvad was favored by the Seleucid kings of Syria and mentioned in a Roman rescript, 138 BC, as a city of considerable importance which showed favor to the Jews.

Due to the fact that few kings are mentioned in the historical record, mostly Assyrians, it is thought that Arvad may be the world's first republic in which citizens formed the government.

❧

REPUBLIC ALTERNATIVE TO MONARCHY

ISRAEL UNDER THE JUDGES (c.1270-1050 BC)

From the period of Moses and Joshua to the period of Kings Saul, David and Solomon, approximately 1270-1050 BC, Israel was ruled by Judges, and functioned in ways as a constitutional republic.

Richard Pipes wrote in *Communism-A History* (Random House, 2001):

> In the oldest civilizations, dating back 5,000 years – pharaonic Egypt and Mesopotamia – agricultural land belonged to palaces and temples.
>
> Ancient Israel is the first country where we possess firm evidence of private land ownership.
>
> The Lord in the Hebrew Bible casts a curse on anyone who tampers with boundary stones ("Cursed be he that removeth his neighbor's landmark," Deuteronomy 27:17), and several biblical books tell of families as well as individuals holding land and pasture in private possession."

Approximately 1300 BC, the children of Israel left Egypt and sojourned in the wilderness 40 years till they entered the land of Canaan, where they were ruled by Judges: Joshua, Othniel, Ehud, Shamgar, Deborah, Barak, Gideon, Abimelech, Tola, Jair, Jephthah, Ibzan, Elon, Abdon, Samson, Eli, and Samuel.

These judges were raised to leadership from any background, usually in times of crises. They defended Israel from external attacks, and judged internal disputes.

Though somewhat disorganized in appearance, this system functioned well to provide protection, yet maximize personal freedoms. Judges did not establish royal monarchies or dynasties. A story of how this system could be abused was when Abimelech took money from a temple treasury to buy supporters:

> Judges 9:4-5 And they gave him threescore and ten pieces of silver out of the house of Baal-berith, wherewith Abimelech hired vain and light persons, which followed him. And he went unto his father's house at Ophrah, and slew his brethren...And all the men of Shechem gathered together...and made Abimelech king.

The Book of Samuel recorded how people finally grew discontented with this system and complained to the prophet Samuel that they wanted a king like the other nations. He warned them that a king would concentrate power, take away individual rights, and that would eventually regret this.

The people of Israel persisted and Samuel relented, anointing Saul as their first king. King Saul was followed by King David and King Solomon, after which the nation was split between the Kingdom of Israel in the north and the Kingdom of Judah in the south.

The Book of First Samuel, chapter 8:4-20 recorded:

> Then all the elders of Israel...came to Samuel...And said unto him, Behold, thou art old, and thy sons walk not in thy ways: now **make us a king to judge us like all the nations.** But the thing displeased Samuel, when they said, **Give us a king...**And Samuel prayed...**and the LORD said unto Samuel...they have not rejected thee, but they have rejected me,** that I should not reign over them...Howbeit...show them the manner of the king that shall reign **over them.**
>
> And Samuel told all the words of the LORD

unto the people that asked of him **a king.** And he said, **This will be the manner of the king that shall reign over you:**

He will take your sons, and appoint them for himself, for his chariots, and to be his horsemen; and some shall run before his chariots.

And **he will appoint** him captains over thousands, and captains over fifties; and will set them to plow his ground, and to reap his harvest, and to make his instruments of war, and instruments of his chariots. And **he will take** your daughters to be confectioneries, and to be cooks, and to be bakers. And **he will take** your fields, and your vineyards, and your oliveyards, even the best of them, and give them to his servants. And **he will take** the tenth of your seed, and of your vineyards, and give to his officers, and to his servants. And **he will take** your menservants, and your maidservants, and your goodliest young men, and your asses, and put them to his work. **He will take** the tenth of your sheep: and ye shall be his servants.

And ye shall cry out in that day because of your **king** which ye shall have chosen you; and the LORD will not hear you in that day.

Nevertheless the people refused to obey the voice of Samuel; and they said, **Nay; but we will have a king over us; That we also may be like all the nations.**"

In the *Memoirs of Benjamin Franklin*, vol. 2 (William Temple Franklin, McCarty & Davis, Philadelphia, 1834, p. 211), Benjamin Franklin compared opposition to the U.S. Constitution to the Ancient Israelites' opposition to Moses, and later the Messiah:

A zealous advocate for the proposed Federal Constitution in a public assembly said, that the repugnance of a great part of mankind to good government was such, that he believed, that **if an angel from heaven was to bring down a constitution, formed there for our use,** it would nevertheless meet with violent opposition...

It might not have immediately occurred to him, **that the experiment had been tried, and that the event was recorded in the most faithful of all histories, the Holy Bible...**

The Supreme Being had been pleased to nourish up a single family, by continued acts of his attentive providence, till it became a great people: and having rescued them from bondage by many miracles, performed by his servant Moses, he personally delivered to that chosen servant, in presence of the whole nation, **a constitution and code of laws for their observance, accompanied and sanctioned with promises of great rewards, and threats of severe punishments, as the consequence of their obedience or disobedience...**

Yet there were, in every one of the thirteen tribes, some discontented, restless spirits, who were continually exciting them to reject the proposed new government, and this from various motives...

After many ages...as they had accused Moses of the ambition of making himself a prince, and cried out, stone him, stone him; So, excited by their high-priests and scribes, they exclaimed against the Messiah...crucify him, crucify him.

REPUBLIC
ALTERNATIVE TO MONARCHY
_
GREEK CITY-STATES (c.650-336 BC)

THEBES
CORINTH
SPARTA
ATHENS

Another departure from monarchy were the Greek city-states, called "polis." Greek city-states were originally ruled by some form of monarchy, with a king being the leader of a landowner class of warrior aristocracy which fought frequent wars with other Greek city-states.

After about 680 BC, a mercantile class arose, as seen in the introduction of coinage, which replaced aristocracies with populist leaders, called "tyrranoi" or tyrants. Thebes, Corinth, Sparta, and Athens emerged as the dominant Greek city-states.

THEBES – was ruled by an oligarchy. Attributed by legend to have been founded by Cadmus, King of Tyre (Lebanon) and brother of Queen Europa. He is credited with introducing the written Phoenician alphabet to Greece. Thebes was a dominat city in Greece, playing roles in the Persian Wars and the Peloponnesian Wars. Philip of Macedon studied in Thebes, but his son, Alexander the Great leveled the city in 335 BC.

CORINTH – Dorians began settling in Corinth around 1100 BC, at the end of the Mycenaean period, most notably under their leader, Aletes. In 747 BC, the Bacchiad clan abolished monarchy and established an aristocratic oligarchy. Corinth developed into a major mercantile and maritime power, being a continual rival of Athens.

SPARTA – Beginning around 650 BC, Sparta was ruled by the constitution of Lycurgus, which maintained a permanent military regime with power retained by the landed aristocracy under a dual monarchy. Sparta grew to dominate the smaller city-states of the Greek Peloponnese and formed alliances with Corinth and Thebes, resulting in a generational rivalry with Athens.

Sparta did not believe in individual rights. A person's worth was only in their value to the State. Children born defective were left to die. Boys were taken from their families and trained to serve the State in the military. It was totalitarian in nearly all respects.

Aristotle criticized the Sparta's government in his work, *The Politics: On the Lacedaemonian (Spartan) Constitution*, as it mixed monarchical, oligarchic and democratic components:

> Monarchical: Two kings, hereditary monarchs, one from each of the Agiad and Eurypontid families, who had priestly obligations and the power to make war.

> Oligarchic: A Gerousia council of 28 elders picked for life, which included the two kings, and was controlled by five ephors, chosen annually by popular election.

> Democratic: The Assembly was made up of those with full Spartan citizenship over 18 years of age.

Aristotle warned in *The Politics: On the Lacedaemonian (Spartan) Constitution*, that Sparta's government was liable to being controlled by the poor, who were more susceptible to taking bribes:

> The Lacedaemonian constitution is defective in another point; I mean the Ephoralty. This magistracy has authority in the highest matters, but the Ephors are chosen from the whole people, and so the office is apt to fall into the hands of very poor men, who, being badly off, are open to bribes.

ATHENS - In Athens the monarchy was abolished in 683 BC. Solon (638–558 BC) established a semi-constitutional system of aristocratic government. Solon repealed the laws of Draco (621 BC), because of the harsh "draconian" death penalty imposed for even minor offenses.

After setting up Athens' government, Solon voluntarily stepped down and left the country. He sailed to the Kingdom of Lydia, where he advised King Croesus, who was the first to introduce the use of gold and silver coins (the world's principal means of exchange till the early 20th century). Though Croesus became the richest man in the world, as the saying goes "rich as Croesus," Solon warned: "Count no man happy until he be dead." The Kingdom of Lydia was soon conquered in 546 BC by King Cyrus of Persia, who burned King Croesus to death on a funeral pyre as he cried out "Solon."

Pisistratus (600-527 BC) and his sons, ruled by tyranny and made Athens a great naval and commercial power.

Cleisthenes, around 500 BC, established the world's first "democracy" with power being held by an assembly of free male citizens over 18 years old who had served in the military, called the ecclesia. In the Greek language, "demos" means "people" and "cratos" means "power or rule." Athenian Democracy was an actual form of government where the people ruled themselves through a complex system of power balanced between three political bodies: the Legislative Assembly, the Executive Council and the Courts. Because of the fear of being ruled by another tyrant, popular citizens were often accused by the ecclesia and, upon a vote of 6,000 citizens, ostracized (banished for ten years).

In 490 BC, the 60,000 strong Persian Army under King Darius I attacked Greece at Marathon, but was defeated by the Athenian army led by Miltiades. Over 6,400 Persians were killed compared to only 192 Greeks. A messenger ran non-stop the 26 miles to Athens, and upon delivering the news of this great victory, fell dead. His run is commemorated by the popular race known as "the Marathon."

In 480 BC, another Persian army numbering in the hundreds of thousands attacked Greece, led by King Xerxes I, son of Darius I. King Leonidas of the Greek city-state of Sparta, with 300 Spartans and 700 Thespians, held back the entire Persian army for seven days at the narrow pass of Thermopylae. Though the Persians eventually won, they were later defeated at sea in the Battle of Salamis, and at the Battle of Plataea (479 BC).

An example of one who was ostracized was Themistocles, a politician who campaigned among the poor as well as the rich. He was elected Eponymous Archon - the effective head of Athenian government. He built Athens' navy and several strategic port cities, and was responsible for the key victory over the Persians at the Battle of Salamis. Jealous citizens, particularly Cimon, were successful in having Themistocles ostracized in 472 BC.

Following the defeat of Persia, Athens allied itself with several independent Greek city-states called the Delian League (478-404 BC), and Sparta allied with other cities to form the Peloponnesian League. War between the two Leagues began in 460 BC.

Pericles (495-429 BC) was a popular general during the First Peloponnesian War (460-445 BC) between Athens' Delian League and Sparta's Peloponnesian League.

Pericles had charisma and was a persuasive speaker, sometime verging on manipulation. He was able to convince the ecclesia to ostracize his rival, Cimon. When historian Thucydides was asked by Sparta's king, Archidamus, whether he or Pericles was the better fighter, Thucydides answered that Pericles was better, because even when he was defeated, he could convince the audience that he had won.

Pericles ushered in what was considered the Golden Age of classic Greece, building temples, public buildings, and advancing arts and theater plays.

Will and Ariel Durant wrote *The Story of Civilization* (Vol. 2-The Life of Greece, Simon & Schuster, 1939, p. 233):

> The realization of self-government was something new in the world; life without kings had not yet been dared by any great society. Out of this proud sense of independence, individual and collective, came a powerful stimulus to every

enterprise of the Greeks; it was their liberty that inspired them to incredible accomplishments in arts and letters, in science and philosophy.

Jefferson wrote to Mr. Coray, 1823 (*The Jeffersonian Cyclopedia*, John P. Foley, ed., New York & London, Funk & Wagnalls Co., 1900, No. 3602, vii, 318):

Greece was the first of civilized nations which presented examples [in government] of what man should be.

In a democratic society, to get an agenda implemented required influencing large numbers of citizens. Greek theater became a remarkable tool to accomplish this, particularly plays called tragedies, or comedies of political satire.

In Athens, government was controlled by laws, and laws are controlled by voters, and voters were influenced by public opinion, and public opinion is molded by media/entertainment in the short run and education in the long run.

Pericles brought more cities into alliance with Athens, creating a kind of imperial empire. He promoted a populist social policy, permitting the poor to watch theatrical plays with the state paying their admission fees. He enacted legislation granting lower classes access to the political system. He lowered the property requirement to hold civil office (archonship) and had the government pay generous wages on citizens who served on the jury.

Athenian private citizens who did not take seriously their duty to educate themselves on the issues and participate in politics were called 'idiotes.' In his Funeral Oration, Pericles states: "It is only we who regard the one, not participating in these duties, not as unambitious but as useless."

Historian Plutarch mentions criticism of Pericles: "many others say that the people were first led on by him into allotments of public lands, festival-grants, and distributions of fees for public services, thereby falling into bad habits, and becoming luxurious and wanton under the influence of his public measures, instead of frugal and self-sufficing". Historian Thucydides wrote that Athens was "in name a democracy but, in fact, governed by its first citizen" - Pericles.

Athens sent its navy to help Egypt in an attempt to rebel from Persia, but it was defeated. After this, several cities tried to leave the Delian League, but Pericles laid siege to them and forced them to capitulate. A tax was placed on the allied cities to provide for their common defense and the money was placed in the alliance's treasury at Delos. Pericles moved the treasury to Athens and withdrew large amounts for his ambitious building projects, including the Acropolis, the Parthenon and a golden statue of Athena, considered to be some of the most artistic creations of the ancient world. A Greek academician, Angelos Vlachos, wrote that Pericles' use of the alliance's treasury was, in a sense, one of the largest embezzlements in human history.

When accusations against Pericles grew, with the threat of being ostracized, it is speculated he allowed relations with Sparta to deteriorate so that another war could begin, turning public attention away from him.

During the Second Peloponnesian War (431-404 BC) Athens was superior at sea, but Sparta was superior on land. Pericles evacuated rural residences from the Attica countryside around Athens and packed them into city. The crowded conditions caused a plague to break out, which first killed Pericles's sons, and eventually Pericles himself. The Spartans eventually won and the Delian League was dissolved.

The Spartan's authoritarian rule ruined the economy and they were eventually overthrown. Sparta resorted to making a treaty with the enemy, the Persians. Athens and Thebes began to regain prominence.

Socrates (469-399 BC) the philosopher, lived during this time. He was a popular leader in Athens, who unsuccessfully stood against a passionate vote to kill some generals who, after a victory against Sparta at sea, failed to collect all the survivors in a storm. Socrates' criticism of the State resulted in his trial, and sentence of execution in 399 BC.

Socrates' student, Plato (428-347 BC), became critical of democracy. Will and Ariel Durant wrote in *The Lessons of History* (p. 74):

> By the time of Plato's death, his hostile analysis of Athenian democracy was approaching apparent confirmation by history. Athens recovered wealth, but this was now commercial rather than landed wealth; industrialists, merchants, and bankers were at the top of the reshuffled heap...The poor schemed to despoil the rich by legislation, taxation, and revolution; the rich organized themselves for protection against the poor...
>
> The poorer citizens captured control of the Assembly, and began to vote the money of the rich into the coffers of the state, for redistribution among the people through governmental enterprises and subsides. The politicians strained their ingenuity to discover new sources of public revenue.

In *The Story of Civilization* (Vol. 2-The Life of Greece, Simon & Schuster, 1939, p. 554), Will and Ariel Durant describe what happened in Athens:

> The class war had turned democracy into a contest in legislative looting.

Jefferson wrote in his Notes on Virginia, 1782 (*The Jeffersonian Cyclopedia*, John P. Foley, ed., New York & London, Funk & Wagnalls Co., 1900, No. 25, viii, 362; Paul Leicester Ford, ed., iii, 224):

Mankind soon learns to make interested uses of every right and power which they possess, or may assume. **The public money...will soon be discovered to be sources of wealth** and dominion to those who hold them; distinguished, too, **by this tempting circumstance, that they are the instrument, as well as the object of acquisition.**

Edmund Burke stated in *A Letter to a Member of the National Assembly,* 1791:

What is liberty without wisdom and without virtue? It is the greatest of all possible evils; for it is folly, vice, and madness, without restraint.

The poor controlling Athens' democracy was described as "empowered envy" by the Durants in *The Lessons of History* (p. 74):

The middle classes, as well as the rich, began to distrust democracy as empowered envy, and the poor distrusted it as a sham equality of votes nullified by a gaping inequality of wealth. The rising bitterness of the class war left Greece internally as well as internationally divided when Philip of Macedon pounced down upon it in 338 BC...Athenian democracy disappeared under Macedonian dictatorship.

President Andrew Jackson warned in his *8th Annual Message to Congress,* December 5, 1836:

No people can hope to perpetuate their liberties who long acquiesce in a policy which taxes them for objects not necessary to the legitimate and real wants of their Government.

Greeks considered Macedonia – an area north of Greece, as barbarian. Phillip of Macedon (382-336 BC) began to seize Greek cities and gained control of the gold and silver mines. With his great wealth, Philip bribed Greek politicians and created a "Macedonian party" of propagandists in every Greek city. These "traitors of Greece," acting as the biased media of the day, thwarted and confused efforts to rally against Philip. The freedoms allowed by the Athenian Democracy were misused as these paid propagandists spoke in Athens' meeting place, the Agora, exclaiming that Philip was not conquering, but liberating the other city-states. These paid propagandists gather around themselves people who believed their lies, whom Lenin later termed "useful idiots."

Thomas Sowell, in his article "Degeneration of Democracy" (6/22/2010), wrote:

> "Useful idiots" was the term supposedly coined by V.I. Lenin to describe similarly unthinking supporters of his dictatorship in the Soviet Union.

These paid propagandists were later termed "the fifth column," as a typical battle array consisted of two columns and two flanks. The "fifth column" were in essence traitors within a democracy who, for personal gain, spread lies to breed confusion.

Gathering around themselves "useful idiots," the result was citizens were so divided in their opinions they could not muster an adequate defense of the city. Franklin D. Roosevelt stated in a Fireside Chat, May 26, 1940:

> Today's threat to our national security is not a matter of military weapons alone. We know of new methods of attack. The Trojan Horse. The Fifth Column that betrays a nation unprepared for treachery. Spies, saboteurs and traitors are the actors in this new strategy.

In a Fireside Chat, Dec. 29, 1940, Franklin D. Roosevelt stated:

> Their secret emissaries are active in our own country… They exploit for their own ends our natural abhorrence of war. These trouble-breeders have but one purpose. It is to divide our people into hostile groups and to destroy our unity and shatter our will to defend ourselves.

Joseph Goebbels, the Nazi Minister of Propaganda, advised:

> The most brilliant propagandist technique will yield no success unless one fundamental principle is borne in mind constantly…it must confine itself to a few points and repeat them over and over.

Athens' internal problems distracted them from preparing to fight external threats. Will and Ariel Durant wrote in *The Story of Civilization* (Vol. 1-Our Oriental Heritage, Simon & Schuster, 1935, p. 463):

> The bitter lesson that may be drawn from this tragedy is that eternal vigilance is the price of civilization. A nation must love peace, but keep its powder dry.

Once Phillip of Macedon won the Battle of Chaeronea in 338 BC, and took control of Athens, the era of Athens as a self-ruling democracy was over. The Greek city-states were no longer capable of forming any lasting federation, and were controlled by Alexander the Great, the son of Philip of Macedon, followed by the Carthaginians, the Romans and then the Muslim Turks.

Of Greece's conquest by Rome in 168 BC, Will and Ariel Durant wrote in *The Story of Civilization* (Vol. 2-The Life of

Greece, Simon & Schuster, 1939, p.659):

> The essential cause of the Roman conquest of Greece was the disintegration of Greek civilization from within. No great nation is ever conquered until it has destroyed itself.

Greece was not free again until the 19th century AD. Historian Sir Alexander Fraser Tytler (1747-1813), in his thesis *Cycle of Nations,* described the Decline and Fall of the Athenian Republic. He is attributed with the statement:

> A democracy cannot exist as a permanent form of government. It can only exist until the voters discover that they can vote themselves money from the public treasury.
>
> From that moment on, the majority always votes for the candidates promising the most benefits from the public treasury, with a result that a democracy always collapses over loose fiscal policy, always followed by dictatorship.
>
> The average age of the world's greatest civilizations has been 200 years.
>
> These nations have progressed through the following sequence:
> -From bondage to spiritual faith;
> -From spiritual faith to great courage
> -From courage to liberty
> -From liberty to abundance;
> -From abundance to selfishness;
> -From selfishness to complacency;
> -From complacency to apathy;
> -From apathy to dependency;
> -From dependency back into bondage.

CHANGE TO CHAINS - WILLIAM J. FEDERER

REPUBLIC ALTERNATIVE TO MONARCHY - NORTH INDIA'S CITY-STATES

KURU OF HASTINAPUR, INDIA (c.600-400 BC) -
Though ruled as a monarchy in previous times, the Kurus are known
to have switched to republic form of government during 6th-5th
century BC. During this Vedic period of India's history, prior to the
rise of Buddhism in Northern India, there were 16 great kingdoms,
called Mahajanapadas.

The Kuru republic, with its capital of Hastinapura, is listed
in history by the Indian poet Panini (Astadhyayi 4.1.168-75) alongside
of the powerful monarchies of the Kshatriya Janapadas. In the 4th
century BC, Kautiliya's Arthashastra recorded that the Kurus
followed a constitution called Rajashabdopajivin (king consul).

LICCHAVI OF VAISHALI, INDIA (c.600-500 BC) - The
Licchavis people settled on the north bank of the Ganges River near
ancient Nepal in what is now Bihar state. Unlike their neighbors, the
Licchavi did not have a monarch, but instead were governed by a
republican government consisting of a general assembly of 7,707
raja - the male heads of households of the leading Kshatriya varna-
caste families. Eminent individuals, called gana mukhyas, were selected
from each district (khandas) to represent their city or village in the
people's council (gana parishad).

The head of the people's council was the Ganapramukh (head
of the state). He and his council of nine assistants, were elected each
year by the raja. Their capital, Vaishali, grew into a prosperous city
of considerable importance, which even the religious leader Buddha
visited. For a time, the Licchavis and other tribal groups formed the
Vaishali confederacy which rivaled the rising power of India's
Magadha rulers.

&

REPUBLIC ALTERNATIVE TO MONARCHY
–
ROMAN REPUBLIC (509-27 BC)

"SPQR" - Senatus Populusque Romanus, or Senate & People of Rome. Rome was a Republic from 509 until 27 BC, when it became an Empire under Julius Caesar's grandnephew, Augustus Caesar.

The word "republic" is from the Latin phrase "res publica," which means "a public affair." A republic is a form of government where representatives are trusted by the people to protect their interests, while the people are busy supporting their families.

The Roman Republic began with the help of Publius (died 503 BC), who ended the reign of the 7th King of Rome, the brutal Tarquinius Superbus, (literally meaning Tarquin the Proud). The king's son, Sextus, had raped Lucretia, wife of the Roman Cousul, Collatinus, and she subsequently committed suicide. This sparked a revolt which led to the founding of the Roman Republic – a government without a king. The rape of Lucretia has been referred to in Saint Augustine's *The City of God* (5th century), Geoffrey Chaucer's *The Legend of Good Women* (1385), William Shakespeare's *The Rape of Lucrece*,1593, and Rembrandt's painting *Lucretia* (1664).

When Publius was building a grand house, he was accused of aspiring to make himself monarch. When he heard this, he destroyed his own house in one night.

Publius instituted policies in the Roman Republic, such as:
ANYONE who attempted to reestablish the monarchy could be executed by any citizen without trial;
ANYONE who seized an office without popular vote would suffer execution;
ANY Roman could be appointed a Consul;
DECISIONS of the Consuls could be appealed;
NEEDY Romans were exempt from taxation;

PATRICIANS would be punished more severely than plebs for disobeying a Consul; and CONTROL of the treasury was removed from the Consuls to the **Temple of Saturn**, under administration of quaestors.

When the United States Constitution was being considered for ratification by the original 13 States, 1787-1788, Alexander Hamilton, John Jay and James Madison wrote a collection of 85 essays in favor of it called the *Federalist Papers,* which they collectively signed "Publius" in honor of the role Publius had in founding Rome's Republic.

The Roman Republic's constitution had a separation of powers with checks and balances, reflecting the tensions between the aristocracy (patricians) and the common people (plebeians).

The Roman Republic eventually had around 600 Senators, who were descendants of founders of the Republic, and two executives, called consuls, who were appointed for one year terms by the Senate. During their respective one year terms of consulship, each consul took turns being head of state, one month on-one month off, thus alternating the office.

During the period of the Republic, Rome expanded from Italy to controlling the entire Mediterranean, North Africa, the Iberian Peninsula, Greece, Gaul (France) and much of the middle east.

A famous early Roman leader was Cincinnatus (519–438 BC). In 458 BC, the Aequians, Sabinians and Volscians were attacking in the Alban hills southeast of the city of Rome. The Roman Senate sent messengers to Cincinnatus, who was plowing his field, requesting him to be dictator and lead the Roman troops. Cincinnatus won the victory, then immediately resigned and went back to his farm. In 439 BC, when the conspiracy of Spurius Maelius, threatened Rome, Cincinnatus was again called out of retirement to save Rome, only to again resign and return to his farm.

Cincinnatus' willingness to relinquish his absolute authority when the national crisis was over was an example of civic virtue to the Roman Republic, as well as early American leaders, like George

Washington. After the victory over the British, officers and soldiers stationed in Newburgh, New York, who had not been paid for years, threatened not to disband. Some suggested Washington declare himself king and they would support him.

At a private meeting, March 15, 1783, Washington urged them to oppose anyone "who wickedly attempts to open the floodgates of civil discord and deluge our rising empire in blood." Many were brought to tears as Washington fumbled to put on his new glasses, saying: "Gentlemen, you will permit me to put on my spectacles, for I have not only grown gray but almost blind in the service of my country."

Later that year, Washington resigned his commission and returned to his farm. After serving two terms as President, Washington again returned to his farm. Every President since honored his example of only serving two terms until Franklin D. Roosevelt, who got himself elected four times. This resulted in Congress passing the 22nd Amendment limiting a President to only two terms.

In May of 1783, Major General Henry Knox and Lieutenant Colonel Alexander Hamilton organized the first meeting of the Society of Cincinnati, honoring the example of Roman Dictator Cincinnatus, who resigned to return to farming. In 1790, a member of the Society, Arthur St. Clair, governor of the Northwest Territory, named the city of Cincinnati, Ohio.

In the early 1780's, while having his portrait painted, King George III asked his American-born painter, Benjamin West, what General Washington would do after winning independence. West replied: "They say he will return to his farm." King George responded: "If he does that, he will be the greatest man in the world."

In a world where kings killed to get power and kings killed to keep power, George Washington had power and gave it up. President Harry S Truman recorded in a personal memorandum, April 16, 1950:

There is a lure in power. It can get into a man's blood just as gambling and lust for money have been known to do. This is a Republic. The greatest in the history of the world. I want this country to continue as a Republic.

Cincinnatus and **Washington** pointed the way. When Rome forgot Cincinnatus, its downfall began. When we forget the examples of such men as Washington, Jefferson and Andrew Jackson, all of whom could have had a continuation in the office, then **will we start down the road to dictatorship and ruin**.

Towards the end of the Roman Republic, popular leaders forgot Cincinnatus and dominated the political scene, usurping and exceeding their constitutional limitations.

Though from an aristocratic family, Julius Caesar was greatly in debt. He escaped his debtors by serving in the military. Becoming a successful general, he positioning himself as a champion of the people, called "populares," against the aristocracy, called "optimates." In 59 BC, Caesar formed an informal alliance, called the First Triumvirate, with the famed Roman general Pompey the Great, and the immensely rich Crassus, with whose money they could buy supporters to challenge the powerful senatorial elite. Caesar realized early on that money was the key to Roman politics. Julius Caesar also wanted to extend citizenship to those living outside of Italy to increase his support base.

When Crassus died in 53 BC, contention grew between the two survivors of the First Triumvirate: Caesar and Pompey. The Durants wrote in *The Lessons of History* (p. 76):

> In Italy...rival factions competed in the wholesale purchase of candidates and votes; in 53 BC, one group of voters received ten million sesterces for its support...

When money failed, murder was available; citizens who had voted the wrong way were in some instances beaten close to death and their homes were set on fire.

Antiquity had never known so rich, so powerful, and so corrupt a government.

In 49 BC, after being victorious in Gaul, Caesar disobeyed the Senate's order to disband his legions before returning to Rome. Caesar crossed the Rubicon River with his legions, and headed toward Rome. Pompey withdrew to a defensive position south of Rome.

Without Crassus' money, Caesar needed another source of money to pay his supporters. Caesar did the unimaginable by raiding the public treasury kept in the **Temple of Saturn**. Treasure that had accumulated since the Temple's founding in 497 BC vanished in an instant: 15,000 gold ingots, 30,000 silver ingots, and 30 million sesterces in coin. Lucan wrote in *The Civil War* (3.153-8; 161-2; 167-8): "Then for the first time was Rome poorer than a Caesar."

As Abimelech in the time of Israel's judges took pubic money from the city of Shechem's temple treasury to buy "vain" supporters, and as Pericles withdrew public money from the Greek treasury, Caesar raided the Roman treasury kept in the Temple of Saturn and used Rome's public money to buy supporters.

Jefferson wrote in his Notes on Virginia, 1782 (*The Jeffersonian Cyclopedia*, John P. Foley, ed., NY & London, Funk & Wagnalls Co., 1900, No. 25, viii, 362; Paul L. Ford, ed., iii, 224):

With money we will get men, said Caesar, and with men we will get money.

Pompey lost to Caesar at the Battle of Pharsalus and fled to Egypt, where he was assassinated. Now, instead of 600 Senators deciding the fate of Rome, there was only one.

Julius Caesar had the Senate declare him dictator for life in 44 BC, then deify him, giving him his own cult, with Caesars's General, Mark Anthony, serving as high priest.

Julius Caesar even changed the calendar and named a month after himself - "July."

William Henry Harrison warned in his *Inaugural Address*, 1841:

> The danger to all well-established free governments arises from the unwillingness of the people to believe in [the] existence...of designing men...
>
> This is the old trick of those who would usurp the government of their country. In the name of **democracy** they speak, warning the people against the influence of wealth and the danger of **aristocracy**. History, ancient and modern, is full of such examples.
>
> **Caesar became the master of the Roman people and the senate under the pretense of supporting the democratic claims of the former against the aristocracy of the latter.**

The Roman Senate realized Julius Caesar was becoming too powerful and plotted to assassinate him on the Ides of March (March 15), 44 BC. The Durants wrote in *The Lessons of History* (p. 76):

> The **aristocrats** engaged Pompey to maintain their ascendancy; the **commoners** cast in their lot with Caesar; ordeal of battle replaced the auctioning of victory; **Caesar won**, and established a popular **dictatorship.**
>
> Aristocrats killed him, but ended by accepting the **dictatorship** of his grandnephew and stepson Augustus (27 BC).
>
> **Democracy** ended, **monarchy** was restored, the Platonic wheel had come full turn.

When Mark Anthony spoke at Caesar's funeral, instead of restoring order to the Roman Republic, he stirred the people into a frenzied mob which burned and rioted on the rich Senators.

In 43 BC, Mark Anthony formed a military dictatorship, called the Second Triumvirate, with Lepidus, a wealthy patrician who had been Caesar's strongest supporter, and Caesar's 20 year old grandnephew, Octavius.

Their official purpose was to be a "three-man commission for restoring the constitution of the republic," yet they were given the power to make or annul law without approval from either the senate or the people, and their judicial decisions could not be appealed.

Octavius forced Lepidus to resign, and the contest for power in Rome was between Octavius and Mark Anthony. President Harrison continued in his *Inaugural Address*, 1841:

> "In the Roman senate Octavius had a party and Antony a party, but the Commonwealth had none."

> Yet the senate continued to meet in the temple of liberty to talk of the sacredness and beauty of the Commonwealth and gaze at the statues of the elder Brutus and of the Curtii and Decii, and **the people assembled in the forum, not,** as in the days of Camillus and the Scipios, **to cast their free votes** for annual magistrates or pass upon the acts of the senate, **but to receive from the hands of the leaders of the respective parties their share of the spoils** and to shout for one or the other, as those collected in Gaul or Egypt and the lesser Asia would furnish the larger dividend.

Mark Anthony conquered much of the Middle East, installed Herod as King in Judea, and fell in love with Cleopatra IV of Egypt.

The power struggle between Octavius and Mark Anthony ended with the sea Battle of Actium, September 2, 31 BC.

Mark Anthony lost and Octavius took the title, "Augustus (divine) Caesar." Shortly after, Mark Anthony and Cleopatra committed suicide in Egypt, and the Roman Republic was ended. Augustus Caesar was now the undisputed Emperor of Roman Empire. In *The Lessons of History* (p. 69), Will and Ariel Durant wrote:

> After the breakdown of Roman **democracy** in the class wars of the Gracchi, Marius, and Caesar, Augustus organized, under what in effect, was **monarchical rule**.

Augustus Caesar also named a month after himself, "August." The Rome Empire became thoroughly a "patronage" or "bribery" system, where each person was indebted to the next wealthier and more politically connected patron, who was indebted to the next wealthier and more politically connected patron, on up the ladder, till the patron was dependent on a Senator, and ultimately the Emperor's favor.

This state of affairs is present in many countries where the middle class in a society is squeezed out of existence and common people are encumbered with debt. A culture develops where each person is expected to give a bribe to their boss or superior.

Benjamin Franklin warned at the Constitutional Convention in Philadelphia, 1787, in an address "Dangers of a Salaried Bureaucracy" (*The World's Famous Orations*, America: I, 1761–1837, 1906, III):

> There are two passions which have a powerful influence in the affairs of men. These are ambition and avarice—**the love of power and the love of money.**
>
> Separately, each of these has great force in prompting men to action; but, when united in view of the same object, they have, in many minds, the most violent effects.

Place before the eyes of such men a post of honor, that shall, at the same time, be a place of profit, and they will move heaven and earth to obtain it...The struggles for them are the true source of all those factions which are perpetually dividing the nation, distracting its councils, hurrying it sometimes into fruitless and mischievous wars, and often compelling a submission to dishonorable terms of peace.

And of what kind are the men that will strive for this profitable preeminence, through all the bustle of cabal, the heat of contention, the infinite mutual abuse of parties, tearing to pieces the best of characters?

It will not be the wise and moderate, the lovers of peace and good order, the men fittest for the trust. **It will be the bold and the violent, the men of strong passions and indefatigable activity in their selfish pursuits. These will thrust themselves into your government and be your rulers.**

࿔

FALL OF THE ROMAN EMPIRE

In 395, after the death of Emperor Theodosius I, the Western Roman Empire was permanently divided from the Eastern Roman Empire. On the other side of the world, the Han Dynasty was building the Great Wall of China along its Mongolian border, which resulted in the Huns attacking west instead of east. This caused a domino effect of tribes across Central Asia migrating west and overrunning the Western Roman Empire.

Illegal immigrants poured in across the Roman borders: Visigoths, Ostrogoths, Franks, Anglos, Saxons, Alemanni,

Thuringians, Rugians, Jutes, Picts, Burgundians, Lombards, Alans, Vandals, as well as African Berbers and Arab raiders. At first they assimilated, learned the Latin language, and worked as servants, but then they came so fast they did not learn the Latin language, and the unity of the Roman Empire dissolved.

Will and Ariel Durant wrote in *The Story of Civilization* (Vol. 3-Caesar and Christ, Simon & Schuster, 1944, p.366) :

> If Rome had not engulfed so many men of alien blood in so brief a time, if she had passed all these newcomers through her schools instead of her slums, if she had treated them as men with a hundred potential excellences, if she had occasionally closed her gates to let assimilation catch up with infiltration, she might have gained new racial and literary vitality from the infusion, and might have remained a Roman Rome, the voice and citadel of the West.

Roman borders became overextended and the military defending them was cut back to dangerously low ranks. The highly disciplined Roman Legions, possessing the most advanced weapons of the day and marching rapidly on advanced road systems, were strained fighting conflicts on numerous fronts worldwide.

The Durants wrote in *The Story of Civilization* (Vol. 3-Caesar and Christ, Simon & Schuster, 1944, p.90):

> The new generation, having inherited world mastery, had no time or inclination to defend it; that readiness for war which had characterized the Roman landowner disappeared now that ownership was concentrated in a few families, and a proletariat without stake in the country filled the slums of Rome.

The entire city of Rome was on welfare, starting in 123 BC, when Caius Gracchus secured a monthly dole of grain for the citizens living within the city. Government jobs exploded. One Roman commented:

> Those who live at the expense of the public funds are more numerous than those who provide them. (Gerald Simons, *Great Ages of Man-Barbarian Europe*, NY:Time-Life Books, 1968, p. 39).

Crowds in the city of Rome were appeased in the Coliseum and the Circus Maximus with violent entertainment, games, chariot races, and until 404 AD, gladiators fighting to the death, "in the causal brutality of its public spectacles, in a rampant immorality that even Christianity could not check." (*Great Ages*, p. 20).

Roman poet Juvenal (circa 100 AD) described how Roman emperors controlled the masses by keeping them ignorant and happy, more obsessed with self-indulgence and distraction than understanding what was really happening in the Empire:

> Already long ago, from when we sold our vote to no man, the People have abdicated our duties; for the People who ONCE UPON A TIME handed out military command, high civil office, legions - everything, NOW restrains itself and anxiously hopes for just two things: **bread and circuses.**

The Durants wrote in *The Lessons of History* (p. 92):

> The concentration of population and poverty in great cities may compel a government to choose between enfeebling the economy with a dole or running the risk of riot and revolution.

Huge bureaucratic machinery was unable to govern the empire effectively with the enormous, out-of-control debt. The educated and skilled pursued business and financial success to the neglect of their involvement in politics.

Richard A. Todd wrote in "The Fall of the Roman Empire" (*Eerdmans' Handbook to the History of Christianity*, Grand Rapids, MI: Wm. B. Eerdmans Co., 1977, p. 184):

> The church, while preaching against abuses, contributed to the decline by discouraging good Christians from holding public office.

Taxes became unbearable, as "collectors became greedy functionaries in a bureaucracy so huge and corrupt." Tax collectors were described by the historian Salvian as "more terrible than the enemy." (*Great Ages*, p. 20).

Roman families had fewer children. Some would sell unwanted children into slavery or, up until 374 AD, leave them outside exposed to the weather to die. Will and Ariel wrote in *The Story of Civilization*, Vol. 3-Caesar and Christ, Simon & Schuster, 1944, p.134):

> Children were now luxuries which only the poor could afford.

Rome had large government bureaucracies and a trade deficit which caused economic stagnation. Rome had outsourced its grain production to North Africa, and when the Vandals captured that area, Rome did not have the resources to retaliate.

Attila the Hun, "The Scourge of God," committed terrorist attacks, wiping out entire cities, such as the city of Aquileia in Italy, which had been listed as the 9th greatest city in the world. Residents fled to lagoons by the sea and hammered trees into the watery mud to create ground, founding the city of Venice. Attila was barely persuaded from sacking Rome by Pope Leo who rode out to meet him in 452 AD.

Court favoritism, injustice in the legal system, loss of patriotism, infidelity, exposure of unwanted infants, homosexual bathhouses, sexual immorality and gymnasiums ("gym" is the Greek word for naked), led 5th-Century historian Salvian to write:

> O Roman people be ashamed; be ashamed

of your lives. Almost no cities are free of evil dens, are altogether free of impurities, except the cities in which the barbarians have begun to live...

Let nobody think otherwise, the vices of our bad lives have alone conquered us...

The Goths lie, but are chaste, the Franks lie, but are generous, the Saxons are savage in cruelty...but are admirable in chastity...What hope can there be for the Romans when the barbarians are more pure than they?

The value of human life was low. Slavery abounded, especially of the captured peoples from Eastern Europe. "Slavs," which meant "glorious" came to have the inglorious meaning of a permanent servant or "slave." (*Great Ages*, p. 18).

City centers were abandoned by the upper class who turned rural farms into in palatial suburban estates. Inner cities were also plagued with lead poisoning, as water was brought in through lead pipes. ("plumb" or "plumbing" is the Latin word for "lead.")

Out of Money - "The Western Roman economy, already undermined by falling production of the great Roman estates and an unfavorable balance of trade that siphoned off gold to the East, had now run out of money." (*Great Ages*, p. 20)

Dependence of Foreign Trade - "As conquerors of North Africa, the Vandals cut off the Empire's grain supply at will. This created critical food shortages, which in turn curtailed Roman counterattacks." (*Great Ages*, p. 39).

President William Henry Harrison, in his *Inaugural Address*, 1841, described that in Rome:

> The spirit of liberty had fled, and, avoiding the abodes of civilized man, had sought protection in the wilds of Scythia or Scandinavia; and so under the operation of the same causes and influences it will fly from our Capitol and our forums.

A calamity so awful, not only to our country, but to the world, must be deprecated by every patriot and every tendency to a state of things likely to produce it immediately checked. Such a tendency has existed—does exist.

John F. Kennedy observed a similar trend, January 6, 1961:

Present tax laws may be stimulating in undue amounts the flow of American capital to industrial countries abroad.

Rome was sacked for the first time by the Visigoth King Alaric in 410, then by the Vandal King Genseric in 455, and finally by the Ostrogoth King Theodoric on September 4, 476, which is considered the official date of the fall of Rome, though Rome was conquered many more times before 563.

Samuel Adams wrote to John Scollay of Boston, April 30, 1776:

The diminution of public virtue is usually attended with that of public happiness, and the public liberty will not long survive the total extinction of morals. **'The Roman Empire,'** says the historian, **'must have sunk,** though the Goths had not invaded it. Why? **Because the Roman virtue was sunk.'**

As a result of Rome being attacked, legions were withdrawn from frontier settlements. As a result, Britain was attacked by raiders who carried thousands away as slaves.

One of those carried away from Britain and sold as a slave in Druid Ireland was Patrick. In an inspiring story of courage, Saint Patrick eventually converted 120,000 Irish to Christianity before his death, March 17, 461. In the following century, Irish missionaries went back to Europe and evangelized the heathen hordes which had overrun the Roman Empire.

REPUBLIC ALTERNATIVE TO MONARCHY
-
CARTHAGE OF NORTH AFRICA (308-146 BC)

Carthage, situated on the North African Mediterranean Coast, was the Roman Republic's greatest rival for centuries. Founded by Phoenicians, it was ruled by monarchs until their kings lost most of their power to an aristocratic Council of Elders after Hamilcar I's death in 480 BC. In 308 BC, Bomilcar attempted a coup to restore the monarch's power, but failed, resulting in the Republic of Carthage.

Though Carthage was controlled by oligarchs, there were democratic elements, such as elected legislators, trade unions and town meetings. Carthaginian heads of state were called Suffets, meaning "judges," a name similar to the Hebrew title Shophet meaning "Judge." Two Suffets were elected annually from wealthy and influential families and ruled together, similar to Roman consuls (as described by the historian Livy).

This practice descended from the first Phoenician cities which were ruled as aristocratic oligarchies, called "plutocracies." Wealthy families were represented in a supreme council, similar to the Roman Senate or Greek Gerousia-Council of Elders.

The Suffets were either elected by this supreme council or by an assembly of the people. They held judicial and executive power, but not military. Aristotle wrote in his *Politics*, that if the Suffets and the Council could not reach a decision, the Carthaginian popular assembly voted.

The historian Polybius wrote in his History, book 6, that during the Punic Wars between Carthage and Rome (264-

146 BC), the Carthaginian public held more sway over the government than the people of Rome held over theirs.

The military was directed by The Hundred and Four judges, which Aristotle described as being similar to Sparta's ephors. These judges oversaw the generals, who were sometimes sentenced to crucifixion.

During the crisis of the First Punic War with Rome (264-241 BC), political power in Carthage gravitated to the Barcid family, led by Hamilcar Barca. Hamilcar raised a mercenary army, promising them rewards for being loyal, and fought valiantly against the Romans in Sicily.

Following the war, Carthage's aristocratic Republic removed Hamilcar and refused to pay the soldiers, resulting in the Mercenary War. In this crisis, Hamilcar was reinstated and subsequently order was restored, consolidating his control. Hamilcar Barca then conquered large areas of Spain, (Barcelona is said to have been founded by him), which led to the Second Punic War (218-201 BC).

Hamilcar Barca's son was Hannibal the Great, who fought victoriously during the Second Punic War, crossing the Alps with his army and elephants, and ravaging Italy. The Carthaginian Republic voted not to send reinforcements, which, if they had, may have resulted in the end of Rome. When Rome retaliated and won the Third Punic War (149-146 BC), the Carthaginian Republic was completely destroyed, with salt being plowed into the ground so they could no longer grow crops.

REPUBLIC ALTERNATIVE TO MONARCHY
DORIC CITY-STATES OF CRETE (259-183 BC)

Small, independent cities on the Island of Crete entered into agreements with each other which resembled republics, as listed in the Decree of Knossos (259 BC); the Pythian Games (230 BC); and the Treaty of King Eumenes II with the Cretan League.

Cities included:

Apollonia (North coast of Crete),
Apollonia (South coast of Crete),
Aptera,
Biannos,
Chersonesos,
Cythera,
Dreros,
Eleutherna,
Eltynia, Elyros,
Gortyn,
Herakleion,
Hierapytna,
Istron,
Itanos,
Knossos,
Kydonia,
Lappa (Rethymno),
Lasaea,
Lato,
Lissos,
Lyctus,
Milatos,
Oaxos,
Oleros,
Olous,
Pelkis,
Petra,
Phaistos,
Phalanna,
Phalasarna,
Polychna,
Polyrrhenia,
Priansos,
Psycheion,
Rhaukos,
Rhithymna,
Rhizenia,
Rhytion,
Syia,
Tarra,
Tylissos,
Yrtakina.

REPUBLIC ALTERNATIVE TO MONARCHY -
BURMA'S CITY-STATE OF PYU (100 BC-840 AD)

Pyu was a language and a collection of city-states found in central and northern regions of modern-day Burma (Myanmar) from 100 BC to 840 AD.

Remnants of the Pyu civilization are known from two main historical sources: stone inscriptions (some in written in the Pali language, but rendered in the Pyu script, or the Gupta script); and brief accounts of Chinese travelers and traders, preserved in the Chinese imperial history.

The people of Pyu are believed to have been an ethnic group distinct from the Bamar (Burmans), although they may have intermarried with Sino-Tibetan migrants who later became part of the Bamar ethnicity.

REPUBLIC ALTERNATIVE TO MONARCHY
-
ITALY'S CITY-STATES

AMALFI (600-1131)
AMBROSIAN MILAN (1447–1450)
CORSICA (1755-1769)
COSPAIA (1440-1826)
FLORENCE (1115-1532)
GAETA (830-1140)
GENOA (1005-1815)
LUCCA (1160–1805)
NAPLES (1799)
NOLI (1193-1797)
PISA (1005-1406, 1494-1509)
SAN MARINO (301-present)
SIENNA (1000-1555)
TRANI (999-1073)
VENICE (697-1797)

Most of the Italian city-states trace their beginnings to the weakening Roman Empire or the later declining Byzantine Empire. They became prosperous through trade or manufacturing, with banking houses, like in Genoa, that lent money to European monarchs. They fought the Muslim Saracen invaders and, in many instances, welcomed the Normans (Christian Vikings) who helped resist the Muslims raiders. The unfortunate warring amongst the Italian city-states was the impetus for Machiavelli writing "The Prince" (1513).

Several Italian city-states became powerful maritime republics: Amalfi, Pisa, Gaeta, Genoa, Noli, Trani, and Venice, alternating between fighting the Ottoman Muslims to trading with them.

A few city-states lasted till they were conquered by Spain, Napoleon, or Garibaldi. One, the Apennine Mountain enclave of San Marino, continues to the present day. The constitution of San Marino, enacted in 1600, is the world's oldest constitution still in effect.

Italian city-states had various republican forms of government. They viewed themselves and their institutions as the heirs of the city-states of ancient Rome and Greece, despite considerable differences. A series of interlocking councils made major decisions in the Italian city-states. Leading adult male citizens, except for clergy, were elected or chosen through lot to fill seats on executive and legislative councils. Terms of office ranged from two months to one year. The franchise and the right to hold office was broad but did not extend to all the inhabitants of the town.

The Republic of Venice had a unique form of government. Only adult male nobles whose legitimate ancestry could be traced back to 1297 were eligible to hold office. But this still included about 2,000–2,500 men in a total population of about 175,000 in the late sixteenth century. The elder council form of Venetian politics further encouraged consensus.

A young noble began the climb to high political office in his early twenties under the watchful eyes of his elders and, if found able, reached the most important councils in his mid-fifties.

In Genoa a number of prominent families shared governmental responsibility. Both Venice and Genoa elected doges to be ceremonial heads of government with limited authority.

Florence was more democratic. In the years between 1498 and 1512, about 3,000 adult males were eligible for public office in a population of about 70,000.

The smaller Siena and Lucca were ruled by relatively broad oligarchies drawn from the leading citizens.

However, none of the Italian republican city-states offered significant political rights to the inhabitants of their subject territories outside the capital city.

Some city-states were already losing their independence in the sixteenth century.

In 1532 the Florentine Republic became the Duchy of Tuscany, ruled by the Medici family.

Spain conquered Siena in 1555 and then sold the city to Florence in 1557.

Genoa became a subservient ally of Spain in 1528, a move that enabled it to survive until 1798. By the eighteenth century the remaining independent city-states were fewer in number and weaker in every way compared with their condition in 1500.

Venice, the largest and most important city-state, lost Cyprus in 1571 and Crete and the rest of its eastern Mediterranean Empire in a series of wars with the Turks between 1645 and 1718. But it remained independent and the ruler of a sizable part of northeastern Italy. Although its commerce waned, Venice remained a major European cultural, intellectual, artistic, and musical center through the eighteenth century.

Then in 1797 the 28-year-old Napoleon Bonaparte, no respecter of age, conquered the 1,000-year-old Most Serene Republic of Venice. The much smaller Lucca emerged from the Napoleonic period still an independent city-state in 1817, but it was ruled by members of the Bourbon family, until it voted to join the Kingdom of Italy in 1860.

When the Holy Roman Empire was formally abolished in 1806, the free German city-states hardly existed except in law. Many Swiss city-states, though, maintained their independence.

In 1500 the city-states played essential roles in European politics, economy, and culture. But they could not afford the money and manpower to defend themselves against aggressive territorial monarchies and princedoms.

They could not compete against national economies. And with the exception of Venice, their artistic and intellectual greatness faded.

The city-states were major losers in the centuries between the Renaissance and the French Revolution.

Will and Ariel Durant wrote in *The Story of Civilization* (Vol. 5-The Renaissance, Simon & Schuster, 1953, p.39):

> Venetian merchants invaded every market from Jerusalem to Antwerp; they traded impartially with Christians and Mohammedans, and papal excommunications fell upon them with all the force of dew upon the earth.

Will and Ariel Durant wrote in *The Story of Civilization* (p.67):

> But it took more than a revival of antiquity to make the Renaissance. And first of all it took money—smelly bourgeois money:...of careful calculations, investments and loans, of interest and dividends accumulated until surplus could be spared from the pleasures of the flesh, from the purchase of senates, signories, and mistresses, to pay a Michaelangelo or a Titian to transmute wealth into beauty, and perfume a fortune with the breath of art. Money is the root of all civilization.

REPUBLIC ALTERNATIVE TO MONARCHY

INDIA'S SMALL REPUBLICS (700-1526)

Small republics in India included: the Malavas, Arjunyas, Yaudhyas, Kushans, Saka Satraps, Guptas, Hunas and Rajasthan, which functioned as a republic until around 700 AD. Northeastern and northwestern Rajasthan, known in ancient times as Jangladesh, was inhabited by Jat clans and ruled by their own chiefs and customary laws until the Muslim invasion of India.

Between 1398, when India was invaded by Timur, a Muslim Mongolian descendant of Genghis Khan, and 1526, when Timur's descendant, Babur, conquered India and founded the Mughal Muslim Dynasty, the area of Jangladesh had 2200 villages which were under the rule of the Jat people.

Jat republics in Jangladesh included: Bhadu; Bhati (on route from Central Asia to India); Bhukar; Chahar; Jakhar; Sangwan, Sahu.

Jat republics in Marwar had included: Dhaulya; Dudi; Gaina; Jewlia; Karwasra; Kulhari; and Moond.

Jat republics in Matsya included: Katewa; Khoja; and Vijayrania.

Jat republics in southern Rajasthan included: Jatrana - an ancient people who fought against Alexander the Great; Gora; Nagil; Ranthambore; Sheoran; and Chandlai.

Jat people held administration in their own traditional fashion till their conquest by the powerful ruling clan of Rathores. After the 17th century, due to internal rivalries among the Jat people, most of Jat clans in Rajasthan had to accept control by the Rathores, who were submitted to the Muslim Mughal Emperors, such as Shah Jahan, thus ending the Jat republics.

ॐ

REPUBLIC ALTERNATIVE TO MONARCHY
-
ICELAND'S COMMONWEALTH (930-1262)

Iceland was initially established by immigrants from Norway who had fled the unification of that country under King Harald Fairhair. They formed an Icelandic Commonwealth which existed from 930 until 1262, when they had to make a pledge of fealty to the Norwegian King.

Iceland was divided into numerous clans run by chieftains. The chieftains provided for defense and appointed judges to resolve disputes between clan members. The clans together formed the medieval Icelandic Commonwealth, which had no king or other central executive power, but was ruled by the Althing - a court and legislature.

Clans were not necessarily geographical districts and individuals could switch membership to a different clan. If a person wanted to appeal a decision made by his clan court or if there was a dispute between members of different clans, the case would be referred to higher-level courts, leading up to the four regional courts which made up the Althing, which consisted of the goðar of the Four Quarters of Iceland.

The Althing eventually created a national "fifth court", as the highest court of all, and more goðar to be its members. The Althing was moderately successful at stopping feuds, as described by Magnus Magnusson, it was "an uneasy substitute for vengeance."

At the conversion of Iceland to Christianity in 1000, the Althing decreed in order to prevent an invasion, that all Icelanders must be baptized. The Althing forbade the public, and later the private, celebration of pagan rituals.

In 1117 the laws were put into writing, called the Gray Goose Laws. The operation of this system is the subject of many Icelandic sagas, such as Njáll's Saga, which describes the Christianisation of Iceland, and the Laxdaela Saga. The followers of the goðar owed them military service. They were organized into platoons or companies based on their social status and equipment, which formed expeditionary armies or leiðangrs.

Icelandic military tradition of the time followed closely practices in Norway. There were no cavalry formations or projectile weapons, but instead light, medium and heavy infantry, with bowmen and rock throwers among them. At least 21 castles and fortresses were built during the Icelandic Commonwealth.

During the Age of the Sturlungs (1220-1264), the Icelandic Commonwealth began to suffer serious internal strife and discontent. This resulted in many battles, though the average battle involved fewer than 1000 men, with only around 10 percent being killed, as the Icelandic blood-feud mentality was that the defeated army could not be slaughtered.

In 1262, the King of Norway pressured his Icelandic vassal chieftains to sign the Gamli sáttmáli ("Old Covenant"), and accept Norway's Haakon IV as their king. This effectively ended Iceland's Commonwealth.

REPUBLIC ALTERNATIVE TO MONARCHY
-
EUROPE'S FREE CITIES (962-1806)

FREE AND HANSEATIC CITY OF BREMEN
(1806–1811, again 1813–1871)
FREE AND HANSEATIC CITY OF HAMBURG
(1806–1811, again 1814–1871)
FREE AND HANSEATIC CITY OF LUBECK
(1806–1811, again 1813–1871)
FREE CITY OF FRANKFURT AM MAIN
(1815–1866)

Charlemagne, Emperor of the Holy Roman Empire, required his aristocratic vassals to be personally responsible for the defense, health and welfare of the people living in their domains, which contributed to towns being more autonomous.

Eventually, dozens of cities of the trans-alpine part of the Holy Roman Empire, in what is now Germany and Switzerland, enjoyed the privileges of being free imperial cities. They were not ruled by a prince or bishop, but instead were self-governing states who only recognized the remote overlordship of the Holy Roman emperor.

Imperial free cities, as well as trading cities and rural communities, adopted republican forms of governments. Notable examples were the medieval city-states of Bremen, Hamburg, and Lübeck.

The city of Lübeck, in Schleswig-Holstein, became a free city in 1226 and created the Lübeck law, which was adopted by other free cities.

It was a municipal constitution for self-government which replaced the personal rule of tribal monarchs which descended from ancient times.

The Lübeck Law in theory made the cities to which it applied independent of royalty.

Some cities were also members of other confederacies. Many cities, mostly along Northern Europe's coast from the Baltic Sea to the North Sea, formed a Hanseatic League - an economic alliance of trading cities and their guilds. Hanseatic cities had some political autonomy with their own legal system and provided for their own defense.

Free imperial cities sent their own representatives to meet with princes, prince-bishops, and knights, at the imperial diet, the consultative body which met periodically to discuss imperial affairs and to grant financial support to the emperor.

Many of the most important free cities were located in southwestern Germany.

Augsburg had 50,000 people in the early sixteenth century and held considerable importance as a commercial center, although its territory was small.

Nuremberg had about 20,000 inhabitants inside the city walls and another 20,000 in over 400 villages in the fields and forests ruled by Nuremberg.

Magdeburg, Cologne, Frankfurt am Main, and Strasbourg were other important free cities.

Ulm, much smaller in population than Augsburg, controlled some 500 square miles of territory outside its walls.

Hamburg, with 20,000 inhabitants in 1550, which rose to about 60,000 in the late seventeenth century, was the most important city-state in northern Germany and a center for shipping, publishing, textile production, and banking.

The Hanseatic League cities of Lübeck, Bremen, and Gdansk (Danzig) were also imperial free cities in northern Germany and Poland.

Oligarchical city councils dominated by leading merchants and professional men from wealthy established families governed the free cities. Although some cities had limited-franchise elections, seats in the city council were often hereditary:

When a council member died, his son or nephew succeeded him. By the sixteenth century artisan guilds had almost no formal role in government. Nevertheless, artisans made their views known, and city council members took them into account, because they feared civil unrest.

Because both wealthy merchants and modest artisans saw their personal well-being dependent on that of the city, German free cities had a strong communal identity. City-states approached religious matters collectively. Leaders and people believed that the entire city-state was responsible to God for the actions of its inhabitants.

Plague, flood, and military defeat were seen as God's punishment on the city as a whole for its sins. Consequently, leaders and people sought agreement on religious issues.

This also meant that city-states approached the local church and its clergymen in a possessive way. They believed that the local church should be responsible to them more than to the papacy. In Italian city-states the leaders of the local church came from prominent local families.

In Venice, the Senate chose the Venetian patriarch, the leader of the local church. Occasionally the Senate chose a prominent member of the government, who, upon being designated patriarch, became a clergyman. Once in office, the patriarch was expected to follow the lead of the civil government in disputes with the papacy and matters affecting the civil government.

Before the Protestant Reformation the bishop was often a nonresident outsider, rather than a member of the ruling group of the city. This produced disputes, anticlericalism, and a receptive audience for the first Protestant preachers.

When townspeople began to support the preachers, city councils had to make decisions about the religious direction of the city-states. Since they wished to affirm the unity of the city-state before God and to keep the peace, they often moved the city-state into the Protestant camp. They moved cautiously, usually orchestrating a step-by-step, orderly, and reasonably peaceful transition to Protestantism.

German and Swiss city-states were among the first states to embrace the Protestant Reformation.

Zurich and Nuremberg are much-studied examples. Geneva won its independence from the House of Savoy and its bishop in the mid-1520s, then became Protestant between 1532 and 1536. However, as religious differences generated warfare between Protestant and Catholic states, the German free imperial cities were vulnerable.

Religious and political warfare was a three-way struggle between empire, princes, and cities. The cities that became Protestant were obliged to form alliances with German Protestant princes, who ruled stronger states and commanded larger armies. These alliances also incurred the vengeance of the emperor, who retaliated against Protestant cities.

The free cities that remained Catholic also became weaker, because they had to rely on the emperor for protection and were bled white to support him. After the sixty-year truce following the Religious Peace of Augsburg of 1555, the free cities again suffered during the Thirty Years War (1618–1648).

An imperial army brutally sacked the free city of Magdeburg and murdered twenty thousand of its inhabitants in 1631.

Münster and Erfurt were not imperial free cities, even though their bishops exercised no control and they lost their independence to nearby princes. Strasbourg came under French domination in the later part of the seventeenth century. Swiss city-states retained their independence mainly because they were difficult to invade.

REPUBLIC ALTERNATIVE TO MONARCHY
—
RUSSIA'S REPUBLIC OF NOVGOROD (1136-1478) & PSKOV (1268-1510)

Novgorod, meaning "new town" in Russian, is considered the first city of the Rus, founded in 859. It served as the capital of the Rus until 882 when Oleg made Kiev the capital. During the Middle Ages, Novgorod was the second main city in Russia after Kiev, and controlled an area as large as Sweden.

A main port city, Novgorod's economy was based on Baltic sea trade, being part of the Hansa Union of rich Baltic ports. It was situated on one of the main travel routes from Northern Europe to Rome and Constantinople.

At its beginning, Russia was divided into small princedoms which fought against each other. Novgorod supported Vladimir the Great of Kiev, who converted to Christianity and proceeded to have all Kievan Russian baptized. When relations with his son, Yaroslav I the Wise, became strained, the citizens of Novgorod supported Yaroslav against Vladimir and another son, Svyatopolk the Accursed. When Yaroslav I the Wise won in 1019, he rewarded the loyal citizens of Novgorod with privileges and freedoms, which effectively laid the foundation for Novgorod's Republic.

Novgorod became a rich state, built stone walls and erected the Church of Saint Sofia, the main cathedral of the Russian North. In 1136, merchants accumulated enough power to remove the nobles and proclaimed Novgorod a republic, the first and only in Russia.

The city of Pskov was founded in 903 and adhered politically to the Novgorod Republic. Novgorod and Pskov were the only major cities in Russia to escape destruction when the Mongols invaded in 1222, led by Batu Khan, the grandson of Genghis Khan.

In 1240, Novgorod invited Prince Alexander to protect it from the Swedish army, which Alexander defeated near the Neva River, resulting in his title - Alexander Nevsky (the main avenue in St. Petersburg is named for him: Nevski Prospekt). In 1242, Alexander Nevsky saved Novgorod from the nearby State of Teutonic Knights, and then recaptured Pskov in a legendary campaign which included the Battle of the Ice on the frozen Lake Peipus, memorialized in Sergei Eisenstein's 1938 movie, "Alexander Nevsky."

As the Mongols became the most powerful foe, Alexander Nevsky met in 1262 with the ruler of the Mongol "Golden Horde," Sartaq Khan, who was a Christian convert and the great-grandson of Genghis Khan. Sartaq Khan granted Alexander Nevsky vassalage to become Grand Duke of Vladimir. Sartaq Khan died mysteriously in 1256, in what was suspected to have been poisoning by his uncle Berke Khan, a Muslim convert, who took control of the Golden Horde and spread Islam throughout the Mongolian Empire. The Muslim Tartar army then captured most of the land of Rus, with the exception of Novgorod, as it was surrounded by swamps.

The Novgorod Republic had elections in a big square where people gathered and shouted for their candidates. The candidate with the loudest supporters became ruler. Princes were still present, but only as hired military leaders to protect the city.

Ivan III of Moscow became more powerful and in 1478 he took the city, massacred its population and destroyed its library, ending the Novgorod Republic. Afterwards the city became less and less powerful till finally, when St. Petersburg was built, Novgorod lost its position of being the only Russian port near the Baltic Sea.

જી

REPUBLIC ALTERNATIVE TO MONARCHY
-
CROATIA'S CITY-STATE OF DUBROVNIK (1358-1808)

Dubrovnik's motto was "Non bene pro toto libertas venditur auro" which is Latin for "Liberty is not well sold for all the gold." Dubrovnik, also known by the Latin name Ragusa, was a maritime republic in Dalmatia on the opposite side of the Adriatic Sea from Italy.

After the fall of Rome and the subsequent Ostrogothic Kingdom, Dubrovnik functioned as an independent city-state under the Byzantine Empire. After the Crusades, it was under Venice, till 1358 when it became a vassal-state of Hungary, operating for all practical purposes as an independent city-state republic till 1808.

Dubrovnik had a population of about 30,000, with strict social classes, and was ruled by local aristocracy in two city councils. It ceased its slave trade in the 15th century, and continually had to balance its independence with Venice on one side and the Ottoman Muslims on the other. An earthquake in 1667 weakened Dubrovnik, and in 1699, land had to be sold to the Ottoman Muslims, which became the countries of Bosnia and Herzegovina.

Dubrovnik's city-state republic ended in 1806 when Napoleon Bonaparte's French Navy blockaded the harbor and fired 3,000 cannonballs into the city.

The only state with similar political history was the Republic of San Marino.

REPUBLIC ALTERNATIVE TO MONARCHY

POLAND & LITHUANIA'S COMMONWEALTH (1569-1791)

The Polish-Lithuanian Commonwealth operated as a "crowned" Republic, beginning when the Kingdom of Poland and the Grand Duchy of Lithuania formed the Union of Lublin in 1569.

In 1653, Tsar Alexis of Russia declared war on the Commonwealth, followed by the Swedish invasion, in which 4 million died. The Commonwealth survived and became the largest and one of the most populous countries of 16th and 17th century Europe.

The Polish-Lithuanian Commonwealth had a unique "Noble's Democracy," with strict checks upon monarchical power enacted by a legislature of nobility, and served as a precursor to modern democracies, constitutional monarchies and federal governments. The Polish–Lithuanian Commonwealth was ethnically diverse, unusually tolerant religiously, and able to defend itself against Sweden, Russia, and the Ottoman Empire.

It declined due to protracted political dissension and growing economic and military weakness, which invited aggression by Austria, Prussia and Russia. Political dissensions were resolved in 1791 with the Polish-Lithuanian Commonwealth reforming and enacting Europe's first and the world's second codified national Constitution in modern times (after the U.S. Constitution). Unfortunately, this was short-lived, as the next year the Russo-Polish War of 1792 began, resulting in the Commonwealth being divided between Russia, Prussia and the Hapsburg Dynasty of Austria.

ھ

REPUBLIC ALTERNATIVE TO MONARCHY
–
SEVEN UNITED NETHERLANDS' REPUBLIC (1581-1795)

Dutch Crowned Republic of the Seven United Netherlands began with independence from Spain after Eighty Years War in 1581, and ended when conquered by Napoleon in 1795.

The Dutch Crowned Republic was one of the major seafaring and economic powers in the world from 1581 to 1795. It operated as a confederation of different Dutch cities, with a "Stadtholder," a royal head-of-state, who was a de-facto hereditary medieval peacekeeper or steward. Since 1747, the Stadtholder was a member of the House of Orange-Nassau.

The Golden Age of the Dutch was a period between 1650-1672, when power was decentralized and there was no "Stadtholder." The powerful military merchant fleet of the Dutch establishment settlements around the world, from New Amsterdam (New York), to the Cape Colony of South Africa, from Dutch Guiana (Suriname) of South America, to Aruba and the Netherlands Antilles Caribbean Islands, from Jakarta, Indonesia, to exploring New Zealand and Tasmania.

With 16,000 merchant ships, including those of the Dutch East India Company and Dutch West India Company, the Dutch homeland, Netherlands (Holland) became the first thoroughly capitalist country in the world, with Amsterdam being the wealthiest trading city. Rembrandt painted masterpieces and the English Separatist Pilgrims fled there for 12 years before sailing to settle Massachusetts.

The Dutch East India Company, established in 1602, had a monopoly on the spice trade and became the first multinational corporation in the world and the first company to issue stock. It was also arguably the world's first megacorporation, possessing quasi-governmental powers, including the ability to wage war, imprison and execute convicts, negotiate treaties, coin money, and establish colonies.

During its Golden Age, the Dutch dominated European affairs and fought two major wars with England. England's noted naval defender was Admiral William Penn (1621-1670), father of Pennsylvania's founder. The Dutch fought several minor wars with other European powers, imposing what was called a "pax neerlandica" in Scandinavia. The Dutch defeated Portugal in a war, resulting in the Dutch East India Company taking over the remnants of the Portuguese empire in Ceylon and South India.

In 1648, when the Dutch war with Spain brought an end to the Spanish trade embargo, Dutch commerce exploded worldwide, from the Iberian Peninsula, the Mediterranean, the Levant, to the Baltic. The Dutch textile industry experienced an economic boom.

Netherlands created the first full-time stock exchange in the city of Amsterdam when a large shipping company was in permanent need of funds to finance the shipping of goods from the Far East.

In 1611, an Amsterdam Stock Exchange Building was opened for daily trading.

In 1614, the Dutch founded the Colony of New Netherlands in America. The Colony's main city, New Amsterdam, was surrounded by a wooden stockade, surrounded by a 12 foot high wall to protect them from the Indians. The Dutch settlers began to trade stocks along what was called Wall Street. When the British defeated the Dutch in the Third Anglo-Dutch War in 1674, they renamed New Amsterdam to New York, and Wall Street became the New York Stock Exchange.

The Dutch traders in Amsterdam developed insurance and retirement funds. They experienced the modern world's first boom-bust cycle, an asset-inflation bubble led by a "Bernie

Madoff" style investment manipulator named Isaac le Maire, as recorded by Murray Sayle. Called the world's first bear raider, Isaac le Maire dumped stock to force prices down, then bought them back at a discount.

The Dutch experienced the first "stock market crash" with the tulip mania of 1636–1637. Tulips, which originally came from the Crimea on the Black Sea, became a luxury status-symbol item in the Netherlands. Certain varieties of tulip bulbs, such as the Viceroy and the Semper Augustus, were so beautiful that the price for a single bulb inflated to 6,000 guilders.

As flower-growers were still cultivating and growing the bulbs, anxious traders would sell them in advance with promissory notes. Buyers of the promissory notes would resell them at higher prices, in what was termed tulpenwindhandel, "tulip wind trade." When the tulip bulbs were finished growing and delivered, the final owner was stuck with the actual bulb and could not resell them.

After many lost money in this scheme, Dutch citizens printed pamphlets and pressured the Dutch government, who responded by concentrating control over the stock market.

The Dutch Republic had flourished under the ruling Dutch Regents (memorialized by Rembrandt's painting *The Dutch Masters,* De Staalmeesters, 1662, in the Rijksmuseum, and on a box of cigars).

The Golden Age of the Dutch ended when power was reconcentrated back to the European model of monarchical absolutism. The Dutch Regents were opposed and eventually defeated by the adherents of the House of Orange, who wanted to restore the young Prince of Orange to the hereditary position of royal Stadtholder.

Capitalizing on the internal political divisions in Holland, the English increased economic competition and began the third Anglo–Dutch Wars in 1674, which resulted in Britain dominating the seas and controlling many Dutch colonies, including New York.

The Dutch Empire was still one of the major seafaring and economic powers up until World War II.

೩

REPUBLIC ALTERNATIVE TO MONARCHY

–

FRANCE'S CITY-STATE OF GOUST (1648-1900)

Goust was a self-governing hamlet in the Pyrenees Mountains in Southwest France, near Spain. Located high on a mountain plateau, it was accessible only by a narrow mountain footpath across the Pont d'Enfer ("Bridge of Hell").

The nearest town was Laruns in the valley below. Goust's independence was recognized by France and Spain in 1648, though it is now considered part of France.

The community consisted of around 150 residents and its government consisted of a Council of Ancients composed of 3-12 citizens, who elected a President every five years.

REPUBLIC ALTERNATIVE TO MONARCHY
-
CONFEDERATION OF SWISS CANTONS (1648-1848)

Switzerland's Confederation of Cantons traces its origins to the early 1300's, though it did not receive official recognition until 1648 when the Holy Roman Empire agreed to the Peace of Westphalia, ending the destructive 30 Years War between the Protestants and Catholics, and ending the 80 Years War between Spain and the Dutch Republic.

The 26 cantons of Switzerland forming the Swiss Confederation, were fully sovereign states, operating as republics with their own borders, army and currency. The German word for confederation, "Eidgenossenschaft," means "oath fellowship of equal partners," in contrast to the vassal-lord relationship in feudal states.

The Swiss Confederacy began with a series of overlapping pacts and bilateral treaties between various members, such as the Pfaffenbrief of 1370, a treaty among eight Cantons. It grew after the victory over the Austrian army at the Battle of Sempach in 1386.

The communal movement in medieval Europe often led to similar alliances or leagues, called conjurationes in official Latin documents. The city alliances (Städtebünde) in the medieval Holy Roman Empire, in which the member cities also were equal, can be regarded as Eidgenossenschaften, though they were less stable, partly due to their fragmented territories.

The best known of these city alliances was the Hanseatic League, but many others existed in the 13th and 14th century. An early example is the Lombard League at the time of Frederick I "Barbarossa"; an example from Switzerland would be the "Burgundian Confederacy" of Berne.

In the Holy Roman Empire, emperor Charles IV outlawed

any such conjurationes, confederationes, and conspirationes in his Golden Bull of 1356. Most Städtebünde were subsequently dissolved, sometimes forcibly, and where refounded, their political influence was much reduced. On the Swiss Eidgenossenschaft, however, the edict had no such effect as Charles IV, who was of the House of Luxembourg, regarded the Swiss as potential useful allies against his rivals, the Hapsburgs.

The Swiss Confederacy lasted until Switzerland was conquered by Napoleon, and not restored as a Federal Republic until 1848.

The 13 independent cantons of the Swiss Confederation made up the third group. The Swiss Confederation grew from the three original forest cantons of Uri, Schwys, and Unterwalden, then added Lucerne (1332), Zurich (1351), Glarus (1352), Zug (1352), and Bern (1353). Solothurn and Fribourg were added in 1481, then Basel and Schaffhausen in 1501, and Appenzell in 1513.

Geneva won its independence from the House of Savoy in the sixteenth century but did not become a member of the Swiss Confederation until the end of the eighteenth century. Swiss cities and towns were small in population: Geneva had 13,000 people, Basel had 10,000, and Zürich had 7,000 in the early sixteenth century. In comparison with the German free cities, Swiss Cantons controlled considerable surrounding territory. The cantons of Glarus, Grisons, Schwyz, Unterwalden, Uri, and Zug were rural, mountainous, and forested, with tiny, isolated populations.

Some cantons ruled additional lands outside their borders, while the Swiss Confederation as a whole also held land. The Confederation was only a loose association organized to pursue common interests, such as defense against invaders, rather than a central government. It could not prevent wars between cantons.

By 1500 the Swiss cantons enjoyed de facto independence from the Holy Roman Empire, a condition recognized in 1648. Councils composed of prominent citizens, either elected or semi-hereditary, ruled individual cantons. The independent city-state of Geneva elected its officials.

இ

REPUBLIC ALTERNATIVE TO MONARCHY

ENGLAND'S PURITAN COMMONWEALTH (1649-1660)

Anglican England persecuted Puritans, who fled to Massachusetts. An English Civil War broke out and Puritans, under Oliver Cromwell, defeated King Charles I.

A Commonwealth was established which operated as a "crowned" Republic from 1649 to 1660, under Lord Protector Oliver Cromwell, and his son Richard. Anglicans and Catholics in England were discriminated against, resulting in George Washington's Anglican great-grandfather, John, immigrating to Virginia. Cromwell punished Catholic Ireland, which had earlier made alliances with Catholic Spain, killing over a half million in Ireland and selling 300,000 into slavery in the West Indies, Jamaica, Virginia and New England. In the 1600's, more Irish were sold into slavery than Africans.

William Henry Harrison wrote in 1841:

> The danger to all well-established free governments arises from the unwillingness of the people to believe in its existence or from the influence of designing men..This is the old trick of those who would usurp the government of their country. In the name of democracy they speak, warning the people against the influence of wealth and the danger of aristocracy. History, ancient and modern, is full of such examples...**Cromwell, in the character of protector of the liberties of the people, became the dictator of England.**

REPUBLIC ALTERNATIVE TO MONARCHY
\-
THE UNITED STATES OF AMERICA (1776-PRESENT)

"And to the Republic for which it stands..."

-Pledge of Allegiance

Dr. Benjamin Franklin stated during the Constitutional Convention, June 28, 1787:

> We have gone back to ancient history for models of Government, and examined the different forms of those Republics which, having been formed with the seeds of their own dissolution, now no longer exist.

After the final day of deliberation at the Constitutional Convention in Philadelphia, Ben Franklin was asked by a lady as he left Independence Hall:

> "Well, Doctor, what have we got - a Republic or a Monarchy?"
> Franklin replied:
> "A Republic, if you can keep it."
> (Notes of Dr. James McHenry, published in *The American Historical Review*, vol. 11, 1906, p. 618. Records of the Federal Convention of 1787, ed. Max Farrand, vol. 3, appendix A, p. 85, 1911, reprinted 1934. *Respectfully Quoted: A Dictionary of Quotations*. 1989. No.: 1593.)

In writing to the Senate, May 18, 1789, George Washington referred to the United States as: "this confederated Republic."

In 1776, the United States of America became independent from the British Empire and, under the Articles of Confederation and then in 1789 under the U.S. Constitution, grew into the longest-lasting, most prosperous, Republic in world history.

The United States of America, under the Articles of Confederation, 1776–1789, and under U.S. Constitution 1789-Present, was a republic.

As most previous examples in history of republics operating successfully were on small city-state level, the question during America's early years was, will it work on a larger scale.

Thomas Jefferson addressed this in his *Second Inaugural Address*, March 4, 1805:

> I know that the acquisition of Louisiana has been disapproved by some from a candid apprehension that the enlargement of our territory would endanger the union, but who can limit the extent to which the federative principle may operate effectively?

On October 3, 1789, just one week after Congress approved the Bill of Rights to the Constitution, President George Washington issued the first *Proclamation of a National Day of Thanksgiving and Prayer*:

> We may...unite in most humbly offering our prayers and supplications to the great Lord and Ruler of Nations...and beseech Him to pardon our national and other transgressions...[and] to render our national government a blessing to all the People, by constantly being a government of wise, just and constitutional laws.

George Washington thanked God for the Constitution in his Proclamation, January 1, 1795:

> I...recommend... a day of public thanksgiving... to the great Ruler of nations... particularly for the

possession of Constitutions of government which unite and, by their union, establish liberty with order...establish habits of sobriety, order, and morality and piety, and finally to impart all the blessings we possess or ask for ourselves to the whole family of mankind.

Prior to the Constitution of the United States of America, 1787, out of the hundreds of governments over previous six thousands of years, there were only a few dozen examples of alternatives to monarchy that existed in world history, and most were relatively small city-states.

The seeds of America's unique experiment were planted during the Renaissance and Reformation, when the middle-class began to read. They became educated, gradually gained financial independence, then challenged the power of monarchs.

∾

CONCENTRATED POWER IS BAD

As the colonies in America were thousands of miles away from the centralized power of European Kings, colonists were provided a rare opportunity to experiment with capitalism and self-government.

James Madison, at the Constitutional Convention, 1787, stated:

All men having power ought to be distrusted.

Jefferson is credited with the statements:

The strongest reason for the people to retain the right to keep and bear arms is, as a last resort, to protect themselves against tyranny in government.

Jefferson wrote in the Declaration of Independence, 1776:

The history of the present King of Great Britain is a history of repeated injuries and usurpations, all having in direct object the establishment of an absolute Tyranny over these States.

After the Continental Army was driven out of New Jersey, an article titled "The American Crisis" was published in the *Pennsylvania Journal*, December 23, 1776. Written by an aide-de-camp to General Nathanael Greene named Thomas Paine, General Washington ordered it read to the troops:

These are the times that try men's souls. The summer soldier and the sunshine patriot will, in this crisis, shrink from the service of his country...

Tyranny, like hell, is not easily conquered; yet we have this consolation with us that the harder the conflict, the more glorious the triumph...What we obtain too cheap, we esteem too lightly...

Heaven knows how to put a price upon its goods; and it would be strange indeed if so celestial an article as freedom should not be highly rated...

God Almighty will not give up a people to military destruction...who have so earnestly... sought to avoid the calamities of war...

The whole English army, after ravaging the kingdom of France, was driven back...by a few broken forces headed by a woman, Joan of Arc. Would that heaven might inspire some Jersey maid to spirit up her countrymen...

'Show your faith by your works,' that God may bless you...I thank God, that I fear not.

American political self-government and financial capitalism was the creation of an educated and religious middle-class, sometimes called the "second sons," as the entitled "first sons" stayed in Europe enjoying their inheritances.

≈

CONSTITUTION - AN ATTEMPT TO HARNESS SELFISHNESS

America's founders understood the inherent selfishness in man. They believed men could have redemption, but would always be subject to being tempted by their fallen nature, a residual effect of man's original sin. Since they had a bad experience trusting a monarch, King George III, and since there were no angels on earth to run the government, the only ones who could keep a check on men were...other men.

Jefferson, in his *First Inaugural Address,* March 4, 1801, stated:

> Sometimes it is said that man can not be trusted with the government of himself. Can he, then, be trusted with the government of others? Or have we found angels in the forms of kings to govern him? Let history answer this question. Let us, then, with courage and confidence pursue our own federal and republican principles.

Here is the problem:

Human beings can yield to their selfish side and become criminals breaking into homes, stealing and killing. **Citizens, therefore, have to relinquish enough of their liberty to create a government with a police and military force that can keep them secure from attacks from criminals on the street and criminals in others nations.**

Jefferson wrote in the Declaration:

That to secure these rights, governments are instituted among men.

Ronald Reagan said:

Government's first duty is to protect the people, not run their lives.

But if individuals have the capacity to yield to their selfish side, what happens when those men who have been entrusted with government yield to their selfish side and use the power of government to break into homes, steal and kill?

Niccolo Machiavelli wrote:

Princes and governments are far more dangerous than other elements within society.

In that case, citizens have to retain enough power to keep the government in check.

James Madison wrote of this dilemma in *Federalist Paper No. 51:*

In framing a government which is to be administered by men over men, the great difficulty lies in this: **you must first enable the government to control the governed;** and in the next place oblige it to control itself.

It is a balancing act. Give up enough power to create the government; retain enough power to control the government. In other words, if you let the tiger out of the cage, you have to keep handy a whip, a chair and a pistol.

The U.S. Constitution was an unprecedented attempt to separate the power of ruling through an elaborate system of checks and balances designed with one overarching purpose - to prevent power from reconcentrating into the hands of a king.

Its expressed purpose was to secure the rights of the individual, to maximize individual liberty.

∾
WHY THREE BRANCHES?

George Washington stated November 13, 1787:

> Government...is force. Like fire, it is a dangerous servant and a fearful master.

Jefferson told Lydia Huntley Sigourney at Monticello, July 18, 1824:

> We have the wolf by the ear and feel the danger of either holding or letting him loose.

Government was viewed a necessary evil, but how should it work?

Since politicians are liable to yield to temptation and become corrupt, a committee needs to be set up to watch over them.

But the committee itself is made up of men, who themselves can be tempted and become corrupt, so a second committee needs to be set up to watch the first committee as it watches the politicians.

But that second committee is also made of up men who can be tempted, so a third committee needs to be set up to watch the second, as it watches the first, as it watches the politicians, and so on, and so on. The problem seems to be unfixable.

The Constitution was a brilliant answer to this age old problem. The power of ruling was divided into three distinct branches – writing the laws, enacting the laws and judging the laws.

Each of these branches, comprised of selfish men, would always try to take power from the other two.

This constant tug of war, with each branch wanting to be "king-of-the-hill," would be a continual dynamic tension keeping power in check.

James Madison (1751-1836), called the "Father of the Constitution," explained in *Federalist Paper, No. 51*:

> But the great security against a gradual concentration of the several powers in the same department, consists in giving to those who administer each department, the necessary constitutional means, and personal motives, to resist encroachments of the others.
>
> The provisions for defense must in this, as in all other cases, be made commensurate to the danger of attack. Ambition must be made to counteract ambition. The interest of the man must be connected with the constitutional rights of the place.

Madison continued:

> It may be a reflection on human nature that such devices should be necessary to control the abuses of government.
>
> But what is government itself but the greatest of all reflections on human nature?
>
> If angels were to govern men, neither external or internal controls on government would be necessary.
>
> In framing a government which is to be administered by men over men, the great difficulty lies in this: you must first enable the government to control the governed; and in the next place oblige it to control itself.
>
> A dependence on the people is, no doubt, the primary control on the government; but experience has taught mankind the necessity of auxiliary precautions.

The U.S. Constitution stretched power apart like a rubber band into three branches: executive, legislative and judicial, and each branch selfishly protected what was under its jurisdiction against encroachment by the other branches.

Throughout history, the selfish ambition of human nature concentrated power into the hands of a king. Under the Constitution, the selfish ambition of human nature was harnessed so that each of the three branches would selfishly fight to prevent the other two branches from accumulating too much power, thereby preventing power from concentrating into the hands of a king.

Greed checked greed. Ambition checked ambition. It was a stroke of genius. The selfish human nature which normally resulted in a monarchy was now put to work preventing a monarchy.

The Constitution attempted to prevent the concentration of power by pitting the selfishness in one branch against the selfishness of the other two branches. But, as George Washington warned, when one political party controls all three branches, this check is effectively short-circuited.

∾

SELFHISHNESS
TO CHECK SELFISHNESS

Montesquieu presented the premise that mankind is basically selfish, and opportunity allowed, individuals would accumulate more and more power unto themselves, eventually becoming despots.

This concept of the fallen nature of man is expressed in Jeremiah 17:9: "The heart is deceitful above all things and desperately wicked: who can know it?"

In order to prevent the accumulation of power, Montesquieu proposed separating the powers of a monarch into three branches and pitting them against each other, allowing the greed and ambition of one to check the greed and ambition of the others. Each branch would try to push down the other two.

Interestingly enough, this idea of Judicial, Legislative and

Executive branches is reflected in a verse in Isaiah 33:22: "For the Lord is our Judge, the Lord is our Lawgiver, the Lord is our King."

An allegory to illustrate Montesquieu's proposal to separate power into branches is to imagine three hungry boys and a chocolate pie.

Left to their greedy nature, the biggest bully would take the biggest piece.

But supposes you gave them different responsibilities:

The first boy's jobs was to lay out the lines on top of the pie where the pieces should be cut. He doesn't know which piece he will get, so he is careful to draw the pieces equal.

The second boy's job is to take the knife and cut the pie. He doesn't know which piece he will get so he is careful to cut the pieces equal.

The third boy's job is to judge who gets which piece. Thus the hungry, fallen nature of the boys, checked by their legislative, executive and judicial roles, caused them to be honest. This idea was a stroke of genius!

To appreciate the uniqueness of this, imagine a Sunday school teacher giving an assignment to her class: "design a system of government where sinners keep other sinners from sinning."

That is what our Constitution was intended to do. Selfish men in one branch of government keeping selfish men in the other two branches from being selfish.

ఞ

DANGERS OF
THE PARTY SPIRIT

The design of three branches works effectively, except in one instance. If the same political party controls all three branches, the check would be short-circuited. There would not be the greedy pull of one branch against another, as all of them would be following the same party agenda set by the same party head.

Montesquieu warned against any two branches being

controlled by the same group:

> Nor is there liberty if the power of judging
> is not separated from legislative power and from
> executive power. If it [the power of judging] were
> joined to legislative power, the power over life
> and liberty of the citizens would be arbitrary, for
> the judge would be the legislator. If it were joined
> to executive power, the judge could have the force
> of an oppressor.
>
> All would be lost if the same...body of
> men...exercised these three powers.

This is why George Washington, in his *Farewell Address*,
September 19, 1796, warned several times of the political "party
spirit" which was developing in the infant nation:

> Let me...warn you in the most solemn
> manner against the baneful effects of the spirit of
> Party...This spirit, unfortunately, is inseparable
> from our nature, having its roots in the strongest
> passions of the human mind...
>
> You cannot shield yourselves too much
> against the jealousies and heart burnings which
> spring from these misrepresentations...
>
> A just estimate of that love of power, and
> proneness to abuse it, which predominates the
> human heart is sufficient to satisfy us of the truth
> of this position...
>
> It gives to ambitious, corrupted, or deluded
> citizens...facility to betray, or sacrifice the interests
> of their own country, without odium, sometimes
> even with popularity: gilding with the appearances
> of a virtuous sense of obligation, a commendable
> deference for public opinion, or a laudable zeal

for public good, the base or foolish compliances of ambition, corruption or infatuation.

Internal divisions, what George Washington called the "party spirit," is a key ingredient in the fall of many cities and empires, such as:

431 BC - divisions between Athens and Sparta allowed Philip of Macedon to conquer.

70 AD – division between factions in Jerusalem facilitated the Roman conquest by Titus.

622 AD - divisions in Medina between Jewish tribes Banu Nadir, Banu Qaynuqa and Banu Qurayza facilitated Mohammed's conquest.

627 AD – divisions in Arabia between Arab pagan tribes facilitated Islamic conquest.

642 AD – divisions in Egypt between Coptic Christians and Byzantine Christians facilitated Muslim conquest by Amr ibn al-Aas.

711 AD - divisions in Visgothic Spain facilitated the Arab/Berber Muslim conquest of Tariq ibn-Ziyad.

1337-1453 AD divisions between France and England during the Hundred Years War enticed Sultan Mehmet II to conquer Constantinople without fear of retaliation.

1453 AD – division in Constantinople between Emperor John Paleologus' sons over who should succeed him weakened the city and facilitated the Muslim conquest by Sultan Mehmet II.

1689 AD division between Catholics and Protestants in England allowed Holland's William of Orange to assume the British throne with his English wife Mary.

FEDERALIST VERSUS ANTI-FEDERALIST

America was a balancing act.

America's founders wanted to separate power as much as possible, but not completely, as that would result in disorder within and vulnerability without. The ditch on one side of the road was tyranny and the ditch on the other side was anarchy. A despotic dictator on one side, and an unrestrained mob on the other, as was witnessed in looting which took place in New Orleans after Hurricane Katrina, August 29, 2005. Mercy Otis Warren wrote in *Observations on the new Constitution, and on the Federal and State Conventions*, 1788:

> Save us from anarchy on the one hand,
> and the jaws of tyranny on the other.

Total government on one extreme and no government on the other. This balancing act was expressed in the debates between the Federalists and the Anti-Federalists during the time of the ratification of the U.S. Constitution.

Federalists wanted a stronger central government, so they could have a navy to protect the country from outside attack, and authority to keep peace internally, overseeing inter-state disputes.

Washington leaned toward the Federalist views, as he remembered his soldiers fighting during the Revolutionary War without being paid for years because the Federal Government had no power to raise revenue. John Adams also held this view, advocating for a U.S. Navy, as did Alexander Hamilton, who was promoting a U.S. Treasury and a central bank.

The Anti-Federalists wanted less concentrated power, so as to prevent a repeat of the abuses of King George III's totalitarian government. King George was the king of their country, the commander of their military and the head of their church.

The Federalists eventually formed the Whig Party, and the Anti-Federalists formed the Democrat-Republican Party.

The large government versus small government tug-of-war has continued ever since.

This balancing of power can be compared to a nuclear reactor. As the radioactive rods are pulled out with calculated precision, a powerful heat is generated within the core which can boil water, turn huge electric turbines, and be a great benefit by providing electricity to many.

But if the radioactive rods are pulled out too much or too fast, the heat in the core builds to an uncontrollable level and melts down the entire reactor, becoming a great threat by spreading contaminating radiation to many.

In addition to separating power into three branches, the founders separated power again from Federal to State jurisdictions, limiting the Federal Government with the 10th Amendment.

The founders then chained this new federal Frankenstein with ten handcuffs, called the First Ten Amendments, before they threw the switch giving it life. They wanted to make absolutely sure the central government knew its limits.

President William Henry Harrison stated in his *Inaugural Address*, March 4, 1841:

> Republics can commit no greater error than to adopt or continue any feature in their systems of government which may be calculated to create or increase the love of power...It is the part of wisdom for a republic to limit the service of that officer...to whom she has intrusted the management...so...as to prevent his forgetting that he is the accountable agent...the servant, not the master....
>
> The great dread...seems to have been that the reserved powers of the States would be absorbed by those of the Federal Government and a consolidated power established, leaving to

the States the shadow only of that independent action for which they had so zealously contended...

There is still an undercurrent at work by which, if not seasonably checked, the worst apprehensions of our Anti-Federal patriots will be realized, and not only will the State authorities be overshadowed by the great increase of power in the Executive department of the General Government, but the character of that Government, if not its designation, be essentially and radically changed.

This state of things has been in part effected by...the never-failing tendency of political power to increase itself...

The Executive department has become dangerous...by the use which it appears may be made of the appointing power to bring under its control the whole revenues of the country...There was wanting no other addition to the powers of our Chief Magistrate to stamp monarchical character on our Government, but the control of the public finances...

The first Roman Emperor, in his attempt to seize the sacred treasure, silenced the opposition of the officer to whose charge it had been committed by a significant allusion to his sword...

I know the importance which has been attached by men of great abilities and patriotism to the divorce, as it is called, of the Treasury from the banking institutions...It was certainly a great error in the framers of the Constitution not to have made the officer at the head of the Treasury

Department entirely independent of the Executive.

President Andrew Jackson, in his *Eighth Annual Message to Congress*, December 5, 1836, stated:

> Congress is only authorized to levy taxes 'to pay the debts and provide for the common defense and general welfare of the United States.'
>
> There is no such provision as would authorize Congress to collect together the property of the country, under the name of revenue, for the purpose of dividing it equally or unequally among the States or the people. Indeed, it is not probable that such an idea ever occurred to the States when they adopted the Constitution.

Dwight Eisenhower described the Federal Government at the Governors' Conference, June 24, 1957:

> The national government was itself the creature of the States...Yet today it is often made to appear that the creature, Frankenstein-like, is determined to destroy the creators.

JUDEO-CHRISTIAN INGREDIENT KEY TO SUCCESSFUL REPUBLIC

President Franklin D. Roosevelt stated on October 6, 1935:

> In the formative days of the Republic the directing influence the Bible exercised upon the fathers of the Nation is conspicuously evident...We cannot read the history of our rise and development as a Nation, without reckoning with the place the Bible has occupied in shaping the

advances of the Republic. Its teaching is ploughed into the very heart of the race.

The different Christian denominations that settled the various colonies had different forms of church government that influenced America's development of civil self-government (ie. Congregational, Presbyterian, Baptist, Quaker, etc.)

Dolly Madison, wife of James Madison, reported that in 1774 Jefferson dined with Baptist Pastor Andrew Tribble (1741-1822) at Monticello, where Jefferson commented that Baptist church government:

> ...was the only form of pure democracy that exists in the world...It would be the best plan of government for the American colonies.

The Durants wrote in *The Lessons of History* (p. 76):

> In America, Protestantism...had opened the way to religious and mental liberty.

On August 1, 1776, Samuel Adams addressed the Continental Congress assembled at the State House in Philadelphia:

> This day, I trust, the reign of political protestantism will commence. We have explored the temple of royalty, and found that the idol we have bowed down to, has eyes which see not, ears that hear not our prayers, and a heart like the nether millstone. **We have this day restored the Sovereign, to whom alone all men ought to be obedient. He reigns in Heaven, and with a propitious eye beholds his subjects assuming that freedom of thought, and dignity of self-direction which He bestowed on them...**
>
> We are now on this continent to the astonishment of the world three millions of souls

united in one common cause...

We have fled from the political Sodom; let us not look back, lest we perish and become a monument of infamy and derision to the world!

Edmund Burke was a renowned British Statesman in the English Parliament. Just prior to the outbreak of the Revolutionary War, Edmund Burke referred to the influence of Protestant Christianity on the American Colonies in his *Second Speech on the Conciliation with America*, March 22, 1775:

> Religion, always a principle of energy, in this new people is no way worn out or impaired; and their mode of professing it is also one main cause of this free spirit. The people [colonists] are Protestants; and of that kind which is the most adverse to all implicit submission of mind and opinion. This is a persuasion not only favorable to Liberty, but built upon it...
>
> All Protestantism, even the most cold and passive, is a sort of dissent. But the religion most prevalent in our Northern Colonies is a refinement on the principle of resistance; it is the dissidence of dissent, and the protestantism of the Protestant religion.

Samuel Adams continued, referencing the Protestant Reformers:

> Providence is yet gracious unto Zion, that it will turn away the captivity of Jacob.
>
> Our glorious reformers, when they broke through the fetters of superstition, effected more than could be expected from an age so darkened.
>
> But they left much to be done by their posterity. They lopped off, indeed, some of the

branches...but they left the root and stock when they left us under the domination of human systems and decisions, usurping the infallibility which can be attributed to Revelation alone.

They dethroned one usurper only to raise up another... And if we now cast our eyes over the nations of the earth we shall find, that instead of possessing the pure religion of the gospel, they may be divided either into infidels who deny the truth, or politicians who make religion a stalking horse for their ambition, of professors, who walk in the trammels of orthodoxy, and are more attentive to traditions and ordinances of men than to the oracles of truth.

Thus by the beneficence of Providence, we shall behold our empire arising, founded on justice and the voluntary consent of the people, and giving full scope to the exercise of those faculties and rights which most ennoble our species.

Besides the advantages of liberty and the most equal constitution, Heaven has given us a country...pouring forth in abundance...and you will want nothing from the rest of the world.

British Prime Minister Margaret Thatcher noted the uniqueness of how America was started in an interview with Joseph A. Cannon, *Human Events*, 1996:

The Decalogue- Ten Commandments- are addressed to each and every person. This is the origin of...the sanctity of the individual...

It is personal liberty with personal responsibility. Responsibility to your parents, to your children, to your God...

If you accept freedom, you've got to have principles about the responsibility. You can't do this without a biblical foundation.

Your Founding Fathers came over with that. They came over with the doctrines of the New Testament as well as the Old. They looked after one another, not only as a matter of necessity, but as a matter of duty to their God. There is no other country in the world which started that way.

President, Calvin Coolidge addressed the Holy Name Society in Washington, DC, September 21, 1924:

The Declaration of Independence... claims...the ultimate source of authority by stating...they were...'appealing to the Supreme Judge of the World for the rectitude of' their 'intentions.'...

The foundation of our independence and our Government rests upon basic religious convictions. Back of the authority of our laws is the authority of the Supreme Judge of the World, to whom we still appeal...

It seems to me perfectly plain that the authority of law, the right to equality, liberty and property, under American institutions, have for their foundation, reverence for God.

If we could imagine that to be swept away, these institutions of our American government could not long survive.

EQUALITY BEFORE THE LAW

President Calvin Coolidge stated on the 150th Anniversary

Celebration of the Declaration of Independence, Philadelphia, July 5, 1926:

> Equality, liberty, popular sovereignty, the rights of man -these...have their source and their roots in the religious convictions...We can not continue to enjoy the result if we neglect and abandon the cause.

President Calvin Coolidge addressed the Holy Name Society, September 24, 1924:

> The principle of equality...follows inevitably from belief in the brotherhood of man through the fatherhood of God.

Harry S Truman stated in his *Inaugural Address*, 1949:

> We believe that all men are created equal, because they are created in the image of God.

President William Howard Taft stated at a missionary conference in 1908:

> The spirit of Christianity...is equality of man before God – the equality of man before the law.

James Madison wrote in his *Memorial & Remonstrance,* 1785:

> Before any man can be considered as a member of Civil Society, he must be considered as a subject of the Governor of the Universe...
>
> Much more must every man who becomes a member of any particular Civil Society, do it with a saving of his allegiance to the Universal Sovereign.

Ronald Reagan said:

I know in my heart that man is good. That what is right will always eventually triumph. And there's purpose and worth to each and every life.

President William Henry Harrison stated in his *Inaugural Address*, March 4, 1841:

There are certain rights possessed by each individual American citizen which in his compact with the others he has never surrendered. Some of them, indeed, he is unable to surrender, being, in the language of our system, unalienable...The American citizen....claims them because he is himself a man, fashioned by the same Almighty hand as the rest of his species and entitled to a full share of the blessings with which He has endowed them.

∾
LIBERTY REQUIRES RESPONSIBILITY

British Statesman Edmund Burke wrote in *A Letter to a Member of the National Assembly,* 1791:

Men are qualified for civil liberty in exact proportion to their disposition to put moral chains upon their own appetites...and the less of it there is within, the more there must be without.

Herbert Hoover stated at a reception for his 80th birthday, August 10, 1954, West Branch, Iowa:

The great documents of that heritage are not from Karl Marx. They are from the Bible, the Declaration of Independence and the Constitution...Within them alone can the safeguards of freedom survive.

Mercy Otis Warren quoted Abbe de Mably in *Observations on the new Constitution, and on the Federal and State Conventions*, 1788:

> An heroic love for the public good, a profound reverence for the laws, a contempt of riches, and a noble haughtiness of soul, are the only foundations of a free government.

On May 6, 1982, in a White House ceremony in observance of the National Day of Prayer, President Ronald Reagan stated:

> The French philosopher Alexis de Tocqueville, visiting America a hundred and fifty years ago, marveled at Americans because they understood that a free people must also be a religious people. 'Despotism,' he wrote, 'may be able to do without faith, but freedom cannot.'

&

RELIGION'S ROLE IN A RARE REPUBLIC

America's experiment of men sitting in peace to design their own government was extremely rare, as Will and Ariel Durant wrote in *The Lessons of History* (p. 90), that most States were formed through conquest:

> States took form through conquest of one group by another, and the establishment of a continuing force over the conquered by the conqueror.

James Wilson signed the Declaration and Constitution, and was appointed as Supreme Court Justice by George Washington. He remarked in Pennsylvania's ratifying convention, November 26, 1787 (Jonathan Elliot, ed., *The Debates in the Several State Conventions on the Adoption of the Federal Constitution*, 2d. ed.

Rev. 5 vols., Philadelphia: J.B. Lippincot, 1907, 2:422, 426):

> Governments, in general, have been the result of force, of fraud, and accident. After a period of **6,000 years has elapsed since the creation, the United States exhibit to the world the first instance,** as far as we can learn, **of a nation...assembling voluntarily**...and deciding calmly concerning that system of government under which they would wish that they and their posterity should live.

Rather than leaving it to "chance, war and conquest," the writers of the U.S. Constitution realized they had an unparalleled window of opportunity to create a limited government, as Ben Franklin wrote:

> God governs in the affairs of men. And if a sparrow cannot fall to the ground without His notice, is it probable that an empire can rise without His aid?...
>
> Without His concurring aid we shall succeed in this political building no better than the builders of Babel...
>
> And what is worse, mankind may hereafter from this unfortunate instance, despair of establishing governments by human wisdom and leave it to chance, war and conquest.

America's founders realized the unusual moment they had in choosing a non-monarchical form of government. John Jay had served for a term as President of the Continental Congress, signed the Treaty of Paris with Franklin and Adams, and helped ratify the Constitution by writing the *Federalist Papers* with Madison and Hamilton. George Washington appointed him as the first Chief Justice of the U.S. Supreme Court.

In 1777, John Jay gave the charge to an Ulster County Grand Jury:

> The Americans are the first people whom Heaven has favored with an opportunity of deliberating upon, and choosing the forms of government under which they should live.
>
> All other constitutions have derived their existence from violence or accidental circumstances, and are therefore probably more distant from their perfection, which, though beyond our reach, may nevertheless be approached under the guidance of reason and experience.

On May 17, 1982, in a proposed Constitutional Amendment of Prayer in Schools, President Ronald Reagan stated:

> One hundred fifty years ago, Alexis de Tocqueville found that all Americans believed that religious faith was indispensable to the maintenance of their republican institutions.
>
> Today, I join with the people of this nation in acknowledging this basic truth, that our liberty springs from and depends upon an abiding faith in God.

This has been clear from the time of George Washington, who stated in his *Farewell Address*:

> Of all the dispositions and habits which lead to political prosperity, religion and morality are indispensable supports....And let us with caution indulge the suppositions that morality can be maintained without religion....
>
> Reason and experience both forbid us to

expect that national morality can prevail in exclusion of religious principle.

The government of the United States of America was originally designed to be controlled by the consent of the governed, with the Federal Government being a Republic limited by a Constitution.

As a result, America pioneered the most individual freedoms, rights, equality and opportunities in world history, which sparked enormous creativity and innovation in areas of agriculture, manufacturing, science, aviation, electricity, communications, telegraph, telephone, radio, television, electronics, computers, Internet, transportation, steam engines, railroads, automotive, military, steam boats, ironclad ships, nuclear energy, solar energy, and space flight.

The experiment worked – America won independence and became the most free and most prosperous nation in world history.

The growth of the middle-class contributed to America experiencing more freedom, opportunity and prosperity than any previous civilization, achieving by 1945 a Gross Domestic Product (GDP) larger than any other nation.

America's founders set up a government where the people were the King and the politicians were the servants – public servants - who could be hired or fired, voted in and voted out.

The power of a king was separated into three branches: executive, legislative and judicial.

These three branches were pitted against each other to check power, with each branch trying to be king of the hill, constantly pushing the other two down.

It was a stroke of genius – greedy men keeping other greedy men from being greedy. The natural human selfishness, which in almost every other instance ended in the creation of a monarchy, was harnessed to prevent a monarchy, as each of the three branches selfishly tried to take power from the other two branches, therefore keeping them in check.

On March 4, 1801, in his *First Inaugural Address*, President Thomas Jefferson stated:

> Enlightened by a benign religion, professed, indeed, and practiced in various forms, yet all of them inculcating honesty, truth, temperance, gratitude, and the love of man; acknowledging and adoring an overruling Providence, which by all its dispensations proves that it delights in the happiness of man here and his greater happiness hereafter.
>
> With all these blessings, what more is necessary to make us a happy and prosperous people?
>
> Still one thing more, fellow citizens-a wise and frugal Government, which shall restrain men from injuring one another, shall leave them otherwise free to regulate their own pursuits of industry and improvement, and shall not take from the mouth of labor the bread it has earned...

Jefferson continued:

> You should understand what I deem the essential principles of our Government...
>
> Equal and exact justice to all men, of whatever state or persuasion, religious or political...arraignment of all abuses at the bar of the public reason; freedom of religion; freedom of the press, and freedom of person under the protection of the habeas corpus, and trial by juries impartially selected...
>
> And may that Infinite Power which rules the destinies of the universe, lead our councils to what is best, and give them a favorable issue for your peace and prosperity.

FEWER OUTSIDE LAWS
IF MORE INSIDE LAWS

Where does the idea of a having fewer laws come from?

By reviewing writings of the founders, it appears that American government was designed to govern people who could govern themselves. John Quincy Adams, while serving for a second time as U.S. Ministry in St. Petersburg, Russia, wrote to his son, September 1811:

> So great is my veneration for the Bible...that the earlier my children begin to read it...the more lively and confident will be my hopes that they will prove useful citizens of their country...
>
> It is essential, my son, in order that you may go through life with comfort to yourself, and usefulness to your fellow-creatures, that you should form and adopt certain rules or principles, for the government of your own conduct and temper...
>
> It is in the Bible, you must learn them, and from the Bible how to practice them.
>
> Those duties are to God, to your fellow-creatures, and to yourself.
>
> "Thou shalt love the Lord thy God, with all thy heart, and with all thy soul, and with all thy mind, and with all thy strength, and thy neighbor as thy self."

William Holmes McGuffey, president of Ohio University and professor at the University of Virginia, was the Department Chairman at Miami University of Ohio and formed the first teachers' association in that part of the nation.

His *McGuffey's Readers* were a mainstay in public education, selling over 125 million copies as of 1963. In *McGuffey's Fifth Eclectic Reader* (1879), lesson XCIII, is an essay by William Ellery

Channing entitled: "Religion - The Only Basis of Society":

> Religion is a social concern; for it operates powerfully, contributing in various ways to its stability and prosperity.
>
> Religion is not merely a private affair; the community is deeply interested in its diffusion; for it is the best support of the virtues and principles, on which the social order rests.
>
> Pure and undefiled religion is, to do good; and it follows, very plainly, that if God be the Author and Friend of Society, then, the recognition of him must enforce all social duty, and enlightened piety must give its whole strength to public order.

James McHenry, signer of the U.S. Constitution and U.S. Secretary of War who supervised the establishment of West Point Military Academy, stated to the Baltimore, Maryland, Bible Society, 1813:

> Public utility pleads most forcibly for the general distribution of the Holy Scriptures.
>
> The doctrine they preach, the obligations they impose, the punishment they threaten, the rewards they promise...can alone secure to society, order and peace, and to our courts of justice and constitutions of government...
>
> Without the Bible, we increase penal laws.

Francis Wayland, a Harvard graduate and president of Brown University, 1827-55, was the first president of the American Institute of Instruction, 1830. He stated:

> That the truths of the Bible have the power of awakening an intense moral feeling in every human being;

THAT they make bad men good, and send a pulse of healthful feeling through all the domestic, civil, and social relations;

THAT they teach men to love right, and hate wrong, and seek each other's welfare as children of a common parent;

THAT they control the baleful passions of the heart, and thus make men proficient in self government; and finally

THAT they teach man to aspire after conformity to a Being of infinite holiness, and fill him with hopes more purifying, exalted, and suited to his nature than any other book the world has ever known -

These are facts as incontrovertible as the laws of philosophy, or the demonstrations of mathematics.

๛
INTERNAL OR EXTERNAL LAWS?

A country can get by with few external laws if the people have an internal law. This is the principle of "self-government."

Robert Winthrop, U.S. Speaker of the House in 1849, stated:

All societies of men must be governed in some way or other. The less they have of stringent State Government, the more they must have of individual self-government. The less they rely on public law or physical force, the more they must rely on private moral restraint.

Men, in a word, must necessarily be controlled either by a power within them, or a power without them; either by the word of God, or by the strong arm of man; either by the Bible or by the bayonet.

On August 14, 1796, Vice-President John Adams made the entry in his diary:

> One great advantage of the Christian religion is that it brings the great principle of the law of nature and nations-Love your neighbor as yourself and do to others as you would that others should do to you,-to the knowledge, belief, and veneration of the whole people...
>
> No other institution for education, no kind of political discipline, could diffuse this kind of necessary information, so universally among all ranks and descriptions of citizens. The duties and rights of the man and the citizen are thus taught from early infancy to every creature.
>
> The sanctions of a future life are thus added to the observance of civil and political, as well as domestic and private duties. Prudence, justice, temperance, and fortitude, are thus taught to be the means and conditions of future as well as present happiness.

In 1784, Patrick Henry supported a Bill establishing a "Provision for Teachers of the Christian Religion":

> The general diffusion of Christian knowledge hath a natural tendency to correct the morals of men, restrain their vices, and preserve the peace of society.

Jedediah Morse (1761-1826), called the "Father of American Geography," was the father of Samuel F.B. Morse, the inventor of the telegraph and the Morse Code. In an "Election Sermon," delivered in Charleston, Massachusetts, April 25, 1799, Jedediah Morse stated:

> To the kindly influence of Christianity we

owe that degree of civil freedom, and political and social happiness which mankind now enjoys. In proportion as the genuine effects of Christianity are diminished in any nation, either through unbelief, or the corruption of its doctrines, or the neglect of its institutions; in the same proportion will the people of that nation recede from the blessings of genuine freedom, and approximate the miseries of complete despotism.

I hold this to be a truth confirmed by experience. If so, it follows, that all efforts to destroy the foundations of our holy religion, ultimately tend to the subversion also of our political freedom and happiness.

Whenever the pillars of Christianity shall be overthrown, our present republican forms of government, and all the blessings which flow from them, must fall with them."

In an article titled "Advice to the Young," included in his *History of the United States*, 1832, Noah Webster stated:

The brief exposition of the Constitution of the United States, will unfold to young persons the principles of republican government; and it is the sincere desire of the writer that our citizens should early understand that the genuine source of correct republican principles is the Bible, particularly the New Testament or the Christian religion....

The 'Advice to the Young,'...will be useful in enlightening the minds of youth in religious and moral principles, and serve...to restrain some of the common vices of our country....

Republican government loses half of its value, where the moral and social duties are imperfectly understood, or negligently practiced. To exterminate our popular vices is a work of far more importance to the character and happiness of our citizens than any other improvements in our system of education.

Noah Webster wrote to James Madison, October 16, 1829:

The Christian religion, in its purity, is the basis or rather the source of all genuine freedom in government...I am persuaded that no civil government of a republican form can exist and be durable, in which the principles of that religion have not a controlling influence.

In 1832, in his *History of the United States*, Noah Webster wrote:

Almost all the civil liberty now enjoyed in the world owes its origin to the principles of the Christian religion...

The religion which has introduced civil liberty is the religion of Christ and His apostles, which enjoins humility, piety, and benevolence; which acknowledges in every person a brother, or a sister, and a citizen with equal rights. This is genuine Christianity, and to this we owe our free Constitutions of Government...

The moral principles and precepts contained in the Scriptures ought to form the basis of all of our civil constitutions and laws...All the miseries and evils which men suffer from vice, crime, ambition, injustice, oppression, slavery and war, proceed from their despising or neglecting the precepts contained in the Bible.

The preface of Noah Webster's 1833 translation of the *Common Version of the Holy Bible, containing the Old and New Testament, with Amendments of the Language*, reads:

> The Bible is the Chief moral cause of all that is good, and the best corrector of all that is evil, in human society; the best book for regulating the temporal concerns of men, and the only book that can serve as an infallible guide to future felicity....
>
> It is extremely important to our nation, in a political as well as religious view, that all possible authority and influence should be given to the scriptures, for these furnish the best principles of civil liberty, and the most effectual support of republican government.
>
> The principles of genuine liberty, and of wise laws and administrations, are to be drawn from the Bible and sustained by its authority. The man, therefore, who weakens or destroys the divine authority of that Book may be accessory to all the public disorders which society is doomed to suffer....
>
> There are two powers only, sufficient to control men and secure the rights of individuals and a peaceable administration; these are the combined force of religion and law, and the force or fear of the bayonet."

In his 1834 work titled, *Value of the Bible and Excellence of the Christian Religion*, Noah Webster wrote:

> The Bible must be considered as the great source of all the truths by which men are to be guided in government, as well as in all social transactions...The Bible [is] the instrument of all

reformation in morals and religion...

Moral evils constitute or produce most of the miseries of mankind and these may be prevented or avoided. Be it remembered then that disobedience to God's law, or sin is the procuring cause of almost all the sufferings of mankind.

God has so formed the moral system of this world, that a conformity to His will by men produces peace, prosperity and happiness; and disobedience to His will or laws inevitably produces misery.

If men are wretched, it is because they reject the government of God, and seek temporary good in that which certainly produces evil...

Men may devise and adopt new forms of government; they may amend old forms, repair breaches, and punish violators of the constitution; but there is, there can be, no effectual remedy, but obedience to the divine law.

In *A Collection of Papers on Political, Literary and Moral Subjects,* published in New York, 1843, Noah Webster stated:

The virtue which is necessary to preserve a just administration and render a government stable, is Christian virtue, which consists in the uniform practice of moral and religious duties, in conformity with the laws of both God and man.

This virtue must be based on a reverence for the authority of God, which shall counteract and control ambition and selfish views, and subject them to the precepts of divine authority.

The effect of such a virtue would be, to bring the citizens of a state to vote and act for the good of the state, whether that should coincide with their private interests or not.

In *A Manual of Useful Studies*, published in New Haven, 1839, Noah Webster stated:

> Practical truths in religion, in morals, and in all civil and social concerns, ought to be among the first and most prominent objects of instruction.
>
> WITHOUT a competent knowledge of legal and social rights and duties, persons are often liable to suffer in property or reputation, by neglect or mistakes.
>
> WITHOUT religious and moral principles deeply impressed on the mind, and controlling the whole conduct, science and literature will not make men what the laws of God require them to be; and
>
> WITHOUT both kinds of knowledge, citizens can not enjoy the blessings which they seek, and which a strict conformity to rules of duty will enable them to obtain.

In other words, the U.S. Government was designed to govern those who could govern themselves. Order was to be maintained, not so much by relying on external physical restraints, but by internal moral restraints, as Franklin wrote April 17, 1787:

> Only a virtuous people are capable of freedom.

Thomas Jefferson wrote on the Rights of British America, 1774 (*The Jeffersonian Cyclopedia*, John P. Foley, ed., New York & London, Funk & Wagnalls Co., 1900, No. 3476, i, 141; Paul Leicester Ford, ed., i, 446):

> The whole art of government consists in the art of being honest.

Pennsylvania Supreme Court (1824), in the case of *Updegraph v. The Commonwealth*, 11 Serg. & R. 393-394, 398-399, 402-407 (1824), recorded the court's declaration that:

> Christianity, general Christianity, is and always has been a part of the common law...not Christianity founded on any particular religious tenets; not Christianity with an established church...but Christianity with liberty of conscience to all men.

Benjamin Franklin is attributed to have stated in a letter to the French ministry, March 1778:

> Whoever shall introduce into public affairs the principles of primitive Christianity will change the face of the world.

On November 27, 1780, in a letter to Elbridge Gerry, Samuel Adams stated:

> More, in my opinion, is to be done than conquering our British enemies, in order to establish the liberties of our country on a solid basis. Human nature, I am afraid, is too much debased to relish the republican principles in which the new government of the commonwealth of Massachusetts appears to be founded. Mankind is prone to political idolatry....
>
> May Heaven inspire the present rulers with wisdom and sound understanding! In all probability they will stamp the character of the people...if we look into the history of governors, we shall find that their principles and manners have always had a mighty influence on the people.

In 1791, Edmund Burke stated in *A Letter to a Member of the National Assembly*:

> What is liberty without wisdom and without virtue? It is the greatest of all possible evils; for it is folly, vice, and madness, without restraint.
>
> Men are qualified for civil liberty in exact proportion to their disposition to put moral chains upon their own appetites; in proportion as they are disposed to listen to the counsels of the wise and good in preference to the flattery of knaves.
>
> Society cannot exist, unless a controlling power upon will and appetite be placed somewhere; and the less of it there is within, the more there must be without. It is ordained in the eternal constitution of things, that men of intemperate minds cannot be free. Their passions forge their fetters.

Massachusetts Governor Samuel Adams wrote to James Warren, February 12, 1779:

> A general dissolution of the principles and manners will more surely overthrow the liberties of America than the whole force of the common enemy.
>
> While the people are virtuous they cannot be subdued; but once they lose their virtue, they will be ready to surrender their liberties to the first external or internal invader. If we would enjoy this gift of Heaven, let us become a virtuous people.

William Howard Taft speaking at a missionary conference, 1908, stated:

> No man can study the movement of modern civilization from an impartial standpoint,

and not realize that Christianity and the spread of Christianity are the basis of hope of modern civilization in the growth of popular self government.

∽

FUTURE ACCOUNTABILITY

To be a country with "few laws," citizens must have an internal law for there to be order, but an internal law is powerless without a consequence, such as being held accountable to a Supreme Being in some future state.

Daniel Webster, Secretary of State for three U.S. Presidents, was asked what the greatest thought was that ever passed through his mind. He replied:

> My accountability to God.

Franklin wrote to Yale President Ezra Stiles, March 9, 1790:

> The soul of Man is immortal, and will be treated with justice in another life respecting its conduct in this.

Benjamin Franklin believed:

> That there is one God, Father of the Universe...That He loves such of His creatures as love and do good to others: and will reward them either in this world or hereafter,
>
> That men's minds do not die with their bodies, but are made more happy or miserable after this life according to their actions.

John Adams wrote to Judge F.A. Van der Kemp, January 13, 1815:

> My religion is founded on the love of God

and my neighbor; in the hope of pardon for my offenses; upon contrition...in the duty of doing no wrong, but all the good I can, to the creation, of which I am but an infinitesimal part. I believe, too, in a future state of rewards and punishments.

John Adams wrote to Judge F.A. Van der Kemp, December 27, 1816:

Let it once be revealed or demonstrated that there is no future state, and my advice to every man, woman, and child, would be, as our existence would be in our own power, to take opium.

For, I am certain there is nothing in this world worth living for but hope, and every hope will fail us, if the last hope, that of a future state, is extinguished.

John Adams wrote in a *Proclamation of Humiliation, Fasting, and Prayer*, March 6, 1799:

No truth is more clearly taught in the Volume of Inspiration...than... acknowledgment of...a Supreme Being and of the accountableness of men to Him as the searcher of hearts and righteous distributor of rewards and punishments are conducive equally to the happiness and rectitude of individuals and to the well-being of communities.

On November 25, 1862, Abraham Lincoln told Rev. Byron Sunderland of the First Presbyterian Church, Washington, DC:

I believe in the supremacy of the human conscience, and that men are responsible beings, that God has a right to hold them, and will hold them, to a strict account for the deeds done in the body. But, sirs, I do not mean to give you a lecture

upon the doctrines of the Christian religion.
These are simply with me the convictions and realities of great and vital truths.

State oaths of office referred to future accountability. Having few laws because citizens strive to keep an internal law, aware they will be accountable in a "future state," is seen in State Constitutions and Court Decisions.

The *Constitution of Pennsylvania*, 1776, (Chp. 2, Sec. 10), stated:

Each member, before he takes his seat, shall make and subscribe the following declaration, viz:
"I do believe in one God, the Creator and Governour of the Universe, the Rewarder of the good and Punisher of the wicked, and I do acknowledge the Scriptures of the Old and New Testament to be given by Divine Inspiration."

The *Constitution of South Carolina*, 1778, Article 12, stated:

Every...person, who acknowledges the being of a God, and believes in the future state of rewards and punishments...[is eligible to vote].

The *Constitution of South Carolina*, 1790, Article 38, stated:

That all persons and religious societies, who acknowledge that there is one God, and a future state of rewards and punishments, and that God is publicly to be worshipped, shall be freely tolerated.

The *Constitution of Mississippi*, 1817, stated:

No person who denies the being of God or a future state of rewards and punishments shall hold any office in the civil department of the State.

Pennsylvania's Supreme Court stated in *Commonwealth v. Wolf*, 3 Serg. & R. 48, 50 (1817):

Laws cannot be administered in any civilized government unless the people are taught to revere the sanctity of an oath, and look to a future state of rewards and punishments for the deeds of this life.

The *Constitution of Maryland*, 1851, required:

A declaration of belief in the Christian religion; and if the party shall profess to be a Jew the declaration shall be of his belief in a future state of rewards and punishments.

The *Constitution of Maryland*, 1864, required of office holders:

A declaration of belief in the Christian religion, or of the existence of God, and in a future state of rewards and punishments.

The *Constitution of Tennessee*, 1870, Article 9, Section 2, stated:

No person who denies the being of God, or a future state of rewards and punishments, shall hold any office in the civil department of this State.

The idea of an oath was to call a higher power to hold you accountable to perform what you said you would. This accountability is expressed in all three branches of government: The President's oath of office ends with "So Help Me God"; Congressmen and Senators' oath of office ends with "So Help Me God," and Federal Judges' oath of office ends with "So Help Me God."

The traditional courtroom oath for witnesses ended "to tell the truth, the whole truth and nothing but the truth, So Help Me God." The military oath of enlistment and oath for commissioned officers ends with "So Help Me God."

Sir William Blackstone, one of the most quoted authors by America's founders, wrote in his *Commentaries on the Laws of England*, 1765-1770:

The belief of a future state of rewards and punishments, the entertaining just ideas of the main attributes of the Supreme Being, and a firm persuasion that He superintends and will finally compensate every action in human life (all which are revealed in the doctrines of our Savior, Christ), these are the grand foundations of all judicial oaths, which call God to witness the truth of those facts which perhaps may be only known to Him and the party attesting.

It was known that witnesses or politicians would have opportunities to twist the truth and do dirty, back room deals for their own benefit and never get caught. But it was reasoned that if a witness or politician believed God existed and was looking over their shoulder, they would hesitate when presented with the temptation. They would have a conscience.

They would think twice before giving in, considering "even if I get away with this unscrupulous action in this life, I will still be accountable to God in the next."

But if that person did not believe in God and in a future state of rewards and punishments, when presented with the same temptation to do wrong and not get caught, they would give in.

In fact, if there is no God and this life is all there is, they would be a fool not to.

୬

CONSCIENCE

President Reagan referred to this while speaking on the *Equal Access Bill* in Dallas, Texas, August 23, 1984:

Without God there is no virtue because there is no prompting of the conscience.

William Linn, elected unanimously as the first Chaplain of the U.S. House, May 1, 1789, stated:

Let my neighbor once persuade himself that there is no God, and he will soon pick my pocket, and break not only my leg but my neck.

If there be no God, there is no law, no future account; government then is the ordinance of man only, and we cannot be subject for conscience sake.

Linn's observation was demonstrated when, after 80 years of atheism, the countries of the former Soviet Union were given liberty, and the result was that organized crime and the black market took significant control. From Bill Clinton to Enron Corporation, one sees where the absence of an internal law will take a country - crimes are only wrong if one gets caught.

Unfortunately, the less internal moral code a nation has results in the government having to pass more external legal codes to keep order - and each new law takes away another little piece of individual freedom. *McGuffey's Fifth Eclectic Reader* (Cincinnati & NY: Van Antwerp, Bragg & Co., 1879), included lesson XCIII, "Religion The Only Basis of Society" by William Ellery Channing:

How powerless conscience would become without the belief of a God...Erase all thought and fear of God from a community, and selfishness and sensuality would absorb the whole man.

Appetite, knowing no restraint, and suffering, having no solace or hope, would trample in scorn on the restraints of human laws.

Virtue, duty, principle, would be mocked and spurned as unmeaning sounds.

A sordid self-interest would supplant every feeling; and man would become, in fact, what the theory in atheism declares him to be, - a companion for brutes.

Patrick Henry noted:

It is when a people forget God that tyrants forge their chains...A corrupted public conscience is incompatible with freedom.

James Madison stated in his Inaugural, March 4m 1817:

It is only when the people become ignorant and corrupt, when they degenerate into a populace, that they are incapable of exercising the sovereignty. **Usurpation** is then an easy attainment, and an **usurper** soon found. The people themselves become the willing instruments of their own debasement and ruin.

Mercy Otis Warren wrote in *Observations on the new Constitution, and on the Federal and State Conventions*, 1788:

Monarchy is a species of government fit only for a people too much corrupted by luxury, avarice, and a passion for pleasure, to have any love for their country, and whose vices the fear of punishment alone is able to restrain...

[Monarchy is] by no means calculated for a nation that is...tenacious of their liberty — animated with a disgust to tyranny — and inspired with the generous feeling of patriotism and liberty.

John Adams wrote to Jefferson, April 19, 1817:

Without religion, this world would be something not fit to be mentioned in polite company...The most abandoned scoundrel that ever existed, never yet wholly extinguished his Conscience and while Conscience remains, there is some religion.

John Adams wrote to Thomas Jefferson in 1819:

Have you ever found in history, one single

example of a Nation thoroughly corrupted that was afterwards restored to virtue? And without virtue, there can be no political liberty...

Will you tell me how to prevent luxury from producing effeminacy, intoxication, extravagance, vice and folly?...I believe no effort in favor of virtue is lost.

U.S. Supreme Court Justice James Wilson, appointed by George Washington, wrote:

The eminent distinction between right and wrong...[is revealed] by our conscience, by our reason, and by the Holy Scriptures.

Washington, copying the *110 Rules of Civility*, wrote in 1745:

Labor to keep alive in your breast that little spark of Celestial fire called Conscience.

∾

WILL OF THE MAJORITY

George Bancroft, Secretary of the Navy, wrote in *The Progress of Mankind*, 1854:

The many are wiser than the few; the multitude than the philosopher.

Calvin Coolidge stated at the unveiling of Equestrian Statue of Bishop Francis Asbury, October 15, 1924, Washington, DC:

Our country was about to begin the work of establishing a government which was to represent **the rule of the people**, where not a few but the many were to control public affairs, where the vote of the humblest was to count for as much as the most exalted.

In history's timeline of thousands of years of monarchies,

Will and Ariel Durant described "democracies" as "hectic interludes."

Because of the 3,000 mile ocean between the American colonies and their British monarch, King George III, America had a very rare moment to experiment in, what Eisenhower called, "their revolutionary experiment."

As no handbook existed on how to have a government without a king, each colony attempted their own version governance.

There was a mixture of Company colonies, Proprietary colonies and Royal colonies, together with the various forms of church government, as colonies were originally founded by different Christian denominations:

> **Virginia**-Anglican
> **Massachusetts**-Puritan
> **New York**-Dutch Reformed
> **Delaware** & **New Jersey**-Swedish Lutheran
> **Maryland**-Catholic
> **Rhode Island**-Baptist
> **Connecticut** & **New Hampshire**-Congregationalist
> **Pennsylvania**-Quaker
> **Carolinas**-officially Anglican, but populated with others
> **Georgia**-Protestant

America had a unique window of opportunity in self-government, separating the powers of a monarch, making "the people" the king and the politicians the public servants. Alexander Hamilton said in New York's ratification debates, June 21, 1788:

> **The will of the people** makes the essential principle of the government.

Thomas Jefferson wrote in 1816 (A.E. Bergh, *Writings*, 15:32):

> Try...every provision of our Constitution, and see if it hangs directly on **the will of the people.**

Thomas Jefferson wrote to Samuel Kerchival in 1816 (*The*

Jeffersonian Cyclopedia, John P. Foley, ed., New York & London, Funk & Wagnalls Co., 1900, p. 391, No. 3557, vii, 9; Paul Ford, ed., x, 37):

> Governments are republican only in proportion as they embody **the will of the people** and execute it.

James Madison wrote in Philadelphia, January 31, 1792:

> The past frequency of wars [is from] a will in the government independent of **the will of the people.**

Robert La Follette, Sr. (1855-1925), a U.S. Congressman, U.S. Senator, and the Governor of Wisconsin, stated:

> **The Will of the People** is the Law of the Land.

Madison wrote in *Federalist Paper No. 46*, January 29, 1788:

> The ultimate authority...resides **in the people alone.**

Jefferson wrote in his Notes on Virginia, 1782 (*The Jeffersonian Cyclopedia*, Foley, NY:Funk & Wagnalls Co., 1900, No. 3483):

> Civil government being the sole object of forming societies, its administration must be conducted **by common consent.**

Thomas Jefferson referred to the "decisions of the majority" in his First Inaugural Address, March 4, 1801:

> The essential principles of our Government [are]...the right of election **by the people** [and]...**absolute acquiescence in the decisions of the majority,** the vital principle of republics.

In 1973, Ronald Reagan stated:

> The classical liberal, during the Revolutionary time, was a man who wanted less

power for the king and **more power for the people.** He wanted people to have more say in the running of their lives and he wanted protection for the God-given rights of the people.

President John F. Kennedy referred to "the consent of the people" in his *National Day of Prayer Proclamation,* September 28, 1961:

Our founding fathers came to these shores trusting in God, and in reliance upon His grace. They charted the course of free institutions under a government **deriving its powers from the consent of the people.**

Patrick Henry is attributed with the statement:

The Constitution is not an instrument for the government to restrain the people, it is an instrument for the people to restrain the government - lest it come to dominate our lives and interests.

Calvin Coolidge stated at the ceremony unveiling the Equestrian Statue of Bishop Francis Asbury, October 15, 1924:

The history of government on this earth has been almost entirely a history of the rule of force held in the hands of a few. Under our Constitution, America committed itself to the practical application of the rule of reason, **with the power in the hands of the people.**

ʾ

A EUROPEAN'S WARNING TO AMERICA

Daniel Hannan, a member of the European Parliament, wrote "A European's Warning to America-The Perils of Following

Us Toward Greater Regulation, Higher Taxes and Centralized Power," (Encounter Books Broadside, "Why America Must Not Follow Europe," 8/11/11, Wall Street Journal, Dow Jones & Co.):

> Obama would verbalize his ideology using the same vocabulary that Eurocrats do...[but] when you prize away the cliché, what these phrases amount to are **higher taxes, less patriotism, a bigger role for state bureaucracies, and a transfer of sovereignty to global institutions.**
>
> He is not pursuing a set of random initiatives but a program of comprehensive Europeanization: European health care, European welfare, European carbon taxes, European day care, European college education, even a European foreign policy, based on engagement with supranational technocracies, nuclear disarmament and a reluctance to deploy forces overseas. No previous president has offered such uncritical support for European integration...
>
> The U.S. would no longer be the world's superpower, but perhaps that would make it more popular. Is a European future truly so terrible?
>
> **Yes.** I have been an elected member of the European Parliament for 11 years. I have seen firsthand what the European political model means. **The critical difference between the American and European unions has to do with the location of power. The U.S. was founded on** what we might loosely call the Jeffersonian ideal: **the notion that decisions should be taken as closely as possible to the people they affect.**
>
> **The European Union was based on precisely the opposite ideal...**

From that distinction, much follows.

The U.S. has evolved a series of unique institutions designed to limit the power of the state: recall mechanisms, ballot initiatives, balanced budget rules, open primaries, localism, states' rights, term limits, the direct election of public officials from the sheriff to the school board.

The EU places supreme power in the hands of 27 unelected Commissioners invulnerable to public opinion. The will of the people is generally seen by Eurocrats as an obstacle to overcome...The nation-state...is seen as more important than freedom, democracy or the rule of law...

The single worst aspect of Europeanization is its impact on the economy. Many Americans, and many Europeans, have a collective memory of how Europe managed to combine economic growth with social justice. Like most folk memories, the idea of a European economic miracle has some basis in fact. Between 1945 and 1974, Western Europe did outperform the U.S. Europe happened to enjoy perfect conditions for rapid growth. Infrastructure had been destroyed during the war, but an educated, industrious and disciplined work force remained...

Few European leaders attributed their success to the fact that they were recovering from an artificial low. They convinced themselves, rather, that they were responsible for their countries' growth rates. Their genius, they thought, lay in having hit upon a European "third way" between the excesses of American capitalism and the totalitarianism of Soviet communism.

We can now see where that road leads: to **burgeoning bureaucracy, more spending, higher taxes, slower growth and rising unemployment.** But an entire political class has grown up believing not just in the economic superiority of euro-corporatism but in its moral superiority. After all, if the American system were better-if people could thrive without government supervision-there would be less need for politicians. As Upton Sinclair once observed, "It is difficult to get a man to understand something when his job depends on not understanding it."

Nonetheless, the economic data are pitilessly clear. **For the past 40 years, Europeans have fallen further and further behind** Americans in their standard of living. Europe also has become accustomed to a high level of structural unemployment. **Only now, as the U.S. applies a European-style economic strategy** based on fiscal stimulus, nationalization, bailouts, quantitative easing and the regulation of private-sector remuneration, **has the rate of unemployment in the U.S. leaped to European levels.**

Why is a European politician urging America to avoid Europeanization? **As a Briton, I see the American republic as a repository of our traditional freedoms.** The doctrines rooted in the common law, in the Magna Carta, and in the Bill of Rights found their fullest and most sublime expression in the old courthouse of Philadelphia.

Britain, as a result of its unhappy membership in the European Union, has now surrendered a large part of its birthright.

But our freedoms live on in America.
Which brings me to my country's present tragedy...

Colossal sums are being commandeered by the government in order to fund bailouts and nationalizations without any proper parliamentary authorization. Legislation happens increasingly through what are called standing orders, a device that allows ministers to make laws without parliamentary consent-often for the purpose of implementing EU standards.

How aptly the British people might today apply the ringing phrases of the Declaration of Independence against their own rulers, who have "combined with others to subject us to a jurisdiction foreign to our constitution, and unacknowledged by our laws."

So you can imagine how I feel when I see the U.S. making the same mistakes that Britain has made: expanding its government, regulating private commerce, centralizing its jurisdiction, breaking the link between taxation and representation, abandoning its sovereignty. You deserve better, cousins. And we expect better.

&

WILL OF A MINORITY

George Washington warned in his *Farewell Address,* September 19, 1796:

> And of fatal tendency...to put, in the place of the delegated will of the Nation, **the will of a party - often a small but artful and enterprising minority...**Cunning, ambitious, and unprincipled men

will be enabled to subvert the power of the people and to **usurp** for themselves the reins of government.

A minority forcing its will on the majority is a tyranny. Americans experienced this during colonial times when the king of England used his government to enforce his will upon his subjects. The Declaration of Independence, 1776, stated:

> The history of the present King of Great Britain is a history of repeated injuries and **usurpations**, all having in direct object the establishment of **an absolute tyranny over these States**...He has made **judges dependent on his will alone**...A Prince, whose character is thus marked by every act which may define a **Tyrant**, is unfit to be a ruler of a free people.

Franklin D. Roosevelt, in accepting the Democrat Party's re-nomination for President, June 27, 1936, explained that America's founders fought so that "the people" could be their own rulers:

> In 1776, we sought freedom from the **tyranny of a political autocracy** – from the 18th century royalists who held **special privileges from the crown**. It was to perpetuate their privilege that **they governed without the consent of the governed;** that they denied the right of free assembly and free speech; that they restricted the worship of God.

Is the will of the people still reflected in government? Are the people still their own rulers? Polls showed that the people in America did not want the government to control their healthcare, yet backroom arm twisting, pork barrel bribes and disinformation campaigns resulted in the President signing the bill into law.

Another example of the "will of the people" no longer being the law of the land is in the area of religious beliefs.

The CIA.gov website's World Factbook (2007) reported that 80.2 percent of the U.S. population held Judeo-Christian beliefs. The *American Religious Identification Survey* (2001), conducted by The Graduate Center, City University of New York, reported:

> **77.8 percent of the U.S. population held Judeo-Christian beliefs** (52 percent Protestant, 24.5 percent Catholic, 1.3 percent Jewish).
> The rest of the population was:
> 0.5 percent Muslim
> 0.5 percent Buddhist
> 0.5 percent Agnostic
> 0.4 percent Hindu
> 0.3 percent Unitarian-Universalist
> 0.1 percent Wiccan-Pagan-Druid
> 13.2 percent Secular
> 6.3 percent Spiritualist-Native American-Baha'i-New Age-Scientology-Humanist-Deist-Taoist-Eckankar
> only 0.4 percent atheist.

Yet groups like the ACLU, Americans United for Separation, and Freedom From Religion Foundation, are working with liberal judges to discriminate against traditional Judeo-Christian beliefs in favor of atheism, and now Islam. If the will of majority of "the people" is not reflected in the laws, then the country is no longer "democratic." Could it be that the debate over religion in America is not the "religious right" versus the "liberal left," but rather between the will of the majority versus the will of, as Washington called them "an artful and enterprising minority"? Reagan stated Feb. 25, 1984:

> Sometimes I can't help but feel the First Amendment is being turned on its head...The First Amendment of the Constitution was not written to protect the people from religion; **that Amendment was written to protect religion from government tyranny.**

Reagan addressed Alabama's State Legislature, March 15, 1982:

> To those who cite the First Amendment as reason for excluding God...may I just say: **The First Amendment** of the Constitution was not written to protect the people of this country from religious values; it **was written to protect religious values from government tyranny.**

Reagan continued in his radio address, 1982:

> The Constitution was never meant to prevent people from praying; **its declared purpose was to protect their freedom to pray.**

If politicians no longer need "the consent of the people," America could be on the path to "the people" ceasing "to be their own rulers," as Lincoln warned in his Inaugural Address, March 4, 1861:

> I do not forget the position assumed by some that constitutional questions are to be decided by the Supreme Court...If the policy of the Government upon vital questions...is to be irrevocably fixed by decisions of the Supreme Court, the instant they are made...**the people will have ceased to be their own rulers**, having to that extent practically resigned their Government into the hands of the eminent tribunal.

TWO WAYS TO CHANGE LAWS

There are two ways to change laws. The first is based on the will of the people. Time and effort is invested to persuade a majority of citizens to change their views, motivate them to vote, electing a majority of Congressmen and Senators, who in turn must vote in the majority to pass laws which the President, elected by the majority, signs.

The second way to change laws is quick and easy, and needs only a "minority." Simply find a judge who is willing to change the definitions of words that are in existing laws.

Could it be that groups like the ACLU want to take power away from the majority because they hold different beliefs than the majority? A Gallup Poll (2007) reported "9 in 10 Americans believe in God"; a Harris Poll (2003) reported 90% of Americans believe in God; a Newsweek poll (2007) reported 91% of Americans believe in God; and a Fox News poll (2004) reported 92% of Americans believe in God.

America is obviously less Judeo-Christian than it used to be, but on May 9, 1833, Supreme Court Justice John Marshall wrote to Jasper Adams, President of the College of Charleston, South Carolina:

> The American population is entirely Christian, and with us, Christianity and religion are identified. It would be strange, indeed, if with such a people, our institutions did not presuppose Christianity, and did not often refer to it and exhibit relations with it.

The ACLU claims to defend the rights of the people against the government, but in actuality, it is has found an artful way through the courts to use the centralized power of the Federal government to restrict the rights of the majority of the people, developing itself into a premier anti-democratic organization.

The ACLU admitted this on its website in 2008:

> The power even of a democratic majority must be limited, to ensure individual rights.

Limiting "the power...of a democratic majority" may sound noble, until one realizes that to accomplish this, the will of a minority must be forcibly imposed upon the majority. Harry S Truman referred to Communists' minority rule in his *Truman Doctrine*, March 12, 1947:

> One way of life is based upon **the will of the**

majority, and is distinguished by free institutions, representative government, free elections, guarantees of individual liberty, freedom of speech and religion, and freedom from political oppression.

The second way of life is based on **the will of a minority forcibly imposed upon the majority.** It relies upon terror and oppression, a controlled press and radio, fixed elections, and the suppression of personal freedoms.

To prevent the abuse that comes from a concentration of power in "an artful and enterprising minority," America's founders insisted on the rule of law to guarantee power remained with the majority of the people, as the Constitution begins "We the People..."

Where America's founders entrusted the preservation of freedom to the will of the majority of the people, the ACLU, knowingly or unknowingly, is wresting power from the will of the people and concentrating it in the hands of a minority of judges.

The ACLU, in this sense, is an undemocratic organization, posting on its website in 2008:

> *Majority power is limited by the Constitution's Bill of Rights.*

Yet a closer examination of the Bill of Rights reveals their intent was to restrict the Federal Government's power, not the majority power of the people, as Patrick Henry noted:

> The Constitution is not an instrument for the government to restrain the people. **It is an instrument for the people to restrain the government,** lest it come to dominate our lives and interests.

Jefferson wrote to James Madison, December of 1787 (*The Jeffersonian Cyclopedia*, John P. Foley, ed., NY & London, Funk & Wagnalls Co., 1900, No. 822, ii, 330; Paul Ford, ed., iv, 477):

A **Bill of Rights is what the people are entitled to against every government on earth,** general or particular; and what no just government should refuse.

Jefferson wrote of the Bill of Rights to F. Hopkinson, March of 1789 (*The Jeffersonian Cyclopedia*, John P. Foley, ed., NY & London, Funk & Wagnalls Co., 1900, No. 819, ii, 586; Paul Ford, ed., v, 76):

I disapproved from the first moment [in the new Constitution] the want of **a Bill of Rights, to guard liberty against the legislative as well as the executive branches of the government.**

Jefferson wrote to A. Donald, February of 1788, in regards to the Bill of Rights (*The Jeffersonian Cyclopedia*, John P. Foley, ed., New York & London, Funk & Wagnalls Co., 1900, No. 818, ii, 355):

By a Declaration of Rights I mean one which shall stipulate freedom of religion, freedom of the press, freedom of commerce against monopolies, trial by juries in all cases, no suspensions of the habeas corpus, no standing armies. **These are fetters against doing evil which no honest government should decline.**

Jefferson wrote to James Madison in August of 1789 (*The Jeffersonian Cyclopedia*, John P. Foley, ed., New York & London, Funk & Wagnalls Co., 1900, No. 820, iii, 100; Paul Leicester Ford, ed., v, 112):

I like the Declaration of Rights as far as it goes, but I should have been for going further...If we do not have them now...**we shall have them as soon as the degeneracy of our government shall render them necessary.**

If there was any doubt, the 9th and 10th Amendments of the Bill of Rights made this clear:

AMENDMENT IX. The enumeration in
the Constitution, of certain rights, shall not be
construed to deny or disparage **others retained
by the people.**

AMENDMENT X. The powers not
delegated to the United States by the Constitution,
nor prohibited by it to the states, **are reserved to
the states respectively, or to the people.**

The fear of America's founders was to repeat the errors of
Europe, where power was concentrated in the hands of kings and
their appointees and judges.

The Preamble to the Bill of Rights, signed September 25,
1789, by Speaker of the House, Frederick Muhlenberg and
President of the Senate, John Adams, expressed the concern that
the Federal Government might abuse its power, therefore
Amendments were needed to restrict the Federal Government:

A number of the States, having at the time
of **their adopting the Constitution**, expressed a
desire, **in order to prevent misconstruction or
abuse of its powers**, that further declaratory and
restrictive clauses should be added.

The First Amendment states this intent very clearly, by
specifying that it is the Federal "Congress" that is to be limited:

AMENDMENT I. **Congress** shall **make
no law** respecting an establishment of religion, **or
prohibiting** the free exercise thereof; **or abridging**
the freedom of speech, or of the press; **or the right
of the people** peaceably to assemble, and to petition
the Government for a redress of grievances.

The 2nd and 4th Amendments cite "**the right of the people**":

AMENDMENT II. A well-regulated militia,

being necessary to the security of a free state, **the right of the people** to keep and bear arms, shall not be infringed.

AMENDMENT IV. **The right of the people** to be secure in their persons, houses, papers, and effects, against unreasonable searches and seizures, shall not be violated, and no warrants shall issue, but upon probable cause, supported by oath or affirmation and particularly describing the place to be searched, and **the persons** or things to be seized.

In *U.S. v Verdugo-Urquidez* (494 US 247, 288 1990), Justice William J. Brennan, Jr., wrote:

The term **"the people"** is better understood as a rhetorical counterpoint **"to the government"**... The Bill of Rights did not purport to "create" rights. Rather, **they designed the Bill of Rights to prohibit our government** from infringing rights and liberties presumed to be pre-existing.

The 3rd Amendment implies protecting people from the government, as only people live in houses:

AMENDMENT III. No soldier shall, in time of peace be quartered in any house, **without the consent of the owner,** not in time of war, but in a manner prescribed by law.

The 5th, 6th, 7th and 8th Amendments restrict the government from treating unjustly a person who has been accused:

AMENDMENT V. **No person shall be held** to answer for a capital, or otherwise infamous crime, unless on a presentment of indictment of a grand jury, except in cases arising in the land or naval forces or in the militia, when in actual service in time of war or public danger;

nor shall **any person** be subject for the same offense to be twice put in jeopardy of life or limb; nor shall be compelled in any criminal case to be a **witness against himself,**

nor be deprived of life, liberty, or property, without due process of law;

nor shall private property be taken for public use, without just compensation.

AMENDMENT VI. In all criminal prosecutions, **the accused shall enjoy the right to a speedy and public trial,** by an impartial jury or the state and district wherein the crime shall have been committed, which district shall have been previously ascertained by law, and to be informed of the nature and cause of the accusation; to **be confronted with the witnesses against him**; to have compulsory process for obtaining witnesses **in his favor**, and to have the assistance of counsel for his defense.

AMENDMENT VII. In suits at law, where the value in controversy shall exceed twenty dollars, **the right of trial by jury shall be preserved**, and no fact tried by a **jury** shall be otherwise reexamined in any court of the United States, than according to the rules of law.

AMENDMENT VIII. **Excessive bail shall not be required, nor excessive fines imposed, nor cruel and unusual punishments inflicted.**

The whole concept of being tried by a jury is evidence that **the framers of the Constitution trusted the decision of the majority, the 12 jurors, more than one government judge.**

The ACLU incriminates its own activity of filing lawsuits to remedy perceived injustices when it posted on its website (2008):

> *Majority power is limited by the Constitution's Bill of Rights*, which consists of the original ten amendments ratified in 1791, plus the three post-Civil War amendments (the 13th, 14th and 15th) and the 19th Amendment (women's suffrage) adopted in 1920.

It is not "majority power" that is limited by the Constitution's Bill of Rights, but "government power." The Amendments that the ACLU cites were passed by the majority of the people. **How can Amendments ratified by the will of the majority be intended to nullify the will of the majority?** If injustices exist, the Constitutionally prescribed remedy is not to legislate from the bench, but to pass Amendments. To guarantee Amendments are what the people want, the Constitution necessitates a "super-majority" to support them:

> Article V: The Congress, whenever **two thirds** of both Houses shall deem it necessary, shall propose Amendments to this Constitution, or, on the Application of the Legislatures of **two thirds** of the several States, shall call a Convention for proposing Amendments, which, in either case, shall be valid to all intents and purposes, as part of this Constitution, when ratified by the Legislatures of **three fourths** of the several States.

"2/3's," "2/3's" and "3/4's" - these formulas were put in place to **keep power in the hands of majority**. The Constitution and Bill of Rights were designed **not to limit "majority power," but to protect it.** If the ACLU wants to limit power, it should work through the legislative process to pass laws and Amendments, not file lawsuits with the intention to skirt the Constitution by having liberal judges legislate from the bench.

The ACLU's shopping for court venues to file lawsuits where activist judges preside, in order to have them re-interpret the

Constitution's meaning, is not what the founders intended. In *Federalist No. 81*, Alexander Hamilton wrote:

> In the first place, **there is not a syllable** in the plan under consideration **which directly empowers the national courts to construe the laws according to the spirit of the Constitution.**

The ACLU's method has been compared to "legal terrorism" as it threatens local schools, communities, and veterans' organizations, with bankruptcy if they spend the millions of dollars necessary to defend themselves against the ACLU suits.

The article "American Legion Lauds Reintroduction of PERA in 110th Congress" (Indianapolis, January 31, 2007), stated:

> Senate Bill 415...would stop the award of taxpayer dollars in legal fees to groups filing lawsuits against veterans' memorials and public displays of religion.
>
> "Legal attacks against veterans' memorials that display religious symbols must not be rewarded by judges **reaching into taxpayer pockets to enlarge the coffers of organizations such as the ACLU** to encourage more lawsuits against our traditions and memorials," said American Legion National Commander Paul A. Morin...
>
> Most Americans are unaware that **activist groups, such as the ACLU, recover hundreds of thousands of dollars from state and local governments each year**...Rees Lloyd, former ACLU attorney and Department of California District 21 Commander, provided examples of ACLU awards of taxpayer money...**These fees were pure profit to the ACLU...**
>
> "If the ACLU feels it has to bring lawsuits

that most Americans abhor, it should at least have the decency not to assess these to the taxpayers to make a profit," Morin said.

"It is not fair for taxpayers to pay the legal bills for groups like the ACLU," said Senator Sam Brownback, "Currently many towns comply with the demands of the ACLU rather than risk going to trial and paying hundreds of thousands of dollars in legal fees to the ACLU if they lose the case."

Thomas Jefferson wrote in his *Draft Kentucky Resolutions*, 1798, that Federal Courts' power was to be limited:

> **No power over the freedom of religion, freedom of speech, or freedom of the press [was] delegated to the United States** by the Constitution...All lawful powers respecting the same did of right remain and **were reserved to the States or the people.**

Jefferson wrote to William Jarvis, September 28, 1820, of despots with absolute, arbitrary power:

> You seem...to consider the judges as the ultimate arbiters of all constitutional questions; **a very dangerous doctrine indeed**, and one which would place us under the despotism of an oligarchy.
>
> Our judges are as honest as other men, and not more so....and their power [is] the more dangerous, as they are in office for life and not responsible, as the other functionaries are, to the elective control. **The Constitution has erected no such single tribunal**, knowing that to whatever hands confided, with corruptions of time and party, its members would become despots.

❧

POWER GIVEN OVERRUNNING GIVERS

Colonial Leader John Cotton wrote:

> Whatever power is given will certainly over-run those that give it...**It is necessary therefore, that all power that is on earth be limited**.

Eisenhower stated at a Governors' Conference, June 24, 1957:

> The national government was itself the creature of the States...Yet today it is often made to appear that **the creature, Frankenstein-like, is determined to destroy the creators**.

Jefferson warned of the tactics used by the ACLU in his letter to Charles Hammond in 1821 (*The Jeffersonian Cyclopedia,* John P. Foley, ed., NY & London, Funk & Wagnalls Co., 1900, No. 1170, vii.316):

> It has long been my opinion that the germ of dissolution of our federal government is in the Constitution of our Federal Judiciary; an irresponsible body, gaining a little today and a little tomorrow, and advancing its noiseless step like a thief, over the field of jurisdiction, **until all shall be usurped from the states, and the government of all be consolidated into one.**

Jefferson wrote to Elbridge Gerry, 1799:

> I am for preserving to the States the powers not yielded by them to the Union...**I am not for transferring all the powers of the States to the General Government.**

Thomas Jefferson wrote to Charles Hammond in 1821 (*The Jeffersonian Cyclopedia*, John P. Foley, ed., New York & London, Funk & Wagnalls Co., 1900, No. 1170, vii.316):

> **When all government**, domestic and foreign, in little as in great things, **shall be drawn to Washington as the center of all power,** it will render powerless the checks of one government on another, and **will become as venal and oppressive as the government from which we separated.** It will be as in Europe, where every man must be either pike or gudgeon, hammer or anvil...
>
> If the States look with apathy on **this silent descent of their government into the gulf which is to swallow all,** we have only to weep over the human character formed uncontrollable but by a rod of iron, and the blasphemers of man, as incapable of self-government, becomes his true historians.

Mercy Otis Warren warned in *Observations on the new Constitution, and on the Federal and State Conventions*, 1788:

> And when asked, what is become of the rich produce of their farms - they may answer in the hapless style of the Man of La Mancha, "The steward of my Lord has seized and sent it to Madrid." Or, in the more literal language of truth...**Government requires that the collectors of the revenue should transmit it to the Federal City.**

Jefferson wrote to William T. Barry in 1822 (*The Jeffersonian Cyclopedia*, John P. Foley, ed., NY & London, Funk & Wagnalls Co., 1900, No. 1171, vii.256):

> If ever this vast country is brought **under a**

single government, it will be one of **the most extensive corruption...**You will have to chose between reformation or revolution...

Before the canker['s] venom has reached so much of the body politic as to get beyond control, remedy should be applied.

Jefferson wrote to Joseph C. Cabell in 1816 *(The Jeffersonian Cyclopedia,* John P. Foley, ed., New York & London, Funk & Wagnalls Co., 1900, No. 1174, vi.543):

What has destroyed the liberty and the rights of man in every government that has ever existed under the sun? **The generalizing and concentrating of all cares and powers into one body**, no matter whether of the autocrats of Russia or France, or of the aristocrats of a Venetian Senate.

Jefferson wrote to William F. Gordon, in January of 1826 *(The Jeffersonian Cyclopedia,* John P. Foley, ed., New York & London, Funk & Wagnalls Co., 1900, No. 1175; Paul Leicester Ford, ed., x.358):

It is but too evident that the general government...[is] in combination to usurp the powers...of the States, and **consolidate themselves into a single government without limitation of powers**...What is to be done? Shall we give up the ship? No, by heavens, while a hand remains able to keep the deck."

Jefferson wrote to William Branch Giles, 1825:

I see...the rapid strides with which the **Federal branch of our government** is advancing towards **the usurpation of all the rights reserved to the States,** and **the consolidation in itself of all powers.**

Jefferson wrote to John Taylor in 1798 (*The Jeffersonian Cyclopedia,* John P. Foley, ed., NY & London, Funk & Wagnalls Co.):

> Our **General [Federal] Government** has, in the rapid course of nine or ten years, become more arbitrary, and **has swallowed more of the public liberty than even that of England.**

William Henry Harrison stated in his *Inaugural Address,* March 4, 1841:

> Limited are the powers which have been granted, still enough have been granted to constitute **a despotism if concentrated in one of the departments.**

President Harrison continued:

> **The tendency of power to increase itself,** particularly when exercised by a single individual...would terminate in virtual monarchy...
>
> The danger to all well established free governments arises from the unwillingness of the people to believe in [the] existence of designing men...
>
> Like the false Christs whose coming was foretold by the Savior, seeks to, and if it were possible would, impose upon the true and most faithful disciples of liberty...
>
> It behooves the people to **be most watchful of those to whom they have entrusted power.**

Andrew Jackson said in his *Farewell Address,* 1837:

> It is well known that there have always been those amongst us who wish to **enlarge the powers of the General Government...**
>
> Government would have passed from the

hands of the many to the hands of the few.

Franklin Pierce stated in his *Inaugural Address*, March 4, 1853:

> **The dangers of a concentration of all power in the General Government...are too obvious to be disregarded**...The great scheme of our constitutional liberty rests upon a proper distribution of power between the State and Federal authorities.

Andrew Jackson vetoed the *Bank Renewal Bill*, July 10, 1832:

> It is easy to conceive that great evils to our country and its institutions might flow from such **a concentration of power in the hands of a few men irresponsible to the people.**

Woodrow Wilson stated in New York, September 4, 1912:

> When I resist the concentration of power, I am resisting the process of death, because **concentration of power is what always precedes the destruction of human initiative.**

Jefferson wrote in his *Autobiography*, published in 1821, (*The Jeffersonian Cyclopedia*, John P. Foley, ed., New York & London, Funk & Wagnalls Co., 1900, No. 1176, i.82; Paul Leicester Ford, ed., i.113):

> It is not by the consolidation, or concentration of powers, but by their distribution, that good government is effected [brought about].

Woodrow Wilson addressed the New York Press Club, September 9, 1912:

> Liberty has never come from government... **The history of liberty is a history of the limitation of government power**, not the increase of it.

Ronald Reagan said:

Man is not free **unless government is limited.**

Harry S Truman wrote in his *Memoirs - Volume Two: Years of Trial and Hope* (1956):

The men who wrote the Constitution knew...that tyrannical government had come about where **the powers of government were united in the hands of one man.** The system they set up was designed to prevent a demagogue or "a man on horseback" from taking over the powers of the government.

As a young man, I had read Montesquieu's *Spirit of the Laws*...The most important thought expressed in our Constitution is that **the power of government shall always remain limited,** through the separation of powers.

French political philosopher Montesquieu wrote in *The Spirit of the Laws*, 1748:

Constant experience shows us that **every man invested with power is apt to abuse it**...It is necessary from the very nature of things that power should be a check to power.

Washington stated in his *Farewell Address*, September 19, 1796:

The spirit of encroachment tends to consolidate the powers of all departments in one, and thus to create, whatever the form of government, a real despotism...

And of fatal tendency...to put, in the place of the delegated will of the Nation, the will of a party -

often a small but artful and enterprising **minority**...
cunning, ambitious, and unprincipled men will be
enabled to **subvert the Power of the People** and
to **usurp for themselves the reins of Government.**

James Madison stated in the Debates of the Virginia
Constitutional Convention, June 6, 1788:

I believe there are more instances of the
abridgement of the freedom of the people by
gradual and silent encroachments of those in
power than by violent and sudden usurpations.

This is no mystery. The Constitution was written by 55
delegates, but only 39 signed it. Of those who refused to sign was
George Mason of Virginia, called the "Father of the Bill of Rights."
He did not sign because he did not think there were enough limits on
the new Federal Government.

Mason was joined by Sam Adams, Patrick Henry and the
writers of the Anti-Federalist Papers, who insisted a Bill of Rights
be added to the Constitution **to prevent power from being taken
from the majority of the people by the minority in government.**

Communist dictator Joseph Stalin, responsible for over
20,000,000 deaths, stated:

Crisis alone permitted the authorities to
demand – and obtain – total submission and all
necessary sacrifices from its citizens.

Whether a crisis was intentional or not, concentration of power
happend nonetheless, as examined in **Volume II of** *Change to Chains*.

It was great that **Lincoln** ended slavery, but in the
process, power went from the States to the Federal
Government. It was great that **Woodrow Wilson** ended World
War I, but in the process, power was concentrated in the
Federal Government through the Income Tax, Federal Reserve
and 17th Amendment.

FDR, during the Great Depression and WWII, concentrated power in the Federal Government with his New Deal programs. **Lyndon Johnson** concentrated power with his War on Poverty "Great Society" welfare programs. Bush concentrated power with the War on Terror, empowering government to track credit card purchases, read emails and search citizens at the airport.

In each crisis, concentration was to remedy immediate problems, such as ending slavery or preventing terrorist attacks, but over time, power once concentrated seldom returns to the people.

President Obama concentrated power at an unprecedented rate, taking control of banks, car companies, and life-and-death healthcare decisions of every citizen, utilizing some 40 unelected czars.

Whereas America's founders studied political philosophers who took the concentrated power of a king and separated it, other philosophers taught to take separated power and concentrated it.

Machiavelli lived 500 years ago in Italy, which at the time consisted of numerous independent city-states: Florence, Naples, Venice, Milan, Pisa, Genoa, Sienna and others, each with their own army and navy. Due to constant fighting, Machiavelli thought that if one prince could control all of Italy, it would end the in-fighting. He wrote a book, titled "The Prince," in which he advocated "the ends justifies the means." The end - one prince controlling all of Italy - was so good, that any means necessary to get there was justified.

For example, if the prince wanted to conquer a city in his quest to unify Italy, he could pay criminals to create terror, and when the people cried for help, he could arrive and kill the very criminals he hired, and the people, unaware of his subterfuge, would praise him as a hero. It is good marketing, create the need and fill it.

Set the back of the house on fire then go around the front of the house and sell them a fire extinguisher.

This is called **Machiavellianism** – create or capitalize on a crises to consolidate control, or as President Obama's Chief of Staff Rahm Emanuel said: "You never want a serious crisis to go to waste."

Another philosopher was **George Wilhelm Friedrich Hegel**. Hegel's "dialectics" was a triangle, with one corner being a thesis, the opposite corner an anti-thesis, and the top corner the synthesis. The thesis is where the people are at, one then creates the anti-thesis - a problem that is **real bad** - and the people will be happy to settle for the synthesis – the answer that is only **half-as-bad**. This synthesis becomes the new thesis, and the process starts again, with each crisis moving the country from separated power to concentrated power.

Hegel inspired **Karl Marx**, who proposed sending community and labor organizers into countries to create an "antithesis" by organizing those who felt discriminated against, playing upon their lust to have what others have, and stirring them to revolt. When blood flowed in the streets everybody was willing to give up their rights and freedoms to have order restored.

When the dust settles, a communist dictator has taken over, such as Lenin, Stalin, Castro, Mao Zedung, Pol Pot, Ho Chi Min, Kim Jung Il, and other despots.

Marxism does not care who the two sides are: whether Bourgeoisie (property owners) versus the Proletariat (wage laborers), Rich versus Poor, Catholics versus Protestants, Blacks versus Whites, Hutu's versus the Tutsi's in the Congo, or Union Members versus the Governor of Wisconsin, all that matters is that a crisis is created, out of which a dictator can usurp power.

Plato wrote of this in his Republic, 380 BC, that democracy without virtue ends in chaos, out of which a tyrant arises.

Saul Alinsky, a political philosopher in Chicago, taught how to use crisis to seize power. Hillary Clinton wrote her Master's Thesis on Saul Alinsky's "Reveille for Radicals," and Barak Obama taught Alinsky's "Rules for Radicals" when he was a community organizer in Chicago. In Rules for Radicals, 1971, Saul Alinsky wrote:

> The **organizer** must first rub raw the resentments of the people of the community; fan the latent hostilities of many of the people to the point of overt expression...search out controversy and issues, rather than avoid them, for unless there is controversy people are not concerned enough to act...

An **organizer** must stir up dissatisfaction and discontent...The first step in community organization is community disorganization. The disruption of the present organization is the first step...

From the moment the **organizer** enters a community he lives, dreams...only one thing and that is to build the mass power base of what he calls the army. Until he has developed that mass power base, he confronts no major issues...

Until he has those means and power instruments, his 'tactics' are very different from power tactics. Every move revolves around one central point: how many recruits will this bring into the organization, whether by means of local organizations, churches, service groups, labor Unions, corner gangs, or as individuals...The **organizer** helps to lead his forces into conflict...In war the end justifies almost any means...The real arena is corrupt and bloody.

America has experienced crisis after crisis, some preventable and some not: Financial Crisis, Debt Crisis, Sub-prime Mortgage Crisis, Gulf Oil Spill Crisis, Border Crisis, Immigration Crisis, AIDS Crisis, Drug Crisis, Crime Crisis, Avian Flu Crisis, Mad Cow Disease Crisis, Swine Flu Crisis, Weather Crisis, Unemployment Crisis, Healthcare Crisis, Computer Virus Crisis and Terrorism Crisis.

No matter what the crisis, the answer is the same – give government more control and they will take care of everything. As the media whips the country into a frenzy, Congress is pressured to hurry up and pass another huge piece of legislation (which someone has already conveniently written, yet no one has had time to read), and only afterwards do citizens get to "find out what is in it."

MIRACLE OF AMERICA

Dwight Eisenhower referred to the "miracle of America" in an *Episcopal Churchnews* article on the Allied invasion of Normandy in June of 1944:

> My father and mother believed that "the fear of God is the beginning of wisdom."...The history of our country is inseparable from the history of such God-fearing families.
>
> In this fact we accept the explanation of the **miracle of America**...

Eisenhower continued:

> The founding fathers had to refer to the Creator in order to make their revolutionary experiment make sense; it was because "all men are endowed by their Creator with certain inalienable rights" that men could dare to be free...
>
> **Our forefathers proved that only a people strong in Godliness is a people strong enough to overcome tyranny and make themselves and others free**...
>
> What is our battle against communism if it is not a fight between anti-God and a belief in the Almighty?

As Calvin Coolidge explained, October 15, 1924:

> There are only two main theories of government in the world.
>
> One rests on righteousness, the other rests on force. One appeals to reason, the other appeals to the sword. One is exemplified in a republic, the other is represented by a despotism.

The history of government on this earth has been almost entirely a history of the **rule of force held in the hands of a few.** Under our Constitution America committed itself to the practical application of the rule of reason, **with the power in the hands of the people.**

The Durants wrote in *Lessons* (p. 70-72):

Most governments have been ruled by a **minority**... The majority can do no more than periodically throw out one minority and set up another.

Ronald Reagan stated in 1961:

In this country of ours took place the greatest revolution that has ever taken place in the world's history...**Every other revolution simply exchanged one set of rulers for another.**

Yale president Ezra Stiles stated to the General Assembly of Connecticut, *The United States Elevated to Glory and Honor,* May 8, 1783:

All forms of civil polity have been tried by mankind, **except one**, and that seems to have been reserved in Providence **to be realized in America**...
The United States are under peculiar obligations to become a holy people unto the Lord our God.

Reagan stated in *A Time for Choosing,* October 27, 1964:

This idea that government was beholden to the people, that it had no other source of power except the sovereign people, **is still the newest, most unique idea in all the long history of man's relation to man.** For almost two centuries we have proved man's capacity for self-government.

Lincoln stated at Independence Hall, February 22, 1861:

> The Declaration of Independence gave liberty not alone to the people of this country, but **hope to all the world for all future time.**
>
> It was that which gave promise that in due time the weights would be lifted from the shoulders of all men, and that all should have an equal chance...
>
> This is the sentiment embodied in the Declaration of Independence...I would rather be assassinated on this spot than surrender it.

Daniel Webster warned in his *4th of July Oration*, Fryeburg, Maine, 1802:

> We live under the only government that ever existed which was **framed by...deliberate consultations of the people.**
>
> Miracles do not cluster. That which has happened but once in 6,000 years cannot be expected to happen often. Such a government, once gone, might leave a void, to be filled, for ages, with revolution and tumult, riot and despotism.

Like water going down a drain, with every succeeding crisis, freedoms are drawn away from the people and down into the vortex of concentrated State power.

Like gravity eventually pulls a satellite out of orbit crashing down to earth, the gravity of concentrated power is trying to pull the republic of the United States of America out of orbit.

But maybe concerned Americans can fire a booster and propel the nation to stay in orbit one more generation.

Mercy Otis Warren wrote in *Observations on the new Constitution, and on the Federal and State Conventions*, 1788:

> **The origin of all power is in the people,** and they have an incontestable right to check the creatures of their own creation.

For the sake of future generations, Americans must remember the price paid for freedom and call to mind Lincoln's admonition to preserve freedom for future generations. On the Gettysburg Battlefield, November 19, 1863, where over 50,000 casualties occurred, Lincoln stated:

> Fourscore and seven years ago our fathers brought forth upon this continent a new nation, conceived in liberty, and dedicated to the proposition **that all men are created equal.**
>
> Now we are engaged in a great civil war, testing whether that nation, or any nation so conceived and so dedicated, can long endure...
>
> That we here highly resolve that these dead shall not have died in vain-
>
> That this nation, under God, shall have a new birth of freedom-and **that government of the people, by the people, for the people, shall not perish from the earth.**

CHANGE TO CHAINS - WILLIAM J. FEDERER

CPSIA information can be obtained at www.ICGtesting.com
Printed in the USA
BVOW06*0736161016

465159BV00006B/38/P